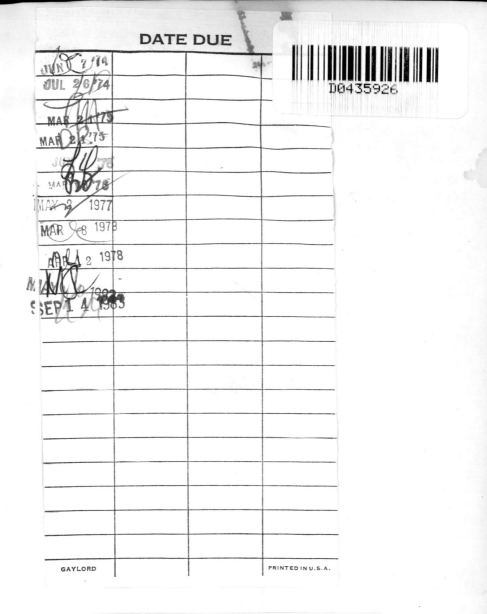

MEASUREMENT
AND
PIAGET

Proceedings of the
CTB/McGraw-Hill Conference on
Ordinal Scales of Cognitive Development

Edited by
Donald Ross Green
CTB/McGraw-Hill
Marguerite P. Ford
Pacific State Hospital
George B. Flamer
University of Minnesota, Morris

McGraw-Hill Book Company
New York, St. Louis, San Francisco, Düsseldorf, Johannesburg, Kuala Lumpur,
London, Mexico, Montreal, New Delhi, Panama, Rio de Janeiro, Singapore,
Sydney, Toronto

Measurement and Piaget

Library of Congress Catalog Card Number 79-153095

07-024307-7

1234567890M A M M 7987654321

This book was set in Univers by Creative Book Services, division of McGregor & Werner, Incorporated, and printed on permanent paper and bound by The Maple Press Company. The designer was Creative Book Services. The editor was William J. Willey. Loretta Palma supervised production.

Acknowledgments

Reference on pages 12 to 28 from B. F. Skinner, "The Science of Learning and the Art of Teaching," *Harvard Educational Review* (Spring 1964), vol. 24, pp. 86-97. Copyright © 1954 by President and Fellows of Harvard College.

Reference on page 97 from John Flavell, *The Developmental Psychology of Jean Piaget.* Copyright © 1963, by Litton Educational Publishing, Inc., by permission of Van Nostrand Reinhold Company.

Reference on pages 153 to 159 from Bärbel Inhelder and Hermina Sinclair, "Learning Cognitive Structures," *Trends and Issues in Developmental Psychology,* P. Mussen, L. Langer, and M. Covington (eds.). Copyright © 1969 by Holt, Rinehart & Winston, Inc. Reprinted by permission of Holt, Rinehart & Winston, Inc.

CONTENTS

PREFACE

The CTB/McGraw-Hill Conference on Ordinal Scales of Cognitive Development was undertaken in hopes that the topic would provide a meeting ground for measurement and developmental psychologists. The theories of Piaget seemed to provide a context in which these long-disparate fields of psychology could converge on common problems to the benefit of both. A theory of cognitive development which postulates an invariant sequence of identifiable stages offers at least partial solutions to many of the dilemmas faced by those endeavoring to provide useful measures of the cognitive status of children. Similarly, the creation of a psychometrically sound instrument which could systematically identify points in this sequence would offer a striking verification of the sequences postulated by Piaget and would open the way for the accumulation of data which might lead to theoretical refinements and elaborations which would otherwise be impossible.

Although the fields of measurement and of development have not paid much attention to each other for many years, there are many reasons why those of the Genevan persuasion and those with a psychometric orientation can interact profitably. The two have typically shared a number of common views on basic issues, as Elkind makes clear in his paper. Secondly, Piaget's studies originated in his work on the measurement of intelligence. Thirdly, there has been growing interest in Piaget's work in the measurement community in recent years, as is illustrated by the British developments discussed by Lovell. And lastly, a number of Piagetian scholars have been working on test development; Tuddenham's work reported here is a prominent example.

The convergence of the two fields has nevertheless not been easily realized since both encounter problems on the way, so to speak. In his opening address at the conference, Piaget gave a clear statement of the problems that become serious issues when attempting to build an ordinal scale based on the theory. Other papers, notably those of Goldschmid and Engelmann, consider one or more of these issues at length. On the other side of the coin are the papers by Bentler and Flavell who discussed very different but important measurement problems.

Thus, the papers fall into three general categories: (a) those that are concerned largely with the theoretical problems in Piaget's system which are not specific to measurement, albeit prerequisite to it—the papers by Piaget, Goldschmid, Engelmann, Beilin, and much of Inhelder's paper; (b) those concerned largely with measurement problems not specific to Piagetian theory—although again, they are logically previous—i.e., the two papers by Bentler (the paper read and his supplementary paper on monotonicity analysis)* and Flavell's paper; and (c) those that dealt directly with both—the papers by Elkind, Tuddenham, Lovell, the supplementary paper by Ayers,* and parts of Inhelder's paper.

---

*The two supplementary papers were not read at the conference but were presented in written and outline form respectively.

Whether or not this mix of views and efforts has led to new or additional fruitful efforts cannot as yet be determined. In any case, we believe that there is a plethora of interesting and thought-provoking ideas in the papers and in the discussions of the papers; each has something of interest and value in its own right quite apart from the interrelationships among the ideas of the several papers. The materials of the conference are presented in the order in which they were given because the discussion material makes more sense that way, even though other arrangements have merit in retrospect. Thus, the first paper is the address by Piaget which was presented in an auditorium to a considerably larger audience than was involved in the remaining sessions during the following 2 days. Unlike the other papers there was no following formal or informal discussion of this address. The fine translation is the work of Miss Sylvia Opper.

We should explain that the content of the open discussions of the papers varied in several ways from session to session, i.e., there were differences in length, interest, emotion, relevance, and clarity of the tape recordings. Consequently we have varied the manner of presentation, some of it being verbatim, some of it summarized, and some of it omitted. Three different editors for different sessions also has added variance. We hope those participating will feel we did their views justice. We wish to thank Peter Bentler for his invaluable assistance in editing the open discussion following his paper. As an aid to identifying those taking part in these discussions, a list of the people who were present at one or more of the sessions can be found in Appendix B.

The paper "Two Approaches to Intelligence: Piagetian and Psychometric" by David Elkind is a modification of his paper "Piagetian and Psychometric Conceptions of Intelligence," which appeared in the 1969 Spring issue of the *Harvard Educational Review* and is presented with their permission. Also the "Learning and Development" section of Inhelder's paper is an adaptation of a portion of the paper "Learning Cognitive Structures" in Mussen, P. H., Langer, J. & Covington, M. (Eds.) *Trends and issues in developmental psychology.* Holt, Rinehart & Winston, 1969. These portions are reproduced with their permission.

The conference and this report of it represent the collaborative effort of many people, most of whom are listed as participants and on the program shown in Appendix B. However, we would also like to thank Archie Lapointe who, as General Manager of CTB/McGraw-Hill, encouraged us and enabled us to take the initial steps in setting up the conference. Joseph Dionne who succeeded Archie Lapointe as General Manager continued this support and has made it possible for this volume to be prepared.

Special thanks for help in assembling the speakers and participants go to Mary Lou Lindquist, and similar thanks go to Anita Endicott who handled the arrangements for the conference itself so well. Finally we should note that Virginia Thompson transcribed all the tapes, the French and the English alike, did most of the collation and copy editing and supervision of the typing. Without her many talents—literary, linguistic, organizational, and problem-solving—the proceedings of this conference would probably have ended up as have so many others, just another set of untranscribed tapes, half finished manuscripts, frustrations, and disappointments. For the manuscript and for the feeling of success and achievement its completion brings, we thank her.

MEASUREMENT
AND
PIAGET

CHAPTER ONE

The Theory of Stages in Cognitive Development

JEAN PIAGET
University of Geneva
Translation by Sylvia Opper, Cornell University

Ladies and Gentlemen:

I should first like to thank the organizers of this small conference on the role of ordinal scales in the problem of development for having invited both my collaborator and friend, Bärbel Inhelder, and me to participate in your meeting. To be quite honest, I am not an expert in ordinal scales. Since you do me the honor of inviting me to address you, however, I feel that the problem of stages is one that should serve as an introduction to the discussions to be held on ordinal scales.

There are two reasons for this. First, a theoretical one: If ordinal scales do indeed have some basis in reality, then a succession of stages must exist in some form or another. And second, as you all know full well, no general agreement has as yet been reached about the existence of these stages. Our own hypotheses about the existence and the necessary sequence of these stages are not accepted by everybody. Consequently, I feel that it might be useful for Bärbel Inhelder and me if I were to discuss the question of stages with you and thus come to know your criticisms, objections, and the problems involved. Generally speaking, however, I feel that it is this working group, whose objective is to study ordinal scales, that will eventually solve the problem of stages. Today, therefore, I shall merely outline the problem and make a few brief comments.

Each time that a specific problem is studied, as for instance that of causality which is currently receiving our attention, the analysis of the responses and reactions of children of different ages seems to point to the existence of relatively well-defined stages in this limited area. The important point, however, is to discover whether there are any general overall stages in development, and whether the different stages found in these more limited and specific areas contain any elements in common. In other words, is it possible to detect broad periods in development with characteristics that can be applied in a general manner to all the events of these periods? This is the hypothesis that we are trying to investigate.

We postulate four major periods in development. First there is a sensorimotor period which occurs before the advent of language. This period is characterized by what we call "sensorimotor intelligence," which is a type of intelligence resulting in a certain number of performances, such as the organization of spatial relationships, the organization of objects and a notion of their permanence, the organization of causal relationships, etc. After the sensorimotor period, at around the age of 2 years, comes another period which starts with the symbolic or semiotic function. This is called the period of "preoperational thought" since the child is now capable of having representational thought by means of the symbolic function. At this stage, though, the child cannot perform operations in the way that I define this term. In my terminology "operations" are internalized actions which are reversible; that is, they can be performed in opposite directions. Finally, they are coordinated into overall structures, and these structures give rise to a feeling of intrinsic necessity.

The third major period starts at around the age of 7 or 8 years and is characterized by the inception of operations. Initially these operations are concrete; that is, they are used directly on objects in order to manipulate these objects. For instance, the child can classify concrete objects, or order them, or establish correspondences between them, or use numerical operations on them, or measure them from a spatial point of view. The operations remain concrete until the child is about 11 or 12 years of age. Then, at approximately this age, the fourth major period begins. This period can be characterized by formal or propositional operations. This means that the operations are no longer applied solely to the manipulation of concrete objects, but now cover hypotheses and propositions that the child can use as abstract hypotheses and from which he can reach deductions by formal or logical means.

If these four major periods do indeed exist, then we should be able to characterize them in a precise manner. What we have tried to do in the past, and what we are still trying to do, is to describe the characteristics of these stages in terms of general overall structures which become integrated. With development, the more elementary structures become incorporated into higher level structures, and these in turn are incorporated into structures of an even higher level.

Not everyone believes that it is necessary to characterize stages in terms of overall structures. For example, Freud's stages of emotional development are characterized by their dominant traits. There is the oral stage, or the anal stage, or the narcissistic or primary stage, and so forth. The different characteristics exist at all the stages, but at any particular moment one of the characteristics predominates. Freud's stages can therefore be described in terms of dominant characteristics.

Such a characterization is not, I believe, adequate for the cognitive functions. In this area we should attempt to go beyond this. If we were to remain satisfied with the notion of dominant characteristics for the cognitive functions, it would always be somewhat arbitrary as to what exactly is dominant and what is not. This is why we are trying to discover the overall structures in cognition rather than specify the dominant characteristics. This means that we are looking for total structures or systems with their own laws, systems which incorporate all their elements and whose laws cover the entire set of elements in the system. It would be these structures which become integrated with development. I shall stop here, but before ending I should like to repeat that this is an important problem, because there is no consensus as to the existence of such structures. I shall therefore try to support my views in the remainder of my address.

The existence of these overall structures raises a problem: do they in fact really exist in the mind of the subject being studied, or are they merely an invention of the psychologist who studies children or adults? The notion of overall structures presents two difficulties. First, the subject is not conscious of the existence of his cognitive structures. For example, he does not know what a seriation is, or a classification, or a relationship of correspondence. He himself has never given a thought to the nature of these overall structures. He acts, he operates, he behaves. And from this behavior we, the psychologists, detect the structures. But the structures are unconscious. They are expressed in regular forms of responses that we believe we are discovering in the subject's behavior. We also feel that if the underlying structures did not exist, we would not be able to explain such behavior. But the subject himself is not aware of these structures. He is neither a professor of psychology nor a professor of logic. He does not reflect upon the structures that he uses. He simply uses them. This, then, is the first difficulty: do the structures really exist in the subject's mind, or have we perhaps invented them?

The second difficulty is this: if we are to be convinced of the existence of these structures, we should be able to formalize them in logical terms. We then try to adapt this formalization to what we are able to observe in the child. But we can never be sure whether we have invented the formalization or whether it really is an expression of what is to be found in the mind of the child. So you see I am very much aware of the various problems involved in the notion of overall structures. Let me, however, deal with some of them by means of a simple example.

I refer here to the example of seriation. Seriation consists of the ordering of a series of sticks from the smallest one to the tallest. Bärbel Inhelder, Mimi Sinclair, and I have once again returned to this problem of seriation in our recent studies on memory, and our findings confirm the stages discovered in our earlier work. For instance, we found that during the initial stage, which we may call stage A, the youngest subjects maintain that all the sticks are of equal length. During the next stage (stage B), the subjects divide the sticks into two categories, large and small, with no ordering of the elements. At stage C, the children talk of the large ones, the middle-sized ones and the small ones. At stage D, the child constructs a series in an empirical fashion, by trial and error, but he is not able to produce immediately a faultless construction. And finally, at stage E, the child discovers a method: he chooses the largest of all the sticks and he sets this on the table, then he takes the largest of all the remaining sticks and places this beside the first stick, then the largest of the remaining ones, until he has placed all the sticks on the table. At this stage, he constructs a correct ordering without any hesitation, and this construction presupposes a reversible relation. That is to say, an element *a* is both smaller than the ones which have gone before it and larger than the ones to follow. This is a good example of what I mean by a structure.

But let us see what the logicians have to say about this problem. What is a seriation from the formal point of view? Can we discover any relationship between the logician's formalization of a seriation and the child's structure of the same notion? For the logician, a seriation is a chaining of asymmetrical, connex, and transitive relations. As far as asymmetry is concerned, this seems obvious in the present example. This means that one element is larger than another. As for connectivity, this means that all the elements are different and that there are no two alike. And lastly, there is the transitivity relationship. This means that if *A* is larger than *B* and *B* larger than *C*, then *A* is automatically larger than *C*. In the above-mentioned seriation problem, we did not see any evidence of transitivity. Is it part of the structure? Does it exist? Here we can do some separate experiments on the problem by taking three sticks of unequal length. We compare the first with the second, and then hide the first under the table. Then we compare the second with the third, and we say to the child, "You saw beforehand that the first was larger than the second, and now you can see that the second is larger than the third. What is the one under the table like compared to the third one? Is it larger, smaller, or just the same?" Experience has shown that very young children are not able to use the deductive method and are thus unable to solve the problem of transitivity. They reply, "I don't know. I haven't seem them next to each other. I need to see all three together at the same time before I can answer your question."

For the older children, however, who use the deductive method, transitivity is evident. Not only is it evident, but it also is necessary. And here we touch upon the real problem of overall structures: the problem of the appearance at a particular point in development of the feeling of necessity. Until this point, a certain occurrence was either absent or simply probable; now it becomes necessary. How can one explain the apparition of necessity from the psychological point of view? This, I feel, is the real problem of overall structures. How is it that a phenomenon which until then had been merely noted empirically, or else had been felt to be simply probable, now becomes logically necessary from the subject's point of view?

One first reply could be to say that it is an illusion. Hume, in his studies on the notion of causality, maintained that the necessary cause-effect relationship was in fact not necessary at all, but simply due to our associations of ideas or to our habits. So one could say that this feeling of necessity is simply a habit. However, the striking thing here is that the child reaches this feeling of necessity as soon as he has understood the phenomenon in question. One can sometimes witness the precise moment when he discovers this necessity. At the beginning of his reasoning, he is not at all sure of what he is stating. Then suddenly he says, "But it's obvious." In another experiment where Bärbel Inhelder was questioning a child on a problem which is not that of seriation but of recurrent reasoning, but which also involves the feeling of necessity, the child was at first very uncertain. Then suddenly he said, "Once one knows, one knows forever and ever." In other words, at one point the child automatically acquires this feeling of necessity. Where does this necessity come from?

My personal feeling is that there is only one acceptable psychological explanation: this feeling of necessity comes from the closure or completion of a structure. One could, of course, also maintain that necessity is simply an awareness of an idea which was predetermined in the mind, an innate or a priori idea. But this is not a true psychological solution, for it defies verification. Also, if this were indeed true, the feeling of necessity would appear much earlier than it actually does.

This is why I believe that the feeling of necessity is neither a subjective illusion nor an innate or a priori idea. It is an idea which is constructed at the same time as the overall structures. As soon as a structure is sufficiently complete for closure to occur or, in other words, once the internal compositions of the structure become interdependent and independent of external elements and are sufficiently numerous to allow for all types of arrangements, then the feeling of necessity manifests itself. I believe that it is this feeling of necessity which constitutes evidence of the existence of the overall structures which characterize our stages.

I do not want to describe here all the overall structures that can be found. They naturally vary according to the four major stages mentioned earlier. At the sensorimotor level we find composite actions which are performed in a step-by-step or contiguous manner, since the child is not capable of representation which would allow for more complex relationships. His compositions are simply actions which are chained to one another but which nevertheless still form some kind of structure. We find, for instance, in the organization of space, an organization of movements and of positions which mathematicians call the group of displacements. This is one example of a structure, with its characteristic of necessity. That is to say, it is possible to return to the point of departure, and this is a necessary return. Also it is possible to reach one point by a variety of different routes, and these are called detour behaviors. So already in these two types of behavior, return and detour, we see the characteristic of necessity and the existence of overall structures.

At the level of preoperational thought we find other overall structures. These are not yet operational structures in the sense that I described earlier; that is, they are not yet reversible, but they are nonetheless structures with their own laws. Take for example the notion of a function. As an example, we have a piece of string, B, which can be pulled over a spring. If you tie a weight to a segment called A, the segment A' will become shorter. When A becomes shorter, A' becomes longer; when A' becomes shorter, A becomes longer. So the lengthening of A is a function of the shortening of A'. At this point of development the child has not yet acquired conservation. If we were to ask the child if the whole string (B) were equal to the sum of the two parts (A and A'), that is, $B = A + A'$, in both cases (when the string has been pulled down with the weight or not), the child would not give the correct answer because he cannot conserve. This is an example of a function but without reversibility.

In other experiments we also find functions, as for instance in the many-to-one relationship, but this is not accompanied by the reverse relationship of one-to-many. In the one-to-many relationship, or the many-to-one, the child reaches only a partial logic; he has not yet acquired the other half of logic which would be reversibility. Other examples of structures at this level are those of qualitative identity. For example, if one pours liquid from one glass to another as in the well-known experiments on conservation, the child at this stage does not accept the conservation of quantity, but he already admits to the qualitative identity. He will say that it is the same water in both cases, but not the same quantity. Qualitative identity is far easier to achieve. All the child needs to do is to isolate the qualities, whereas for conservation the child must construct the quantities, and this is another matter.

I do not need to remind you that at the level of the concrete operations we find a great many overall structures which are much richer than those of the preoperational level and which we have called groupings. Examples are the notion of seriation mentioned previously, classification, one-to-one correspondence, and many-to-one or one-to-many correspondences. At this level quantification becomes possible as a result of the overall structures, and consequently so, too, do the notions of conservation which were lacking at the preoperational level. Even identity changes and becomes operational and additive. For example, in the conservation problem, the child will say, "It's the same quantity, because you haven't added anything or taken anything away." Nothing has been added and nothing taken away; this is an additive identity and therefore a quantitative one, and no longer simply qualitative identity as when the child says, "It's the same water. It's the same color," etc.

There is no need for me to remind you that at the level of formal or propositional operations we also find even richer structures which are a synthesis of the previous ones. For instance, we have the group of four transformations which combines into a single system the structures of inversion $(A - A = 0)$ and the structures of reciprocity $(A = B$ therefore $B = A)$. These formal structures incorporate the preceding ones and constitute the termination of the construction of overall structures which has been going on throughout the entire period of childhood. The stages are therefore characterized by successive structures which do not replace each other, but which are integrated into one another. The simplest ones become incorporated into later, more complex ones. For example, the preoperational functions, or identities, are integrated into the concrete operations; then later, these concrete operational structures become incorporated into the formal operational structures.

At this point of our study I should like to note that these two notions of stages and overall structures, which I believe are necessarily closely bound together, have a meaning which is not only a logical and formal one. Despite their formalization, these structures have essentially a biological meaning, in the sense that the order of the stages is constant and sequential. Each stage is necessary for the following one. If this were not the case, one would be in no position to talk of stages. Naturally, the ages at which different children reach the stages may vary. In some social environments the stages are accelerated, whereas in others they are more or less systematically retarded. This differential development shows that stages are not purely a question of the maturation of the nervous system but are dependent upon interaction with the social environment and with experience in general. The order, however, remains constant.

Furthermore, the accelerations or retardations raise one problem which has not yet been studied sufficiently but which will have to be considered in the future. This is the problem of the optimal speed of development. What advantages are to be gained from speeding up the stages? I am often asked the following question in this country: "Can one accelerate the stages indefinitely?" My reply is to ask: "Is there any advantage to be derived from such acceleration?" Take experiments like those of Gruber where he finds that kittens acquire the requisite reactions towards the permanent object by the age of 4 months; that is, they search for objects hidden under a screen. It takes the human baby 9 months to reach this self-same point of development. One can consequently ask whether it would be advantageous for the human baby to reach this point at 4 instead of 9 months. I do not think so, because the kitten does not go very much further. Once it reaches a certain level, it scarcely progresses beyond this point. The human baby, on the other hand, develops more slowly, but in the long run he goes much further. One must remember that the higher the zoological species the longer is its period of infancy. There is a reason for this, and it may be that there is an optimal speed of development for each species. So we return to biology.

Our stages are very similar to those described by Waddington when he speaks of necessary courses which lead to a certain result. He calls these necessary courses or channels "creodes." He also describes certain forms of equilibrium which occur when there is a deviation from the creode due to unforeseen circumstances. In this case some force acts to bring the development back to its normal course. Waddington calls this "homeorhesis." It is a dynamic equilibrium, as opposed to homeostasis which is static. And finally, Waddington stresses what he calls the "time tally." This particular notion of a time tally raises the problem of the optimal speed of the stages of development. One last point is that the stages in embryology have a sequential ordering, with each stage being necessary for the following one. It is not possible to miss a stage in development.

If this were true of psychology, then there would be a relationship or a very close analogy with embryological development. I repeat that this does not mean that everything is genetically or internally determined within a hereditary program, since accelerations or retardations can occur in mental development which appear to be of an even greater magnitude than in embryology.

The present basic problem in the question of stages is that of the passage from one stage to the next. What mechanisms are responsible for this passage? Bärbel Inhelder and her collaborators have been dealing with this specific problem in their study of the possibility of certain forms of learning. These are not the types of learning that take place as a result of repetition or of the external reinforcements as in habit learning. Rather, she has been studying the type of learning which consists of isolating the factors which we believe are active in normal development in order to show how variations in these factors can produce accelerations in certain areas of development, and, more particularly, can result in certain correlations between the various learning experiences.

But I do not wish to discuss this problem here since it is currently in the process of investigation and the results will shortly be published in a book by Inhelder and her collaborators. What I would like to do is to raise the general problem of the passage from one stage to the next. I should like to approach this problem in the following manner. Three models can be used to describe this passage from one stage to the next. First, one could maintain that the successive acquisitions which characterize the stages mentioned earlier are acquisitions which are purely and simply due to environmental pressures, to experience, or to more or less random encounters with certain aspects of the daily social and physical environment. In this case, the succession of the stages would no longer be necessary. It might be a regular succession, with some regularities being more or less emphasized or attenuated depending upon the environment, but there would be no necessary succession.

The second possibility would be that the stages are internally determined; that is, they are predetermined. The succession of stages would be somehow preformed in the hereditary equipment of each individual. This approach is a return to the conception of innate ideas, and this notion, which was not very popular some years ago, has now become fashionable again. I refer in particular to the work being carried out in psycholinguistics by Chomsky, and to work done by certain psychologists who maintain that they are able to find notions of conservation very early in life, and that these notions then deteriorate—I am not quite sure how—only to reappear eventually at a later stage in development. I would classify this second solution as one of predetermination.

And then there is a third approach which is the one to which we subscribe. This solution is difficult to prove. It is even difficult to express or to explain. But once one has understood it, it seems that it is a compelling one, although it still remains to be proved. This third solution is that the stages result in a certain number of overall structures which become necessary with development, but are not so at the beginning of life. For example, the formal structures become necessary once the child possesses the concrete operations. As soon as he can perform the concrete operations, sooner or later he will begin to coordinate reversibility by inversion with reversibility by reciprocity and hence construct the group of four transformations. Similarly, once he is able to manipulate the classifications, sooner or later he will construct a classification of all the classifications, and thus he will end up by producing the combinatorial, which is a necessary form of formal thought.

Thus stages are characterized by overall structures which become necessary but which are not so initially. Formal structures become necessary when the concrete structures are complete; concrete structures become necessary when the structures of identity, of functions, etc., are complete; and these in turn become necessary when the sensorimotor functions are complete. But nothing is given in an a priori or innate fashion; nothing is preformed or predetermined in the activity of the baby. For instance, we could search far and wide in the behavior of the baby without finding even the rudiments of the group of four transformations, or of the combinatorial. These are all constructed and the construction—this I find to be the great mystery of the stages—becomes more and more necessary with time. The necessity is at the end of development, not at the point of departure. This, then, is the model upon which we are trying to base our work and our experiments.

There are still two more remarks that I should like to add before closing. First, that the stages which I have just discussed are those of intelligence, of the development of intelligence, and more particularly of the development of the logico-mathematical operations. They refer to those operations of which the subject is, in a way, the master or the director and which he can apply at will, in such a manner as he deems suitable, to a particular group of objects. When we study other cognitive functions, things naturally become more complex and the stages may be far less evident. In the field of perception, for example, we find hardly any stages as far as the primary or field effects are concerned. We do find some semistages in the perceptual activities, but these are not nearly as well defined as the stages of intelligence.

With mental imagery, we find essentially two periods. There is one preceding the concrete operations when mental images are mainly reproductory and static. During this period children have great difficulty in representing or imagining transformations or movements. The anticipatory images which are necessary for the representation of transformations only make their appearance at the level of the concrete operations. So here we find the beginnings of a stage, but again far less evident than in the field of intelligence.

In our recent research into memory, we find three distinctions. These are: recognitive memory, which is by far the earliest type of memory to appear and which is found right at the beginning of the sensorimotor level; evocative memory, which only appears with the semiotic function from the age of two or three years onwards; and then, between the two, there is a level of reconstructive memory which is still bound up with movement, with action, but which is more than simple recognition. These are very elementary distinctions which don't go very far in the differentiation of stages.

Even in the area of intelligence, as I mentioned before, the stages which I have just described are those of the logico-mathematical operations. Because here the subject does what he wants, in a manner of speaking. For the notion of causality, on the other hand, which we are studying at present, knowledge is physical and no longer logico-mathematical, and so the resistances of the object present all sorts of new problems. Consequently the stages are far less clear. At first, we had the impression that there were very few stages in the development of the notion of causality. Now we are slowly finding some. However, we are not yet at the point of being able to describe these stages in terms of the characteristics of overall structures such as described earlier. This is the first of my two concluding remarks.

Finally, a fairly important problem for the theory of stages is that of time lags. At certain ages the child is able to solve problems in quite specific areas. But if one changes to another material or to another situation, even with a problem which seems to be closely related, lags of several months are noted, and in some cases even of 1 or 2 years. Let us take one example, the problem of inclusion. The child is given a bunch of flowers, some of which are primroses, while others are tulips, daisies, or any other flowers. If you were to ask the child, "Are all the primroses flowers?" he will reply, "Of course." If you then ask, "Are there more flowers or more primroses in this bunch?" the child, instead of comparing the primroses with all the flowers, will compare them with all the flowers which are not primroses. And he will answer, "There are more," or "There are less," or "There are the same number," depending upon the result of this comparison, as if he were not able to include the part in the whole. This is the problem of class inclusion.

This problem is solved at approximately the age of 8 years for the flowers. But Bärbel Inhelder and I have noted that if one uses animals, for example, the problem becomes more complicated. If one asks the child, "Are all sea gulls birds?" he will reply, "Of course." If you ask, "Are all the birds sea gulls?" he will reply, "Of course not. There are also blackbirds, sparrows, etc." Then if you ask, "If you look out of the window, can you tell me whether there are more sea gulls or more birds in Geneva?" the child finds this more difficult to answer than for the flowers. Why is this? Is it because one cannot make a bunch with the sea gulls as with the flowers? I do not know. But this is one example of the problem. It is possibly a poorly chosen one, but there are any number of these problems of time lags between the solution of a problem with a certain material and the solution of the same problem with another material.

I have often been reproached for not having produced a sufficiently precise theory of these time lags in the same way as one can try to produce a theory of the overall structures or of the positive characteristics of stages. But time lags are a negative characteristic which form an obstacle to the construction of the overall structures. My reply to such a reproach is merely the following: time lags are always due to an interaction between the person's structures on the one hand, and the resistances of the object on the other. The object may be flowers, which offer little resistance; one places them on the table, and one makes a bunch of them. But there are other objects which offer more resistance, as for instance the birds. One cannot put them on the table. Some resistances of objects are unpredictable. When one encounters them, one can explain them, but always after the event. It is not possible to have a general theory of these resistances.

And so, in concluding, I should like to find some sort of an excuse for this failure by a comparison with physics. Physics is a much more advanced science than psychology, a more exact science which permits mathematical theories in almost all areas. But there is one area where physicists have not yet managed to produce a general theory. This is the problem of friction. Friction is the resistance of an object when you make it move along a surface. Physicists explain the role of friction in such and such a situation, but they have not yet come up with a general theory for this phenomenon. Time lags are somewhat analogous; they are comparable to all the concrete situations where friction is involved. Some areas are manipulated with ease; others offer all sorts of resistances. This problem still remains to be solved.

As you see, I have tried to be honest in my address by pointing out the various problems and difficulties which still remain. But I repeat, I am counting especially on the work that you are going to do here in your meeting on ordinal scales to shed some light on the difficult question of stages.

Two Approaches to Intelligence: Piagetian and Psychometric

CHAPTER TWO

DAVID ELKIND
University of Rochester

Within recent years, the rapid growth of interest in the work and theory of the Swiss psychologist Jean Piaget has made imperative the consideration of his conceptions with those widely used in psychology. The need is particularly great with respect to the concept of *intelligence* which is employed both by Piaget as a developmental psychologist and by psychologists and educators whose orientation is the psychometric assessment of individual differences. Accordingly, the present paper will compare and contrast the Piagetian and psychometric conceptions of intelligence. What I plan to do is to discuss, in the first section of the paper, some of the similarities between the Piagetian and psychometric positions. Then, in the second section, some of their differences will be pointed out. Finally, in the third section, I want to consider two related practical issues regarding the modification of intelligence.

CONCEPTUAL SIMILARITIES

What struck me in preparing for this essay, and what had not really occurred to me before, were the many parallels and affinities between the psychometric or mental test approach to the problem of intelligence and the developmental approach as represented by Piaget. It brought to mind the fact that Piaget began his career as a developmental psychologist by working in Binet's laboratory where he sought to standardize some of Burt's (1962) reasoning tests on Parisian children. Indeed, Piaget's "methode clinique" is a combination of mental test and clinical interview procedures which consists in the use of a standardized situation as a starting point for a flexible interrogation. The affinities, however, between the Piagetian and psychometric approaches to intelligence run more deeply than that. In this section I want to discuss such affinities: the acceptance of genetic and maturational determination in intelligence, the use of nonexperimental methodologies, and the conception of intelligence as being essentially rational.

Genetic Determination

Implicit and often explicit in both the psychometric and Piagetian positions is the assumption that mental ability is, in part at least, genetically determined. With respect to the psychometric position, it assumes that at least some of the variance in intelligence test performance is attributable to variance in genetic endowment (Burt and Howard, 1957; Jensen, 1969). Piaget (1967a) also acknowledges the importance of genetic factors for intellectual ability but qualifies this by pointing out that what may be genetic in one generation may not always have been so and could be the partial result of prior environmental influences. So, for Piaget, as for the biologist Waddington (1962a) there is a certain relativity with respect to what is attributed to genetic endowment, because what is genetic now may not always have been genetic in the past.

One consequence of their joint acceptance of the partial genetic determination of intellectual ability, is that both psychometricians and Piaget recognize the importance of maturation in human development. To illustrate their communality in this regard, consider these two passages, one written by Harold Jones in 1954 and the other by Piaget in 1967:

> Dubnoff's work, together with other related studies, may lead to the speculative suggestion that between natio-racial groups, as within a given group, a slight tendency exists for early precocity to be associated with a slower mental growth at later ages and perhaps with a lower average intelligence level at maturity. A parallel situation may be noted when we compare different animal species; among the primates, for example, the maturity of performance at a given age in infancy can be used inversely to predict the general level of adaptive ability that will be attained at the end of the growth span (Jones, 1954, p. 637).

Piaget writes:

> We know that it takes 9 to 12 months before babies develop the notion that an object is still there even when a screen is placed in front of it. Now kittens go through the same substages but they do it in 3 months—so they are 6 months ahead of the babies. Is this an advantage or isn't it? We can certainly see our answer in one sense. The kitten is not going to go much further. The child has taken longer, but he is capable of going further so it seems to me the 9 months were not for nothing (Piaget, 1967b).

Nonexperimental Methodology

In addition to their shared genetic or maturational emphasis, the Piagetian and psychometric approaches to intelligence have still another characteristic in common. This common feature is their failure, for the most part, to use the experimental method in the strict sense of that term. It seems fair to say that most of the studies which attempt to get at the determinants of test intelligence are correlational in nature. By and large, such studies attempt to relate the test scores of parents and their children, of twins or adopted children and their parents, or of the same children tested at different points in time, and so on. Only in rare instances such as the Skeels (1966) study is an attempt made to modify intelligence by active intervention and with the utilization of a control group which does not receive the experimental treatment. While experimental work on human intelligence might well be desirable, such research often raises serious moral and ethical questions.

Piaget, for his part, has not employed the experimental method simply because it was not appropriate for the problems he wished to study. In every science there is a natural history stage of enquiry during which relevant phenomena must be carefully observed and classified. American psychology has often tried to bypass this stage in its headlong rush to become an experimental science. In his studies Piaget has revealed a wide range of hitherto unknown and unsuspected facts about children's thinking, which have in America now become the starting points for a great deal of experimental investigation. What is often forgotten, when Piaget is criticized for not using the experimental method, is that such a method would not have revealed the wealth of phenomena which experimental investigators are now so busy studying.

Rationality as the Definition of Intelligence

There is a third and final communality between the mental test and Piagetian approaches to intelligence which should be mentioned. This communality resides in what these two positions regard as the nature or essence of intelligence. While there is considerable variability among psychometricians in this regard, many agree in general with the position taken by Jensen (1969). Jensen argues that the g factor which is present in all tests of mental ability appears in its purest forms on tests of generalization and abstraction. Spearman (1923) called these activities the eduction of relations (A is greater than B, B is greater than C, so A is in what relation to C?) and of correlates (Complete the series A AB ABC). While intelligence tests contain measures of many different types of mental abilities, including language and perceptual skills, the psychometric approach holds that the most central feature of human intelligence is its rationality, or, as Wechsler put it: "Intelligence is the aggregate or global capacity of the individual to act purposefully, to think rationally, and to deal effectively with his environment" (Wechsler, 1944, p. 3).

For Piaget, too, the essence of intelligence lies in the individual's reasoning capacities. Piaget, however, is more specific in his description of these abilities and defines them in terms of mental operations which have the properties of mathematical groupings in general and the property of reversibility in particular. An operational grouping is present when in the course of any mental activity one can always get back to the starting point. For example, if the class *boys* and the class *girls* are mentally combined to form the class *children,* it is always possible to recapture the subclass by subtraction. That is to say, the class of children minus the class of boys equals the class of girls. Put differently, the operation of subtraction can be used to undo the operation of addition so that each of the combined classes can be retrieved. Verbal material learned by heart is, however, not rationally organized, as is illustrated by the fact that no matter how well a passage is learned, it is impossible, without additional effort, to say it backwards. If an operational system were involved, having learned the passage forward would automatically imply the ability to say it backwards. In Piaget's view, neither perception nor language is truly rational since neither one shows complete reversibility. So while perception and language play an important part in intellectual activity, they do not epitomize that activity.

The psychometric and Piagetian approaches to intelligence thus agree on its genetic determination (at least in part), on the use of nonexperimental methodology, and upon the essentially rational nature of mental ability. After this look at their commonalities, it is perhaps time to look at their differences.

CONCEPTUAL DIFFERENCES
Despite the communalities noted above, the psychometric and developmental approaches to intelligence also differ in certain respects. These differences, however, derive from the unique ways in which the psychometricians and Piaget approach and view intelligence and not from any fundamental disagreements regarding the nature of intelligence itself. In other words, the differences are due to the fact that the two approaches are interested in assessing and describing different facets of intelligent behavior. Accordingly the differences arise with respect to: (1) the type of genetic causality they presuppose; (2) the description of mental growth they provide; and (3) the contributions of nature and nurture which they assess.

Genetic Causality
Although the Piagetian and psychometric approaches to intelligence agree on the importance of genetic determination, at least in part, of human mental ability,

each approach emphasizes a somewhat different mode of genetic determination or causality. In order to make these differences clear, it is necessary to recall some of the basic features of evolutionary theory upon which all modern conceptions of intelligence are based.

Within the Darwinian conception of evolution there are two major phenomena that have to be taken into account: within-species variability and natural selection. For any given species of animal or plant, one can observe a range of variations in such features as color, shape, and size. Among a flock of robins, to illustrate, one can see that some adult birds differ in size, in richness of breast coloration, and that some even manifest slight variations in head and wing conformation. Similar variations can be observed among a group of collies, Persian cats, and even among tomato plants in the garden. This within-species variability, we know today, is due to the chance pairings of parental genes and gene complexes which occur because each parent contributes only half its genetic complement to its offspring. Variations within a given species at a given time are, therefore, primarily due to chance factors, namely, the random genetic assortments provided by the parent generation. One determinant of variability among animals and plants is then, simply, chance.

Now in the psychometric conception of intelligence, this random type of variation is just what is presupposed. Test intelligence, it is assumed, is randomly distributed in a given population at a given time, and such distribution should resemble the bell-shaped curve of the normal probability function. Measurement of human abilities does in fact reveal a tendency for such measurements to fall into normal distributions. In addition, evidence such as "regression toward the mean" (children of exceptionally bright or dull parents tend to be less bright and less dull than their parents) is also characteristic of genetic traits which are randomly determined. In short, when the psychometrician speaks of genetic determination, he is speaking of the chance gene combinations which produce a "normal" bell-shaped distribution of abilities within a given population.

Obviously this description of genetic determination is extremely oversimplified; we know that a test score is a phenotype which is determined by many different factors, not all of which are genetic. Jensen, for example, breaks down the variance of test intelligence into a large number of components such as genotypic variation, environment, environment-genotype interaction, epistasis, error-of-measurement variance and so on. With the exception, perhaps, of the selective mating variable, however, all of these factors can again be assumed to operate in a random manner, so that one might say that the chance distribution of observed test scores is the product of many underlying chance distributions. That the psychometric approach does in general presuppose a random distribution is also shown by the fact that the criterion of a true change in intellectual ability is the demonstration that such a change could *not* be attributed to chance factors.

That variability within a species is in part determined by chance gene and gene-complex assortments has, of course, been demonstrated by Mendel and all of the research which has derived from his theory of genetics. There are, however, other forms of organismic variability which cannot be attributed to chance. Natural selection, the other component of evolution, is never random but always moves in the direction of improved adaptation to the milieu. To illustrate, over the past hundred years there has been a gradual predominance of dark over light-colored moths in the industrial sections of England. Kettlewell (1955) demonstrated the survival value of dark coloration by showing that light moths placed on soot-darkened bark were more readily eaten by insectivorous birds than were similarly placed dark moths. When variations across generations are considered, the variations are not random but rather show a clear-cut direction.

The same holds true within the course of individual development. In the case of individual growth, however, the direction of progress is not determined by mating practices but rather by biochemical mechanisms which are only now in the process of being understood. That these biochemical agents determine the direction of development, however, cannot be doubted. As Waddington (1962b) points out, animals consist of a limited variety of cells such as nerve cells, muscle cells and so on. Similarly, the organs of the body are also distinct from one another in form, composition, and function. What direction particular cells will take as the egg matures will depend upon the action of chemical agents which Speman (discussed in Bertalaffny, 1962) called *organizers* with definite loci in the cell material called *organization centers*. It is the organizer which determines whether particular cells will become nerve, muscle, or organ tissue. Individual development, therefore, is not determined by random factors but rather by biochemical organizers which specify the nature and direction of organismic differentiation.

Now when Piaget speaks of the genetic determination of intelligence, he has in mind not the random factors which determine gene combinations but rather the nonrandom action of biochemical organizers and organization centers. Indeed, this is the kind of determination which Piaget assumes when he argues that the *sequence* in which the child attains the successive components of a concept or in which he acquires systems of mental operations is invariant. In the formation of body organs the order of differentiation is fixed because each new phase of differentiation produces the organizer for the next stage. In Piaget's view this is equally valid for the growth of cognitive structures, because the preceding cognitive structures, say the concrete operations of childhood, are a necessary prerequisite for the elaboration of the more complex formal operational structures of adolescence. For Piaget, then, genetic determination means that there are factors which give development a definite nonrandom direction.

In pointing out that the Piagetian and psychometric approaches to intelligence postulate different forms of genetic determinism, I want to reiterate that these two positions do not contradict each other. The mental test approach to intelligence is concerned with interindividual differences in ability and these are, insofar as we know, largely randomly determined. Piaget, in contrast, is concerned with the intraindividual changes which occur in the course of development, and these, to the best of our knowledge, are not random but rather have a direction given them by specific organizing mechanisms. Accordingly, and this is the genius of evolution, human intelligence manifests both determinism *and* freedom.

The Course of Mental Growth

Let us look now at a somewhat different issue, the agewise course of mental growth. Here again we find a difference in perspective rather than a contradiction in conception as between the two positions. In psychometric terms, the course of mental growth is plotted as a curve which measures the amount of intelligence at some criterion age that can be predicted at any preceding age. As Bloom (1964) has pointed out, when age 17 is taken as the criterion age, some 50 percent of the total IQ at that age can be predicted at age 4, and an additional 30 percent can be predicted from ages 4 to 8. Based on correlational data of this sort, curves of mental growth appear to rise rapidly in early childhood and taper off to a plateau in late adolescence. Such curves, it must be noted to avoid a frequent misinterpretation, say nothing as to the *amount* or *quality* of knowledge at given age levels (see Jensen, 1969).

From the mental test perspective, therefore, intellectual growth is pretty much a statistical concept derived from correlations of test scores obtained at different age levels on the same individuals in the course of longitudinal studies. Such curves can be interpreted as reflecting the rate of mental growth but say nothing as to the nature of what is developing. Indeed, if intelligence is defined in the narrow sense of the abilities to generalize and abstract, then any qualitative differences in these abilities will necessarily be obscured by the curve of mental growth which suggests merely a quantitative increase in mental ability with increasing age.

Looked at from the standpoint of Piagetian psychology, however, mental growth involves the formation of new mental structures and consequently the emergence of new mental abilities. The child, to illustrate, cannot deal with propositional logic of the following sort: "Helen is shorter than Alice and taller than Ethel; who is the tallest of the three?" (Glick and Wapner, 1968), nor can children grasp the metaphorical connotations of satirical cartoons or proverbs (Shaffer, 1930). Adolescents, in contrast, have no trouble with either propositional logic or with metaphor. In the Piagetian view, therefore, mental growth is not a quantitative but rather a qualitative affair and presupposes significant differences between the thinking of children and adolescents as well as between preschool and school-age children.

These qualitative differences are, as a matter of fact, built into the items of mental tests but are masked by the assignment of point scores to successes and failures. On the Wechsler Intelligence Scale for Children, some of the subtests recognize qualitatively different responses only by assigning them additional points (Wechsler, 1949). A child, for example, who says that a peach and a plum are alike because "they both have pits" is given a single point; whereas a child who says "they are both fruit" is given two points. On other subtests, such as the arithmetic subtest, there is no point differential for success on problems which patently require different levels of mental ability. For example, correct answers to the following two problems are both given only a single point: (1) "If I cut an apple in half, how many pieces will I have?" (2) "Smith and Brown start a card game with $27 each. They agree that at the end of each deal the loser shall pay the winner one-third on what he (the loser) then has in his possession. Smith wins the first three deals. How much does Brown have at the beginning of the fourth deal?" Clearly, the items on any given subtest can tap quite different mental processes, but these qualitative differences are obscured by assigning equivalent point scores to the various items regardless of the mental processes involved.

This is not to say that Piaget is right and that the mental test approach is wrong, or vice versa. The quantitative evaluation of mental growth is necessary and has considerable practical value in predicting school success. The qualitative approach is also of value, particularly when diagnosis of learning difficulties and educational remediation are in question. Which approach to mental growth one adopts will depend upon the purposes of the investigation. The only danger in the quantitative approach is to assume that, because subtests include items of the same general type and are scored with equal numerical weights, they therefore assess only quantitative differences in the ability in question.

The Contributions of Nature and Nurture to Intelligence

Still a third way in which the psychometric and Piagetian views of intelligence differ has to do with the manner in which they treat the contributions of nature and nurture to intellectual ability. In the psychometric approach this contribution is treated substantively with regard to the amount of variance in intellectual ability that can be attributed to nature and nurture respectively. Piaget, on the contrary, treats these contributions functionally with respect to the regulative role played by the environment or inner forces for any given mental activity. Both positions now need to be described in somewhat more detail.

The psychometric approach is substantive (and static) in the sense that it regards intelligence as capable of being measured and holds that such measures can be used to assess the extent to which nature and nurture contribute to intellectual ability. In the discussion of genetic causality the various components into which test scores could be analyzed were briefly noted. We are indebted to writers such as Burt and Howard (1957) and Jensen (1969) for making clear the many and complex determinants into which test performance can be analyzed. Without wishing to minimize these other determinants, the needs of the present discussion will be served if we consider only how the psychometric approach arrives at the contribution of the hereditary and environmental factors.

As Jensen (1969) makes clear, *heritability* is the proportion of variability among observed or phenotypic intelligence (test scores) that can be attributed to genotypic variations. Estimates of heritability are obtained from correlational data for subjects with known kinship relations such as parents and children, siblings, and identical twins. The contribution of the environment is arrived at somewhat differently. Variability in intelligence test scores attributable to the environment is estimated from that variability which cannot be attributed to any other factors. It is, in fact, the residual variance, that which is left after all the other factors contributing to intelligence test performance have been accounted for. For the psychometrician, then, nature and nurture are regarded as substantive and static and their contributions are assessed quantitatively with the aid of statistical procedures.

When we turn to the work of Piaget, however, we encounter quite a different conception of the contributions of nature and nurture. In Piaget's view, these contributions must be conceived functionally and dynamically with respect to their regulatory control over various mental activities. In this regard Piaget's views are not unlike those of David Rapaport (1958) who spoke of "the relative autonomy of the ego," a conception which may help to introduce Piaget's somewhat more difficult formulation. Rapaport argued that we are endowed with certain mental processes, such as perception, that are responsive to the environment and so tend to guarantee or ensure a certain independence of the mind from the domination of instinctual drives. Other mental processes, such as fantasy, are most responsive to internal forces and these in turn guarantee a certain independence of the mind from the domination of the environment. The presence and activity of both types of processes thus ensure that the mind is enslaved neither by the environment nor by the drives but retains a "relative autonomy" from both.

Piaget's view (1967c) is roughly similar. He argues that intelligence is an extension of biological adaptation which, in lieu of the instinctive adaptations in animals, permits relatively autonomous adaptations which bear the stamp not only of our genetic endowment but also of our physical and social experience. On the plane of intelligence, what we inherit are the processes of assimilation (processes responsive to inner promptings) and of accommodation (processes responsive to environmental intrusions). Assimilative processes guarantee that intelligence will not be limited to passively copying reality while accommodative processes insure that intelligence will not construct representations of reality which have no correspondence with the real world. To make this functional conception of the contributions of nature and nurture to intelligence concrete, let us consider several different mental abilities which are differently regulated by internal and external forces.

If we look at imitation (Piaget, 1951) it is clear that it is largely accommodative in the sense that it is most responsive to environmental influence and is relatively independent of inner forces. The vocal mimic, for example, is expert to the extent that he can capture the pitch, timbre, and inflections of his model's voice and to the extent to which he can supress those aspects of his own speech which differ from the model's. Play, in contrast, is largely assimilative in that it is most responsive to inner needs and is relatively independent of environmental influence. The child who uses a stick alternatively as a gun, as an airplane, and as a boat has responded to the object largely in terms of his own inner needs and with a relative disregard of its real properties.

Between the two extremes of imitation and play is intelligence, which manifests a balance or equilibrium between assimilative and accommodative activities and is thus relatively autonomous both of inner *and* outer forces. To illustrate, suppose we deduce, from the premise that Helen is taller than Jane and that Jane is taller than Mary, that Helen is the tallest of three girls. We have in so doing attained a new bit of knowledge, an adaptation, but without altering the elements involved (assimilation without transformation of the objects) and without modifying the reasoning processes (accommodation without alteration of mental structures). Reason, or intelligence, is thus the only system of mental processes which guarantees that the mind and the environment will each retain their integrity in the course of their interaction.

Accordingly, for Piaget as for Rapaport, the question is not how much nature and nurture contribute to mental ability, but rather the *extent to which various mental processes are relatively autonomous from environmental and instinctual influence.* Such a conception is functional and dynamic, rather than substantive and static, because it deals with the regulatory activity of nature and nurture upon various mental processes. Those processes which show the greatest independence from environmental *and* internal regulation, the rational processes, are the most advanced of all human abilities. It is for this reason that Piaget reserves for them, and for them alone, the term "intelligence."

In summary then, the psychometric and Piagetian approaches to intelligence differ with respect to: (1) the type of genetic causality which they presuppose; (2) their conceptions of the course of mental growth; and finally (3) the manner in which they conceive the contributions of nature and nurture to intellectual ability. In closing this section on the differences between the two positions I want to say again that the differences arise from differences in perspective and emphasis and are not contradictory but rather complementary. Both the psychometric and the Piagetian approaches to the conceptualization of human intelligence provide useful starting points for the assessment and interpretation of human mental abilities. Let us turn now to a couple of practical issues related to the modification and stimulation of mental abilities.

PRACTICAL ISSUES

In this section I would like to discuss three practical issues related to the modification, stimulation, and assessment of intellectual abilities which seem to involve some misinterpretation of the Piagetian position. First, Piaget's insistence upon the qualitative differences between the modes of thinking at different age levels has been wrongly taken to suggest the need for preschool instruction in order to move children into the concrete operational stage more quickly. Secondly, Piaget's emphasis upon the non-chance or self-directed nature of mental development has mistakenly been taken as justification for the use of methods such as "discovery learning" which supposedly stimulate the child's intrinsic motivations to learn. Finally, Piaget's use of the term "intelligence" to describe what his tasks assess has led to some premature efforts to psychometrize Piagetian materials. I would like, therefore, to try to clarify below what seems to me to be the implications of Piaget's conception of intelligence for preschool instruction, motivation, and mental growth and for the assessment of intelligence.

Preschool Instruction

There appears to be increasing pressure these days in both the popular and academic literature for beginning academic instruction in early childhood, i.e., from 3 to 5 years. Bruner's famous statement that "We begin with the hypothesis that any subject can be taught effectively in some intellectually honest form to any child at any stage of development" (Bruner, 1962), as well as the work of Hunt (1961), of Bloom (1964), of O. K. Moore (1961), of Fowler (1968), and of Skeels (1966) have all been used in the advocacy of preschool instruction. Indeed Piaget and Montessori have been invoked in this connection as well. The argument essentially is that the preschool period is critical for intellectual growth and that if we leave this period devoted to fun and games, we are lowering the individual's ultimate level of intellectual attainment. Parental anxiety and pressure in this regard has been so aroused that legislation has been passed or is pending in states such as New York, Massachusetts, and California for the provision of free preschool education for all parents who wish it for their children.

What is the evidence that preschool instruction has lasting effects upon mental growth and development? The answer is, in brief, that there is none. To prove the point one needs longitudinal data on adults who did not have preschool instruction but who were equal in every other regard to children receiving such instruction. With the exception of the Montessori schools, however, the preschool instruction programs have not been in existence long enough to provide any evidence on the lastingness of their effects. Indeed, most of the earlier work on the effects of nursery school education (see Goodenough, 1940 and Jones, 1954 for reviews of this literature) has shown that significant positive effects are hard to demonstrate when adequate experimental controls are employed. It is interesting that no one, to my knowledge, has done a longitudinal study of adult Montessori graduates. Have they done better in life than children from comparable backgrounds not so trained? In any case, it is such unavailable longitudinal data that is crucial to the proposition that the preschool period is a critical one for intellectual development.

I am sure that someone will object at this point that studies of mental growth such as those of Bloom (1964) suggest that half the individual's intellectual potential is realized by age 4. Does this not mean that the preschool period is important for intellectual growth and that interventions during this period will have lasting effects? Not necessarily, if we look at the facts in a somewhat different way. Bloom writes, "Both types of data suggest that in terms of intelligence measured at age 17, about 50 percent of the development takes place between conception and age 4, about 30 percent between ages 4 and 8, and about 20 percent between ages 8 and 17" (Bloom, 1964). Now an equally feasible implication of this statement is quite in contradiction to that of preschool instruction. If, it might be argued, the child has only 50 percent of his intellectual ability at age 4 but 80 percent at age 8, why not delay his education 3 years so that he can more fully profit from instruction? With 80 percent of his ability he is likely to learn more quickly and efficiently and is not as likely to learn in ways that he will need to unlearn later. That is to say, without stretching the facts, it is possible to interpret the Bloom statement as implying that instruction should *not* be introduced into the preschool program.

Not only is there no clear cut longitudinal data to support the claims of the lastingness of preschool instruction, there is evidence in the opposite direction. The work cited by Jones (1954) and by Piaget (1967b) in the quotations given earlier in this paper are cases in point. This evidence together with more recent data reported in Jensen's paper suggest a negative correlation between early physical maturation and later intellectual attainments. Animals are capable of achieving early some skills (a dog or a chimp will be housebroken before a child is toilet trained) but perhaps at the expense of not being able to attain other skills at all. This data suggests the hypothesis that *the longer we delay formal instruction, up to certain limits, the greater the period of plasticity and the higher the ultimate level of achievement.* There is at least as much evidence and theory in support of this hypothesis as there is in favor of the early instruction proposition. Certainly, from the Piagetian perspective there are "optimal periods" for the growth of particular mental structures which cannot be rushed.

Please understand, I am not arguing against the benefits of preschool enrichment for children. Even preschool instruction may be of value for those disadvantaged children who do not benefit from what Strodtbeck (1967) called the "hidden curriculum of the middle-class home." What I am arguing is that there is no evidence for the *long-term effects* of either preschool instruction or enrichment. Nursery school experience most assuredly has immediate value for the child to the extent that it helps him to appreciate and enjoy his immediate world to the full and to better prepare him for future social and intellectual activities. Everyone, for example, recognizes the value of a vacation without expecting that it will produce any permanent alterations. Isn't it enough that we lighten the burdens of childhood for even a brief period each day without demanding at the same time that we produce permanent results? The contributions of the nursery school, no less than that of the vacation, do not have to be long lived to be of value.

In closing the discussion, I would like to emphasize another side to this issue of preschool instruction. This is the consideration that the emphasis on preschool education has obscured the fact that it is in reality the elementary school years that are crucial to later academic achievement. It is during these years that the child learns the basic tool subjects, acquires his conception of himself as a student, and develops his attitudes towards formal education. In this connection it might be well to quote a less publicized finding of Bloom's (1964) study:

> We may conclude from our results on general achievement, reading comprehension, and vocabulary development, that by age 9 (grade 3) at least 50% of the general achievement pattern at age 18 (grade 12) has been developed whereas at least 75% of the pattern has been developed by age 13 (grade 7) (Bloom, 1964, p. 105).

With respect to the intellectual operations of concern to Piaget, similar trends appear to hold true. While children all over the world and across wide ranges of cultural and socioeconomic conditions appear to attain concrete operations at about the age of 6 or 7 (Goodnow, 1969), the attainment and use of formal operations in adolescence, in contrast, appear to be much more subject to socioculturally determined factors such as sex roles and symbolic proficiency (Elkind, 1961; Elkind, Barocas and Rosenthal, 1968; Goodnow and Bethon, 1966). Apparently, therefore, environmental variation during the elementary school period is more significant for later intellectual attainments of the Piagetian variety. In short, there is not much justification for making the preschool the scapegoat for our failures in elementary education. Like it or not, the years from 6 to 12 are still the crucial ones with respect to later academic achievement.

Motivation and Intellectual Growth

In recent years there has been an increasing recognition among psychologists such as Berlyne (1965), Hunt (1965), and White (1959), that certain mental activities can be self-rewarding and do not have to be externally reinforced. European writers such as Piaget (1954) and Montessori (1964) long ago recognized the existence of this "intrinsic motivation" (to use Hunt's apt phrase), and Montessori in particular gave incomparable descriptions of children who suddenly discover they can read and proceed to read everything in sight. Piaget (1967d) too, has argued that needs and interests are simply another aspect of all cognitive activities.

Educators, however, in their efforts to capitalize upon this intrinsic motivation seem to have missed the point of what Montessori and Piaget had in mind. To maximize intrinsic motivation and to accelerate mental growth we have recently had an emphasis upon "learning by discovery" and upon "interesting reading materials" and so on. These approaches miss the point because they assume that intrinsic motivation can be built into materials and procedures which will in turn maximize mental growth. But as Piaget and Montessori pointed out (Elkind, 1967) intrinsic motivation resides in the child and not in methods and procedures. It is the child who must, at any given point in time, choose the method of learning and the materials that are reinforcing *to him*. Without the opportunity for student choice and the provision of large blocks of time, in which the child can totally engross himself in an activity, the values of intrinsic motivation will not be realized.

Indeed, I am very much afraid that by the time most children have reached the third or fourth grade a good deal of their intrinsic motivation for learning has been stifled. This is because spontaneous interest follows only the timetable of the child's own growth schedule. We can all remember, I am sure, those periods when we were so totally immersed in an activity that we forgot time, food, and rest. During such periods we are at our creative and productive best and afterwards the feeling of exhaustion is coupled with a deep sense of accomplishment. In the school, however, we do not permit children to become totally engrossed in an activity but rather shuttle them from activity to activity on the hour or half-hour. The result is what might be called *intellectually burned children*. Just as the burned child shuns the fire so the intellectually burned child shies away from total intellectual involvement.

How is this condition produced? In clinical practice we often see children (and adults) who are unwilling to form any emotional attachment. In the history of such children one always finds a series of broken relationships due to a wide variety of causes including the death of parents or the forced separation from them. Such children have learned that every time they have reached out and become emotionally involved, rejection, hurt, and misery were the result. Consequently they prefer not to get involved any more because the pain and anguish of still another broken relationship is just too high a price to pay for an emotional attachment. The intellectually burned child is in somewhat the same position. He refuses to become totally involved in intellectual activities because the repeated frustration of being interrupted in the middle is just too much to bear. Our lockstep curricula, 30 minutes for this and an hour for that, have the consequence, I suspect, of producing intellectually burned children who shun the fire of intense mental involvement.

Accordingly, the educational practice which would best foster intrinsically motivated children in the Piagetian and Montessori sense would be the provision of "interest areas" where children could go on their own and for long periods of time. Only when the child can choose an activity and persist at it until he is satisfied can we speak of truly intrinsically motivated behavior. Where such interest areas and time provisions have been made, as in the World of Inquiry School in Rochester, New York, the results are impressive indeed.

The Assessment of Intelligence

As interest in Piaget's work has grown, there has been a corresponding interest in psychometrizing the tasks which he has introduced. Indeed, attempts are currently under way to build scales and intelligence tests with the Piagetian tasks. The idea is attractive because the Piagetian tasks are so much richer than traditional test items in the behavioral data they provide. But, as I have tried to demonstrate in the previous section, the psychometric and Piagetian perspectives with respect to intelligence differ in important ways and tend to complement one another. The question is, therefore, what is to be gained by psychometrizing the Piagetian tasks, and, equally important, what might be lost?

Before attempting to answer this question, it is important to recall the different origins of the mental test and the Piagetian tasks. Intelligence tests and intelligence testing grew out of pressing educational, clinical, and research needs which became evident at the beginning of this century (Goodenough, 1949). From the very first, therefore, mental tests were practical tools whose use could be justified on the basis of the fact that they worked and did the job they were supposed to do. Piaget's tasks, in contrast, were designed to test his hypotheses regarding how the child attains certain concepts. In the case of the Piagetian tasks, therefore, their justification lay in whether or not they revealed developmental trends in the kinds of concepts about which Piaget was concerned.

It is important to keep this difference regarding the origins of mental tests and Piagetian tasks in mind when considering the applicability of Piagetian tasks to practical ends. We can put the question more directly and ask whether Piagetian tasks, converted to a standardized and reliable scale, would serve us better than our existing intelligence, achievement, or clinical tests. I do not believe that this is the case, at least at present, and want to detail my reasons for this belief below. Let us then consider, in turn, the applicability of a Piagetian scale in the assessment of general intelligence, of academic achievement, and of clinical syndromes.

GENERAL INTELLIGENCE   The major use of general intelligence tests such as the Binet (Terman and Merrill, 1960) or the Wechsler Scales (1944, 1949) is to rank individuals of the same age as to their relative brightness. Even though, as I mentioned earlier, Piaget and psychometricians conceive intelligence as essentially rational, psychometricians conceive intelligence more broadly than Piaget. Most general intelligence tests contain measures of language ability, of rote memory, and of perceptual-motor coordination as well as of reasoning ability. Traditional intelligence tests thus sample a much wider range of human abilities than do the Piagetian tasks, which assess primarily reasoning ability. So, while there is no question that a scale of Piagetian tasks could be used to differentiate among individuals, it is questionable whether such a scale would be as useful as one which provides a broader profile of individual performance.

EDUCATIONAL ACHIEVEMENT   Tests of educational achievement are generally geared to the curricula which is taught in the schools. By and large they assess, with some fidelity, the child's progress in academic subjects. The Piagetian tasks, in contrast, assess those concepts that the child has learned more or less on his own and without the benefit of direct instruction. A child's performance on a battery of Piagetian tasks would, therefore, be of little practical value to teachers and school administrators at the present time. Even if she were given the results of the child's performance on Piagetian tasks, the teacher would not know what to do with the information. A great deal of curriculum and other work needs to be done before a child's performance on Piagetian tasks will have relevance for teachers and parents concerned with the child's academic achievement.

CLINICAL PRACTICE   Like it or not, most clinical diagnosis in psychiatry and clinical psychology is based on a Freudian model and Freudian concepts. Clinicians are accustomed to interpreting both objective and projective tests in terms of Freudian conceptions of personality. The clinician, like the teacher, is simply not prepared to use the information given by the Piagetian tests because it is based on an entirely different model and framework. This is not to say that Piagetian tests cannot be used in the clinic, for both Inhelder (1968) and E. J. Anthony (1956a) have shown how valuable the tests can be for the clinician. Both Inhelder and Anthony, however, had to translate clinical problems into cognitive conceptions consonant with the Piagetian scheme of things. Not many clinicians are prepared to do that.

In summary, then, I cannot see, at the present time at least, much point in substituting a scale of Piagetian tasks for intelligence, achievement, or clinical tests that are already in use. A great deal of theoretical and empirical work needs to be done before the information provided by Piagetian tasks will be relevant to laymen, educators, and clinicians. That is to say, until educators and clinicians come to see their problems in cognitive developmental terms, a subject's performance on a scale of Piagetian tasks will have little practical value for them. And, if a test has no practical value, it will not be used.

In summary, then, the Piagetian conception of intelligence provides no real support for those who advocate formal preschool instruction, or for those who suggest that methods and materials in and of themselves will arouse intrinsic motivation, or for those who wish to psychometrize Piagetian tasks for practical educational or clinical purposes. As I tried to show, there is really no evidence as yet for the lastingness of preschool instruction. Likewise intrinsic motivation seems best stimulated by allowing the child to engage in the activity of his choice for unbroken periods of time. Finally, while Piagetian scales could be constructed, their practical usefulness will be dependent upon rather wide ranging changes in orientations of teachers and clinicians. In short, if we really want to use Piaget's conception of intelligence for educational purposes, it will not pay to blink at the facts whether these have to do with the effects of preschool instruction, the nature of intrinsic motivation, or the practicality of Piagetian scales of intelligence.

Comments on Elkind's Paper by Read Tuddenham
University of California, Berkeley

A discussant is often cast in the role of critic. I find this role uncongenial, indeed impossible, because I am in almost total agreement with Elkind's position. As a differential psychologist, I've probably been a little defensive about being concerned with individual differences; a concern which some of the academic colleagues who share my interest in Piaget, but from a normative point of view, tend to regard as not really very fundamental. I've tried in other contexts to point out that the individual is, if not more fundamental, at least more real than the abstracted group average. Nevertheless, I am grateful that Elkind has so eloquently shown that psychometric approaches—i.e., differential psychological approaches—need not be antagonistic to the developmental approach of Piaget, and are in fact complementary to it.

I've sometimes thought that those who focus on the smooth regularity of group means (which tend to foster theory building) and those who are attracted by individual variations (which tend to elude theoretical formulation) are separated by quasireligious differences, like Swift's Big Endians and Little Endians. Here in California where, as you know, it's a standing national joke that our weather is usually unusual, we are daily reminded of the importance of variability as contrasted with the central tendency. Here it can rain for 3 weeks at a stretch or be foggy a month at a time, in spite of the cumulative data that make our weather look so attractive when only averages are taken into account.

Listening to Piaget yesterday, however, I realized that psychometrists have been trying to make discriminations *within* the broad stages that have interested Piaget. *Within* a given stage, we fail to discover smooth ordinal scales, except with respect to particular content domains. Instead, we find "decalages," or as a statistician would say, relative independence of different cognitive tasks. I suspect the reason psychometrists have been notably unsuccessful in producing strictly ordinal scales of general intelligence is because they are concerned with differentiating successive age levels which fall within a single Piagetian stage. At these more closely spaced age levels, the findings fail to demonstrate the invariant sequence in all individuals which Piaget reports for his broader stages.

Some specific points about Elkind's paper which interested me very much:

He remarked that there is a certain relativity with respect to what is attributable to environment and what to genetic endowment, because what is genetic in one generation could in earlier generations have been the partial results of environmental influences. Vandenberg and many others have pointed out the relativity of nature and nurture and the insufficiency of the old attempts to divide up variance once and for all into an heredity component and an environmental component, as for example, in the study by Barbara Burks (1928) which purported to show that 80 percent of the variability in IQ is hereditary. It should have been obvious that such partitioning of variance is specific to a given population. Within pairs of identical twins, for example, all variability is environmental, whereas among foster children reared in the same family, most variability is probably genetic. But Elkind seems to be talking about a different sort of relativity. I wonder if his views imply a Lamarckian position, and propose to ask him.

Next, I'd like to add my voice to Elkind's in congratulating Piaget for not attempting to short circuit the "natural history" stage of psychological inquiry. The premature theorizing and premature experimentation which clog our journals are the direct consequence of an attempt to accelerate the scientific maturation of psychology. And like other attempts at acceleration, it seems to be foredoomed to failure.

Elkind's belief that Piagetian tests are unlikely to prove more useful than conventional IQ measures for ordinary purposes anticipates my own conclusion (see Chapter 4). Some of us have nevertheless devoted considerable effort to converting some of Piaget's experiments into test items meeting psychometric criteria. We have had purposes other than ordinary IQ classification in mind.

First, such tests have a contribution to make to theory. For example, Piaget's practice of using different children for different experiments leaves open the question of how much various problems, presumably measuring the same stage, actually correlate with each other. In other words, how extensive is the problem of horizontal décalages within a given stage? Furthermore, we do not yet know as much as we should like about the transitions from stage to stage *within* a given child. For example, do stages reveal themselves in discontinuities of cognitive development, or is growth smooth and transitions very gradual? Adequate research on this problem must await the development of objective, reliable scales which will permit longitudinal observation of the same children through time.

On a more pragmatic level, many experimental curricula based on Piagetian theory are currently being developed. While I share Elkind's doubts about most current acceleration efforts, I think we will find that Piagetian-inspired tests which are independent, reliable, and objective are indispensable for assessing empirically the special programs of educational intervention which are now so much in vogue.

I would take minor issue with Elkind on one point—the view that unweighted scores necessarily obscure latent scales in the data. It certainly does throw away information to count as equally valuable responses which differ widely in generality or conceptual elegance. In the item "In what way are a peach and plum alike?" the response that both are fruit should be worth more than the response that both have skins or are round. Probably short scales could be founded on the type of response to items of this sort, and variable amounts of credit assigned depending upon the response type.

Variable weighting of responses is not required, however, when the successive items differ very appreciably in difficulty. For example, the item on how many pieces are formed in cutting an apple in half and the card game item mentioned by Elkind, by themselves, or even with well-chosen intervening items, would form a good Guttman scale, because they differ so very much in difficulty. Even if you assign one point for each item, as long as you're giving them in a series, the items generate a Guttman scale. The person who can solve the card game problem can certainly deal with the apple. The person who gets the apple may or may not be able to deal with the card game. There are ordinal scales of this sort latent in traditional psychometric instruments like WISC and WAIS whenever there is a real difficulty dimension, and provided that the steps are large enough that idiosyncratic individual differences in relative item difficulty don't spoil the symmetry of the scale. It seems to me that the trouble with psychometric tools is not so much their lack of scalar properties as it is their lack of any real theory to govern the choice of content.

I must again endorse Elkind's remarks about some current fads and fetishes in education—the enormous preoccupation with discovery learning, with inquiry techniques and the like, which are intended to mobilize intrinsic motivation—in what interests the *instructor*! As Elkind pointed out—and as Montessori and

Piaget have pointed out before him—intrinsic motivation resides in the child and not in methods or procedures of instruction. Attempts to seduce him into being interested in what the adult values are really just the same old shell game. I've been concerned for many years with the Guidance Study at Berkeley, a longitudinal study where we followed from birth people who are now in their forties (which is a little awkward since they live as long as do the experimenters who had rather a chronological head start on them). We found that among middle-class children, after-school time was often totally mobilized. Not only were most sent to preschool, but also after they got into the regular school, many of these children had one or more lessons every single afternoon: they had music lessons, dancing lessons, horseback-riding lessons, skating lessons, art lessons until they had literally no free time. We used to have great difficulty in scheduling two afternoons a year to get them into the Institute because they always had a conflicting lesson. Hence, it is instructive to recall that the current generation of hippies are not, by and large, children of the lower class who were permitted to grow at their own rate. Rather they are hothouse-grown children of the middle class who have been kept learning and working every minute of the day. They now drop out and turn on in the Haight-Ashbury district and thus escape from the zeal of their parents to educate them and accelerate them into positions further up the social scale. The moral is clear: let us teach what we must, but try to keep our interventions to a minimum. Perhaps with people like Elkind to defend and spread Piaget's views, we may yet succeed in saving a small bit of childhood for children.

Open Discussion

The discussion of Elkind's paper focused on two areas: (1) the nature of intrinsic motivation and its relation to learning, and (2) issues related to preschool education and Piagetian training in cognitive skills.

In the opening question of the session Elkind was asked to clarify his statement that intrinsic motivation resides in the child. Elkind replied that some kinds of learning are intrinsically motivated and others are not, and it is necessary to distinguish between the two. Certain rote-learning skills are not intrinsically motivating and require external reinforcements; e.g., learning to read and to do mathematics and other culturally normative skills that the child hasn't developed on his own but develops as a consequence of instruction. Such skills become intrinsically motivating only when the child has attained a certain level of competence. There are other kinds of skills which the child masters on his own, which are built into the system, and which are motivating in themselves.

Following this discussion, Beilin raised the issue of preschool education in relation to Piagetian training in cognitive skills. He noted that most of the preschool programs are designed for disadvantaged children who are ostensibly quite retarded in their achievement by the age of 5 or 6 years. The results from these programs, even those with Piagetian oriented training, have been generally disappointing. He pointed out that for Piagetian psychologists this raises the question of why activity for these children is not resulting in superior achievement relative to what they would have shown without the activity.

In his reply to this question, Elkind noted that Piaget has not dealt with the specifics of how to go about training children except to emphasize that the child's own actions are important. The problem in assessing children from deprived backgrounds is often one of differences in communication between the middle-class adult and the child. The child may have the operation but the adult will not discover this unless he learns how to understand and communicate with the child and to change his assessment approach. Thus, when we say these children are not doing well, there may be a problem with the method of assessment itself. Elkind used two examples to illustrate this point. In giving various types of perceptual tests to Sioux Indian children, he found they performed very poorly. However, when he changed his approach and began encouraging them to talk, they opened up, performed very well, and showed that they had the operations involved. Our traditional testing methods simply do not reach these children and a different approach is called for.

Again, in teaching young black children, the pounding and hitting which are interpreted by the white, middle-class teacher as aggression are for the children a way of relating to another person, of making body contact and showing warmth. The behavior has a very different meaning to the children than to the adult so that we misinterpret a good deal of the nonverbal communication of these children as well as having problems with verbal communication. Such factors make it difficult to get a good assessment of disadvantaged children. However, the cognitive operations may well be there. Our problem is to learn how to assess them through communication of a different sort. We also have to learn the kinds of stimuli which are proving resistant for these children and give them more experience with different kinds of stimuli, rather than training the operations per se.

Kamii commented on the difficulties of trying to run a preschool based on Piaget's theory due to the lack of well-developed techniques. There is a certain amount of trial and error involved. It was only after a visit from Dr. Sinclair that Kamii and her group realized that in the matter of classification it is the child, not the teacher, who determines the rightness or wrongness of the grouping of a set of objects. When this is accepted and the adult does not impose his own ideas, the children make better progress.

The concluding remark was made by Beilin who felt that Kamii was saying in theory it should be possible to improve the acquisitions of children in these circumstances by the general Piagetian approach if it were understood correctly theoretically and if it were pursued correctly in terms of the actual training procedure, and that the reason we do not get the achievements now is due to the need for improvement of techniques. He warned that this was the same kind of argument made by empiricists who claim that all you have to do is improve your techniques and you will be able to get learning in any kind of circumstances at any kind of level, and he would not like to see the Piagetians fall into the same kind of error.

An Implicit Metric for Ordinal Scales: Implications for Assessment of Cognitive Growth

PETER M. BENTLER
University of California, Los Angeles

The general dissatisfaction expressed by test constructors and psychometricians in regard to linear models for analyzing psychological test responses has recently led to a renewed emphasis upon the development of less restrictive models for analyzing multivariate data (e.g., Shepard, 1962a; Lingoes & Guttman, 1967). Monotonicity analysis, an approach developed by the author for the analysis of multivariate data using only rank-order assumptions, similarly represents a technique for analyzing the internal structure of variables with a minimum of assumptions; this procedure is described more fully elsewhere in this volume. Such a multivariate analysis of test or other multivariate data yields information about the degree of rank-order internal consistency among the various variables as well as about the dimensions within which the variables are imbedded. The degree of internal consistency, in the rank order or monotonic sense, among a particular set of test items can thus ultimately be described by a homogeneity coefficient or some other summary statistic. If a data matrix contains a subset of items which are highly monotonically related to one another, it is possible to select those items from the total set, combine them into one single scale, and thus generate a scale or test which can be used for the assessment of individual differences.

It is not inappropriate to inquire whether or not an ordinal scaling procedure such as monotonicity analysis will yield individual difference information only on an ordinal scale, or whether some additional types of analyses can be undertaken to obtain a "higher" scaling level than simple rank order. In particular, the question may be asked whether or not item parameters can be determined, parameters which are determined on a linear, interval scale, or even more hopefully, on a ratio scale. The aim of this paper is to describe a scaling technique which can be applied to binary (dichotomous) data in order to recover a level of scaling which is higher than that of a simple ordinal scale. In particular, I will demonstrate how it is possible to determine parameters for psychological scales whose scaling level is not only a ratio scale, but is indeed an absolute scale. The parameters are absolute parameters in the sense that any transformation of the parameters destroys information about the data matrix which these parameters describe. While the discussion of this paper will focus specifically upon binary scales because of their prevalence in psychology and other disciplines, the scaling techniques described in this paper are actually far more general and apply to quantitative data as well as qualitative data. Not all quantitative data, of course, will fit the models to be described in this paper. Ordinal multicategory items can always be scaled by the procedures to be described in this paper if the items are first broken into derived binary items by cutting the original multicategory items at various category boundaries and generating a dichotomous response to such a breakdown. Descriptions for performing such a breakdown can be found in Torgerson (1958).

The plan of this paper is as follows. The methods for deriving absolute scale parameters from a data matrix are first presented for the error-free case. Procedures for finding least-square estimates of the parameters are then described for the usual case in which the data matrix will contain some error. Our attention then shifts to procedures aimed at describing the parameters not for the observed data matrix, but for a hypothetical latent data matrix which is presumed to underlie the manifest data. Finally, we discuss some implications of the procedures described in this paper for the study of cognitive growth.

THE ABSOLUTE SIMPLEX

An *absolute simplex* is an *n* by *m* data matrix (*n>m*) which can be generated completely from the set of *m variation parameters*. One example of an absolute simplex is the well-known Guttman scale, which is a perfectly homogeneous scale in the internal consistency sense of homogeneity as described in my paper, "Monotonicity Analysis." An example of a perfectly homogeneous absolute simplex is presented in Table 3-1. Table 3-1 indicates the responses of ten persons to five items. It might represent a data matrix which could be derived from a learning task. Each person is given five trials at the task; at each trial, if the person responds incorrectly, he receives the score 0, and if he responds correctly, he receives the score 1. This data matrix represents an absolute simplex, or a perfectly homogeneous scale, because of the particular pattern of zeros and ones observed. A person will fail at the task up to some particular trial, at which point he will succeed. After his initial success, success on further trials will be perfect. Thus, any particular person's responses will be all zeros up to a particular point, and all ones thereafter. Various attributes of the data of Table 3-1 are presented in Table 3-2. Each row of Table 3-2 presents information relevant to describing the data in a particular column of Table 3-1. The first column of Table 3-2, the p_i, represent the *simplicity parameter* for each column of the data matrix. The simplicity parameter simply represents the proportion of subjects obtaining a correct response on a given trial for this binary data matrix. Thus, one-tenth of the subjects were correct on the first trial of the learning task. The next column of Table 3-2, labeled q_i, represents $1 - p_i$. That is, it presents information about the proportion of subjects failing on a particular trial. The next column of Table 3-2 presents the quantities V_i^2. These quantities represent the ratio of the proportion of subjects passing to the proportion of subjects failing on a given trial. Thus, the ratio for the first trial is 1/9. The final column of Table 3-2 presents the quantities V_i, which represent the square roots of the entries in the previous column. It is the quantities V_i which we call the *variation parameters* of an absolute simplex. The variation parameters can be considered to be the fundamental parameters of an absolute simplex. In the general case, they represent the reciprocal of the old-fashioned coefficient of variation. It will be remembered that the coefficient of variation (not the variance or the standard deviation) is defined as the standard deviation of a variable divided by its mean. Then the variation parameter represents its reciprocal, as we see in

$$V_i = \frac{\overline{X}_i}{\sigma_i} . \tag{3-1}$$

It represents the ratio of the mean divided by the standard deviation.

TABLE 3-1   A HOMOGENEOUS SCALE

PERSON	TRIAL NUMBER				
	1	2	3	4	5
1	0	0	0	0	0
2	0	0	0	0	1
3	0	0	0	1	1
4	0	0	0	1	1
5	0	0	0	1	1
6	0	0	1	1	1
7	0	0	1	1	1
8	0	0	1	1	1
9	0	1	1	1	1
10	1	1	1	1	1

TABLE 3-2   SCALE ATTRIBUTES OF TABLE 1

TRIAL NO.	p_i	q_i	$V_i^2 = \dfrac{p_i}{q_i}$	$V_i = \sqrt{\dfrac{p_i}{q_i}}$
1	.1	.9	$\frac{1}{9}$	$\frac{1}{3}$
2	.2	.8	$\frac{1}{4}$	$\frac{1}{2}$
3	.5	.5	1	1
4	.8	.2	4	2
5	.9	.1	9	3

It will now be instructive to determine how the variation parameters describe all the information of the entire data matrix of Table 3-1. In the first place, it is convenient to notice that the item simplicity parameter, p_i, represents a transformation of the variation parameter according to the formula

$$p_i = \frac{V_i^2}{(V_i^2 + 1)} \, . \tag{3-2}$$

Thus a substitution for trial number 5 of $V_i^2 = 9$ into Eq. (3-2) shows that the proportion of subjects responding correctly on trial number 5 is .9. Obviously, once having obtained the item simplicity, it is possible to subtract the item simplicity from unity to obtain the proportion of subjects failing on a particular trial.

The variation parameter, however, has far more significance than only determining item simplicity. It determines all aspects of the covariance and the correlation among the various items, or trials in this particular case. The item or trial variance for dichotomous data simply represents the product of $p_i \times q_i$, and thus, once the simplicity parameter has been determined, the variances of the columns of the data matrix are determined as well. It is then only necessary to describe how the variation parameters generate the intercorrelations among the columns of a data matrix. The Pearson product moment correlation matrix for the data of Table 3-1 are presented in Table 3-3. The correlations of Table 3-3 were obtained by actually performing the calculations required for computing the correlation on the data of Table 3-1. It is far easier, however, to compute the intercorrelations among the trials directly from the variation parameters according to the formula

$$r_{ij} = \frac{V_i}{V_{j'}}, \qquad V_i \leq V_j \, . \tag{3-3}$$

Thus, the correlation between two variables simply represents the ratio of the two variation parameters. As an illustration, we note that the variation parameters for trials 3 and 4 are 1 and 2, respectively. The ratio 1/2 equals .5, which we see to be the product moment correlation between variables 3 and 4. The explanation for this rather fascinating method for generating the intercorrelations among the variables can be seen more clearly in Table 3-4. Table 3-4 shows the bivariate distribution for some pair of items, say items i and j. We will assume that item j is easier than item i, that is, that its simplicity parameter is greater. Then we see from Table 3-4 that for an absolute simplex, all subjects who pass the harder item also pass the easier item. Table 3-5 illustrates this phenomenon for two trials chosen from the data matrix of Table 3-1. Plotting the proportion of subjects obtaining various combinations of 0 and 1 scores, we note that no subjects failed trial 4 if they passed trial 3. In this special circumstance, the Pearson product moment correlation, which is in fact the phi coefficient, can simply be written as

$$\phi_{ij} = \frac{p_i q_j}{\sqrt{p_i q_j p_j q_j}} \quad . \tag{3-4}$$

This simplification for the phi coefficient is possible because of the zero cell entry in the bivariate distribution of items i and j. It is possible to simplify Eq. (3-4) to yield

$$\phi_{ij} = \sqrt{\frac{p_i q_j}{p_j q_i}} \quad . \tag{3-5}$$

which is the well-known expression for the maximum value of the phi coefficient for fixed marginal distributions (Guilford, 1965). If we attempt to write the phi coefficient as the ratio of the two variation parameters, we obtain

$$\phi_{ij} = \frac{V_i}{V_j} = \frac{\sqrt{p_i/q_i}}{\sqrt{p_j/q_j}} = \sqrt{\frac{p_i q_j}{p_j q_i}} \tag{3-6}$$

which represents the phi-maximum value obtained in Eq. (3-5). This concludes the proof of the equivalence of the ratio of the variation parameters and product moment correlation for the absolute simplex.

TABLE 3-3   CORRELATION MATRIX FOR TABLE 3-1

	1	2	3	4	5
1	1.000	.667	.333	.167	.111
2	.667	1.000	.500	.250	.167
3	.333	.500	1.000	.500	.333
4	.167	.250	.500	1.000	.667
5	.111	.167	.333	.667	1.000

TABLE 3-4   BIVARIATE DISTRIBUTION FOR ITEM PAIRS, $p_i \leqslant p_j$

	0	1	
1	$p_j - p_i$	p_i	p_j
0	q_j	0	q_j
	q_i	p_i	

TABLE 3-5   BIVARIATE DISTRIBUTION TRIALS 3 AND 4

		TRIAL 3		
		0	1	
Trial 4	1	.3	.5	.8
	0	.2	0	.2
		.5	.5	

The simplex was originally discovered and described extensively by Guttman (1954a, 1955). A simplex represented for Guttman a set of statistical variables whose intercorrelations revealed a simple order pattern, and whose intercorrelations could be specified according to the set of parameters a_i according to the formula

$$r_{ij} = \frac{a_i}{a_j}, \ a_i \leqslant a_j.$$ (3-7)

Guttman emphasized that the parameters a_i, which he called *complexity parameters*, were determined only up to a ratio scale, for if all the parameters were multiplied by a constant k, the correlations among variables would remain unchanged, since we obtain

$$r_{ij} = \frac{ka_i}{ka_j} = \frac{a_i}{a_j}.$$ (3-8)

Thus, for Guttman, the complexity parameters were determined only up to a constant of proportionality. The variation parameters described for the absolute simplex, however, are a set of parameters which cannot be altered without disturbing their usefulness in describing the original data matrix from which they were generated. While multiplying the variation parameters v_i by a constant k maintains the characteristic ability of the parameters to describe the interrelationships among the variables, as described in Eq. (3-3), such a multiplication destroys the ability of the parameter to generate the simplicity parameter of the data matrix. Thus, multiplying the variation parameter by k yields for the simplicity parameter p_i

$$\hat{p}_i = \frac{k^2 v_i^2}{(k^2 v_i^2 + 1)} , \qquad (3\text{-}9)$$

in which the "hat" over the p_i is meant to indicate an estimate of the simplicity parameter. It is clear that an estimate of the simplicity parameter is inaccurate unless it is made directly from the variation parameter. For example, multiplying the variation parameter of trial 3 (Table 3-2) by the constant $k = 2$, yields as an estimate of the simplicity parameter the value .8, which is far off the correct value of .5. Guttman failed to appreciate that extremely tight restrictions need to be placed upon the ratio scale parameters for them to have any relevance to the data matrix itself. While for Guttman "complexity and difficulty have no necessary connection with each other in our theory" (1954, p. 283), the two concepts are tightly interwoven in the theory of the absolute simplex presented in this paper. In order to distinguish the extremely restricted parameters of the present system from those of Guttman, we have named the fundamental parameter of the absolute simplex the *variation parameter*; it represents an absolute version of Guttman's complexity parameter. Similarly, since the word "difficulty" has a conventional meaning in test theory, as it is related to a group average, we have felt it would be better to rename item difficulty the *simplicity parameter* in order to identify it specifically as a transformation of the fundamental variation parameter of the absolute simplex. While in the error-free case it may not make much difference whether one talks about item difficulty (really "easiness" would be an even better descriptor) or the simplicity parameter, when error contaminates the absolute simplex the concepts of item difficulty and simplicity parameter part company. In this case, item difficulty may still describe the proportion of subjects answering, or failing to answer, a particular item, and the simplicity parameter still represents the transformation of the variation parameter as described in Eq. (3-2). However, as will be seen below, the best estimate of the variation parameter will not simply be the reciprocal of the coefficient of variation, as it was defined in Eq. (3-1), but will depend instead upon the coefficients of variation as well as all the interrelationships among the variables. This problem will be described more fully below.

It may be useful to refer back to Tables 3-1 and 3-2 to clarify the nature of the change in the variation parameter with increased practice on the learning task. It can be seen in Table 3-1 that subjects initially start out naive, usually failing on the task. As trials proceed, they become more competent, and they obtain correct responses. The increment of correct responses with increasing trials represents a change in the "complexity" of the subjects. We will maintain the use of the word complexity to describe the change because the linear factorial complexity of the subjects literally increases, as will be shown in a later section of this paper. On the average, subjects become more and more competent across trials. This gain is represented by the increasing size of the variation parameters, or the square of these parameters, as described in Table 3-2.

In contrast to the learning tasks described above, which have direct developmental implications, another type of situation needs to be described for which the concept of an absolute simplex is applicable. In the learning situation the subjects are changing across trials, and gaining on a latent continuum; the more usual test situation, however, generates a data matrix where the subjects are all assessed at one moment in time. Subjects do not differ in complexity; items, however, do. While the variation parameters for learning tasks describe the subjects across time, the variation parameters at one moment in time instead describe the complexity of the variables. Thus, for example, in the field of mathematics, items which represent addition, multiplication, division, and algebra would be expected to vary in complexity. Each succeeding item in this list is more complex than the previous one. Each succeeding item contains the skill represented in the previous item but an additional skill as well.

When talking about item parameters for a specific set of subjects, the monotonic relationship between the simplicity parameters and the variation parameters should seem to be the reverse of that previously described for learning tasks. For a group of junior high school students, for example, algebra would be the most complex topic, being made up of addition, multiplication, and division, and the most complex topic would have the least proportion of subjects responding correctly. Thus in this usual testing situation, it would seem that the variation parameter, representing an increase in complexity, should be inversely related to the simplicity parameter, representing the ease with which subjects pass a particular item. For this situation, it would seem most reasonable to consider the following definition of the variation parameter:

$$v_i = \frac{\sigma_i}{\overline{X}_i} \cdot$$ (3-10)

The variation parameter in this case is then the reciprocal of that previously defined, and, indeed, represents the traditional coefficient of variation. The corresponding equation for determining the simplicity parameter is

$$p_i = \frac{1}{(v_i^2 + 1)} \, ,$$ (3-11)

reflecting the fact that as the variation parameter increases in size, item simplicity becomes smaller or, to put it differently, the item becomes more difficult. The intercorrelations generated from parameters defined according to Eq. (3-10) again represent a ratio of the two variation parameters.

The possibility of redefining the variation and simplicity parameters is inherent in a certain kind of indeterminacy in the data matrix itself. Suppose that the entire data matrix of Table 3-1 were converted so that every entry currently possessing a zero were replaced by a one, and every entry containing a one were replaced by a zero. The effect of this reorientation would simply be to reverse the roles of p and q in Table 3-2, having the effect of yielding variation parameters which are the reciprocal of the ones described. Equations (3-10) and (3-11) simply formalize this reciprocal relationship. It may thus be said that while the variation parameters are defined on an absolute scale, they are subject to an indeterminacy corresponding to the direction of complexity. There can be no quibble with this point of view when, indeed, the direction of factorial complexity cannot be settled on a priori grounds. For the two major classes of situations in which simplex scaling may be undertaken, however, the direction of complexity can be settled on rational principles. An obvious characteristic of learning tasks, for example, is that growth in skills is one-directional. As subjects proceed through numerous learning trials, their complexity must increase and not decrease. Such a conclusion can be made more graphic by examining the linear decomposition of the variables which enter an absolute simplex.

LINEAR ANALYSIS OF ABSOLUTE SIMPLEXES

A Symmetric Scaling Method

Scaling the correlation matrix of the simplex variables in a particular fashion provides a highly instructive way of looking at simplexes. Instead of factoring the correlation matrix itself, it will be useful to pre- and postmultiply the correlation matrix by a diagonal matrix of variation parameters. Any particular entry in the resulting matrix, then, can be represented as

$$\frac{r_{ij}\sigma_i\sigma_j}{\bar{X}_i\bar{X}_j} = r_{ij}v_iv_j = \frac{v_i}{v_j}\,v_iv_j = v_i^2,\ v_i \leq v_j\ . \tag{3-12}$$

Thus, while the scaling of the matrix is symmetric, in the sense that a particular diagonal matrix is the pre- and postmultiplier of the correlation matrix, as represented in the first two terms of Eq. (3-12), we see that the final product represents the square of the variation parameter for the variable with the smaller variation parameter. Then the whole matrix of Eq. (3-12) will look like the matrix illustrated in Table 3-6. Since this matrix exhibits all variation parameters in the ideal case, we may call it the *parametric covariance matrix*. It should be noted that if instead of scaling the correlation matrix by the variation parameters defined in Eq. (3-10), we had scaled it by the variation parameters defined in Eq. (3-1), a matrix formally equivalent to that of Table 3-6 would be derived. This may be seen in

$$\frac{r_{ij}\bar{X}_i\bar{X}_j}{\sigma_i\sigma_j} = r_{ij}V_iV_j = \frac{V_i}{V_j}\,V_iV_j = V_i^2,\ V_i \leq V_j. \tag{3-13}$$

Again, any particular cell entry would represent the smaller variation parameter of the two variables being compared. What would happen, then, to a matrix such as that in Table 3-6 is that the order of complexity would be reversed from [1, 2, 3, 4] to become [4, 3, 2, 1], and the corresponding rows and columns in that matrix would contain the square of the variation parameters. The column or row averages of a matrix such as Table 3-6 define the order relationships among the magnitude of the parameters for the various variables.

TABLE 3-6   PARAMETRIC COVARIANCE MATRIX

$$(v_1 \leq v_2 \leq v_3 \leq v_4)$$

	1	2	3	4
1	v_1^2	v_1^2	v_1^2	v_1^2
2	v_1^2	v_2^2	v_2^2	v_2^2
3	v_1^2	v_2^2	v_3^2	v_3^2
4	v_1^2	v_2^2	v_3^2	v_4^2

It is now instructive to factor the parametric covariance matrix presented in Table 3-6 so as to yield the triangular component matrix presented in Table 3-7. A number of important features can be discerned from this table. In the first place, for a given component or factor, the loadings are all either exactly equal or else equal to zero. Second, each variable in the sequence from top to bottom is composed of the factor present in the previous variable plus the addition of one new factor. The number of factors comprising a particular variable indexes the *complexity* of each variable. Increases in complexity are reflected in increasing size of the variation parameters as can be seen by the incrementing row sums of squares of the factor matrix. Notice that the variable with the smallest variation parameter is the least complex, in the sense of being made up of only one factor, while the variable with the highest complexity loading is made up of the largest number of linear components or factors. Reversing the orientation of the variation parameters by taking reciprocals of all parameters would generate a triangular factor matrix that was "opposite" to that presented in Table 3-7; the factorial complexity, as represented by the number of nonzero factor loadings for a particular variable, would be in the reverse order. It is the triangular factoring which reveals whether or not the direction of increasing or decreasing size of the variation parameters is arbitrary, or whether the parameters must be unidirectional to be in accord with the nature of the problem. In the case of learning trials, for example, it is most reasonable to assume that the first trial is the least complex (that is, loads positively on only one factor) while successive trials bring into play other and newer factors. It is unreasonable in such a situation to consider the last trial as being the least complex and the first trial most complex. A contrary point of view, however, will be entertained below.

TABLE 3-7   TRIANGULAR FACTORS OF TABLE 3-6

VARIABLES	FACTORS			
	I	II	III	IV
1	v_1	0	0	0
2	v_1	$\sqrt{v_2^2 - v_1^2}$	0	0
3	v_1	$\sqrt{v_2^2 - v_1^2}$	$\sqrt{v_3^2 - v_2^2}$	0
4	v_1	$\sqrt{v_2^2 - v_1^2}$	$\sqrt{v_3^2 - v_2^2}$	$\sqrt{v_4^2 - v_3^2}$

The triangular factor matrix of Table 3-7, when postmultiplied by its transpose, generates the parametric covariance matrix with which we started in Table 3-6. It may be instructive to look at the example of the data matrix of Table 3-1 and its corresponding correlation matrix presented in Table 3-3. Performing the matrix multiplication $D_v R D_v$ leads to the matrix of Table 3-8. Generating the triangular factorization of the matrix in Table 3-8 yields the factor-loading matrix of Table 3-9. The attributes previously described for Table 3-7 are again evident. Trial 1 is the least complex trial and further trials increase in complexity, in the sense that further factors enter into performance on those trials. The operations just performed on the symmetrically scaled matrix may be represented by matrix algebra as the equation

$$D_v R D_v = T T'.\tag{3-14}$$

The correlation matrix R was pre- and postmultiplied by a diagonal matrix, and the result was factored to yield the triangular matrix T. Someone who is more interested in obtaining a factorization of the correlation matrix itself can pre- and postmultiply the matrix of Eq. (3-14) by the inverse of the diagonal matrix to obtain an expression for the original correlation matrix. Thus a triangular factoring of the correlation matrix can be taken as $D_v^{-1} T T' D_v^{-1}$. An example of such an expression for the correlation matrix can be seen in Table 3-10, which represents the triangular factor of Table 3-9 premultiplied by the diagonal matrix of the reciprocals of the variation parameters. For those not acquainted with matrix algebra, this operation amounts to multiplying each element of a given row in Table 3-9 by the reciprocal of the variation parameter shown for that trial in Table 3-2. Table 3-10 results from that multiplication. When the correlation matrix is thus factored (component analysis would be a more appropriate name), the factorial representation is not particularly parsimonious. As many factors appear as there are variables in the analysis. It should be remembered, however, that the variation parameters represent a single set of parameters which generate all information about the original data matrix that may be required.

TABLE 3-8   PARAMETRIC COVARIANCE MATRIX OF TABLE 3-3

	1	2	3	4	5
1	$\frac{1}{9}$	$\frac{1}{9}$	$\frac{1}{9}$	$\frac{1}{9}$	$\frac{1}{9}$
2	$\frac{1}{9}$	$\frac{1}{4}$	$\frac{1}{4}$	$\frac{1}{4}$	$\frac{1}{4}$
3	$\frac{1}{9}$	$\frac{1}{4}$	1	1	1
4	$\frac{1}{9}$	$\frac{1}{4}$	1	4	4
5	$\frac{1}{9}$	$\frac{1}{4}$	1	4	9

TABLE 3-9   TRIANGULAR FACTORS OF TABLE 3-8

TRIAL	FACTORS				
	I	II	III	IV	V
1	$\frac{1}{3}$	0	0	0	0
2	$\frac{1}{3}$	$\sqrt{\frac{5}{36}}$	0	0	0
3	$\frac{1}{3}$	$\sqrt{\frac{5}{36}}$	$\sqrt{\frac{3}{4}}$	0	0
4	$\frac{1}{3}$	$\sqrt{\frac{5}{36}}$	$\sqrt{\frac{3}{4}}$	$\sqrt{3}$	0
5	$\frac{1}{3}$	$\sqrt{\frac{5}{36}}$	$\sqrt{\frac{3}{4}}$	$\sqrt{3}$	$\sqrt{5}$

TABLE 3-10   TRIANGULAR FACTORS OF TABLE 3-3

TRIAL	FACTORS				
	I	II	III	IV	V
1	1	0	0	0	0
2	$\frac{2}{3}$	$\sqrt{\frac{5}{9}}$	0	0	0
3	$\frac{1}{3}$	$\sqrt{\frac{5}{36}}$	$\sqrt{\frac{3}{4}}$	0	0
4	$\frac{1}{6}$	$\sqrt{\frac{5}{144}}$	$\sqrt{\frac{3}{16}}$	$\sqrt{\frac{3}{4}}$	0
5	$\frac{1}{9}$	$\sqrt{\frac{5}{324}}$	$\sqrt{\frac{1}{12}}$	$\sqrt{\frac{1}{3}}$	$\sqrt{\frac{5}{9}}$

It is instructive to look at the column sums of squares for each of the factors in the triangular factoring method of analyzing n-variable simplexes. These column sums of squares, which represent the proportion of variance accounted for by various linear factors, are

$$nv_1{}^2$$

$$(n-1)\,(v_2^2-v_1{}^2)$$

$$(n-2)\,(v_3^2-v_2^2)$$

$$\cdot \qquad \cdot \qquad \cdot$$

$$(n-m+1)\,(v_m{}^2-v_{m-1}^2) \qquad v_{m-1}^2 \leq v^2{}_m \tag{3-15}$$

$$\cdot \qquad \cdot \qquad \cdot$$

$$v_n^2-v^2{}_{n-1} \qquad \cdot$$

The above sums of squares represent the column sums of squares of the original factorization of the matrix of Eq. (3-14).

The Problem of Error

Unless a data matrix is perfectly homogeneous, the variation parameters cannot be estimated accurately using the original formulations presented in Eqs. (3-1) or (3-10). The major characteristic of the variation parameters is that they must fit both the coefficients of variation as well as all the intercorrelations among the variables. A set of estimated variation parameters $\hat{v}_i^2$ must fit the entire intercorrelation matrix as well as the coefficients of variation with minimal error. It is unlikely that the coefficients of variation alone will provide an accurate representation of all the interrelations of the variables. The problem then becomes one of finding estimates of the variation parameters which allow one to generate a close fit both to the correlation matrix, as well as to the coefficients of variation. It is not sufficient simply to find variation parameters which fit the correlation matrix with a reasonable degree of fit, nor to find parameters that fit the coefficient of variation; both must be fitted simultaneously. The symmetric scaling method described in the previous section of the paper provides an avenue for simultaneously fitting the parameters in the senses described. The observed correlation matrix is first pre- and postmultiplied by the diagonal matrix of coefficients of variation. The resulting matrix is similar to that of Eq. (3-14), as illustrated, for example, in Table 3-6. The resulting matrix, a symmetrically scaled correlation matrix, will not look exactly like the ideal seen in Table 3-6. The various terms which are identical in Table 3-6 will only be approximately identical when error contaminates the data. The problem is, then, one of finding best estimates of the variation parameters from the error-contaminated matrix.

The method for doing this is implied directly in the triangular factorization shown, for example, in Table 3-7. The triangular factorization of the symmetrically scaled error-contaminated correlation matrix will look approximately like the factorization shown in Table 3-7. However, the nonzero loadings in a particular column of the factor matrix which, in the ideal case, are all exactly equal will show some degree of variability. The sums of squares of the first factor loading which would, according to Eq. (3-15), equal exactly the number of variables times the square of the first variation parameter, may still provide a basis for getting a best estimate of that variation parameter. A useful technique is to take one nth the sum of squares of the factor loadings for the first factor as an estimate of the squared parameter of variation, as we see in the following equation:

$$\hat{v}_1{}^2 = \frac{1}{n}\Sigma b_1{}^2 .\qquad (3\text{-}16)$$

In general, for any successive squared variation parameter, we may use the relation

$$\hat{v}_m{}^2 = \hat{v}^2{}_{m-1} + \frac{\Sigma b_m{}^2}{n-m+1}\qquad (3\text{-}17)$$

involving a previous variation parameter and the given sums of squares of factor loadings to yield an estimate of the successively higher variation parameter. Equation (3-17) simply represents a rearrangement of the general root described previously in Eq. (3-15). Thus, in this fashion we can obtain successive estimates of all variation parameters.

The Quasisimplex
The problem of error leads to an immediate consideration of what Guttman (1954) has called the quasisimplex, instead of the simplex. Just as traditional common-factor theory would factor a correlation matrix into common parts and unique, uncorrelated error factors, so the simplex correlation matrix can be conceived of as containing a latent perfect simplex plus some error. Thus, it is possible to write the quasisimplex with "the delta law of deviation" in the following fashion:

$$R = DCD + U^2 ,\qquad (3\text{-}18)$$

where R represents the correlation matrix of the manifest variables, C represents the correlation matrix of the latent simplex, D represents a diagonal scaling matrix, and U^2 is the diagonal matrix of unique variances. Then DCD represents the usual covariance matrix of common portions of the variables. It is the internal correlation matrix C, however, which is presumed to have a simplex representation. In order to obtain the latent simplex representation for the matrix C, it is first worthwhile to pre- and postmultiply the correlation matrix by the diagonal matrix of coefficients of variation, as we had done previously in Eq. (3-14). Now we see that Eq. (3-14), when represented as a sum of a common and unique portion, has the same manifest form in the off diagonals but differs in the diagonal. Thus we see

$$D_v R D_v = D_v D C D D_v + D_v^2 U^2 .$$ (3-19)

Where the variables are composed of a common and a unique part, the matrix $D_v R D_v$ cannot be represented as in Table 3-6. The off-diagonal elements of the matrix of Eq. (3-19) would consist of the desired squared *variation parameters* as before. In contrast, however, the diagonal of the matrix would contain the squared *coefficients of variation* (or their reciprocals) rather than the desired simplex variation parameters. It is then immediately apparent that we are dealing here with a communality problem, as in traditional factor analysis. There are, however, some important exceptions. While it is true that the coefficient of variation squared is thus partitioned into common variance and unique variance, the problem posed by this partition is quite different from the usual factor analytic problem. While linear factor analysis attempts to find communalities consistent with lower rank or minimum factor explanations for the interrelations among the common scores, the quasisimplex formulation of the problem requires a solution to the communality problem when the latent common factor space is assumed to be full rank. In other words, as many latent linear factors as variables are assumed. Since no computing procedures have been described for obtaining an exact factor analytic solution while yielding a Gramian residual matrix, I have devised some procedures that will fit the factor model within the limits of computer accuracy. This work, which is as yet unpublished, represents a minimum trace formulation of the communality problem (Bentler, 1968c, 1969a). An alternative minimum rank formulation is presented by the regression procedure (Bentler, 1970). However, under these circumstances both techniques require an artificially constrained high rank. In addition, it may be desirable to allow the unique scores to be correlated in the case of binary variables.

Once having obtained the diagonal elements for the first matrix on the right-hand side of Eq. (3-19), this matrix can be scaled by the procedures described previously for the manifest simplex if desired. That is, a triangular factorization can be found, and latent variation parameters can be determined for the latent perfect simplex. It may be noted, however, that the solution to the problem of finding communalities for the latent simplex is itself a sufficient solution to the problem of finding the variation parameters of the latent simplex. This is because the diagonal elements can themselves be squared variation parameters. The scaled quasisimplex with communalities would look like the matrix in Table 3-6 in the ideal, since diagonal values would be computed to be consistent with the off diagonals. In practice, there will be some variability among the exact values of the off diagonals.

An alternate formulation for scaling the quasisimplex can be made for a data matrix rather than only the covariance matrix of the variables. Once having obtained an estimate of the communalities, it is possible to obtain a least-square estimate of the data matrix of common scores using the procedures of generalized image analysis (Bentler, 1969a). This data matrix is analogous to the raw-score data matrix illustrated in Table 3-1, but unsystematic variance will have been removed from the original data matrix to yield the estimated matrix of common scores. Scaling procedures described above, and others to be mentioned below, can then be applied to this matrix. Details of the image-analysis formulation are too complex to be described here conveniently.

DISTANCE ATTRIBUTES OF THE ABSOLUTE SIMPLEX

The parametric covariance matrix illustrated in Table 3-6 can generate an *absolute distance matrix* for the simplex. Distance will be measured not in the usual Euclidian fashion, but rather by the square of the Euclidian distance. Thus, we shall let the variance of difference scores for the parametric covariances define distance. Specifically,

$$d_{ij} = v_i^2 + v_j^2 - 2r_{ij}v_iv_j \qquad (3\text{-}20)$$

where v_i^2 and v_j^2 are diagonal entries from the parametric covariance matrix and $r_{ij}v_iv_j$ represents the appropriate off-diagonal entry. This definition is a natural one for the absolute simplex, since two variables with the variances v_i^2 and v_j^2 $(v_i^2 \leqslant v_j^2)$ differ in variance by the variance of difference scores. Alternatively stated, $v_i^2 + d_{ij} = v_j^2$. When the variance of a sum equals the sum of separate variances, the variables are independent; thus, difference scores are also seen to be independent increments to initial scores.

When the parametric covariance matrix represents a perfect simplex, as does Table 3-6, the distances (Eq. 3-20) can be seen to be

$$d_{ij} = v_i^2 + v_j^2 - 2v_i^2 = v_j^2 - v_i^2, v_j^2 \geqslant v_i^2 . \qquad (3\text{-}21)$$

For the absolute simplex, these distances obey the usual distance axioms, such as the triangle inequality, so that the variables can be embedded in a space of one dimension. An illustration of the absolute distance matrix obtained from the parametric covariance matrix of Table 3-6 is shown in Table 3-11. The possibility of embedding all the variables in a space of one dimension can be seen in the formula

$$d_{ij} + d_{jk} = d_{ik} \qquad (3\text{-}22)$$

for $v_i^2 \leqslant v_j^2 \leqslant v_k^2$. Thus the distances represent points along a line. For the distances of Table 3-11, for example, one obtains $d_{13} = v_3^2 - v_1^2$, which can also be found from $d_{12} + d_{23} = (v_2^2 - v_1^2) + (v_3^2 - v_2^2) = v_3^2 - v_1^2$.

TABLE 3-11   ABSOLUTE-DISTANCE MATRIX

	1	2	3	4
1	0	$v_2^2 - v_1^2$	$v_3^2 - v_1^2$	$v_4^2 - v_1^2$
2	$v_2^2 - v_1^2$	0	$v_3^2 - v_2^2$	$v_4^2 - v_2^2$
3	$v_3^2 - v_1^2$	$v_3^2 - v_2^2$	0	$v_4^2 - v_3^2$
4	$v_4^2 - v_1^2$	$v_4^2 - v_2^2$	$v_4^2 - v_3^2$	0

PRACTICAL SCALING PROCEDURES

The initial practical problem involved in scaling a simplex or quasisimplex has been described by Kaiser (1962) and Schönemann (1968) as the problem of finding the correct order for the variables. In the case of the absolute simplex, this problem is immediately solved by noting, as in Table 3-6, that the sum of covariance terms for a given variable determines the order of the variables. The ordering of the parameters corresponds to the ordering of the sums. This result holds for the quasisimplex as well. It follows that the covariance of any variable j with the total score t across all variables is given by $C_{jt} = (n-j+1)v_j^2 + \Sigma v_i^2 + u_j^2$, involving the sum of parameters of all variables $i < j$ and the unique variance of variable j. Since the observed variance $\sigma_j^2 = v_j^2 + u_j^2$, the parameters v_j^2 can be estimated successively from $C_{jt} - \sigma_j^2 - \Sigma v_i^2 = (n-j)v_j^2$. The parameter for the nth or last variable cannot be estimated since $(n-j) = n - n = 0$. Consequently, its unique variance may be arbitrarily set at zero, and the parameter v_n^2 taken to be the observed variance σ_n^2. This result for the quasisimplex reflects the fact that there are n variation parameters plus n uniqueness parameters, while only $2n - 1$ parameters are estimable. Since all uniquenesses above equal zero for the simplex, this procedure is applicable to either the simplex or quassimplex. For completeness, additional techniques for scaling the simplex may be mentioned.

The most well-known method for scaling the simplex correlation matrix was published by Kaiser (1962). He proposed taking the logarithms of the matrix R^* $= (r^*_{ij})$, defined as r_{ij} for $i \leqslant j$ or the reciprocal of r_{ij} for $i > j$. This step leads to a skew-symmetric matrix of logarithms, which is then operated upon in a particular fashion to yield estimates of the logarithms of the parameters. Antilogs are then taken to yield estimates of simplex parameters, but these parameters are scaled *arbitrarily* and cannot be assumed to be the absolute simplex variation parameters described in this paper. A feature of Kaiser's solution which makes it generally undesirable is that the parameters which are obtained for a given variable will differ for different orderings of the variables in the correlation matrix. This conclusion results from the lack of symmetry in the matrix R^*. The reader can consult Kaiser's article for further information about the difficulties inherent in applying his estimation method.

A Distance Method

Since entries in the correlation matrix for the absolute simplex can be expressed as the ratio of two numbers v_i/v_j, we can follow Morrison's (1967) suggestion of taking logarithms of the correlations and reversing sign to yield

$$-\log r_{ij} = \log v_j - \log v_i. \tag{3-23}$$

There results a symmetric matrix of nonnegative numbers which obey the distance axioms and the triangle inequality, so that the variables can be embedded in a space of one dimension. Recovery of this dimension can be obtained from the distance matrix using the Young and Householder (1938) scaling method as described by Torgerson (1958). The procedure involves transforming the distance matrix into a matrix of scalar products and performing a principal components analysis on this matrix. The loadings on the principal component represent the logs of an arbitrary rescaling of the variation parameters, so that antilogs of the loadings represent that scale for the variation parameters. This approach has been spelled out by Schönemann (1968), who recommends scaling the scale values to multiply to unity. The resulting estimates are scaled arbitrarily, and do *not* represent the variation parameters.

When the simplex contains error, the distance matrix and its corresponding matrix of scalar products will not be exactly rank 1, and consequently a rank 1 factoring procedure amounts to a least-squares fit to the logs of an arbitrary scaling for the parameters. The arbitrary scale for the parameters can be removed by requiring the average of the logs of the estimated parameters to equal the average of the logs of the coefficients of variation. Antilogs of these values then represent estimates of the variation parameters, i.e., are on the correct scale. This estimation method represents an extension of the previous work cited above. It is still not an ideal procedure because sampling error may generate a few negative correlations, and logarithms cannot be taken of negative numbers. Thus this procedure does not allow the correlations to be taken at face value, and an arbitrary small positive number must be substituted for an observed negative correlation.

Absolute-distance Analysis

The absolute distance matrix generated from the parametric covariance matrix holds the key to the most acceptable method for finding the variation parameters of the absolute simplex, since the absolute distances can be scaled irrespective of the ordering of the variables or the presence of error or negative correlations. The usual methods for multidimensional scaling, as described by Torgerson, are used. The distance matrix is transformed to a scalar product matrix relative to some origin. One principal component is extracted from this matrix, yielding a least squares rank 1 analysis. The ratio of the first root to the trace of the scalar product matrix indicates the goodness of fit of the absolute simplex model. For a centroid analysis, the resulting component loadings must be adjusted to yield the squared variation parameters since the average of the loadings is set to zero in such a solution. A constant then needs to be determined which, when added to the loadings, yields the final squared variation parameters. Output from the component analysis yields loadings a_i which differ by a constant k from the estimated variation parameters v_i^2. Since the ratio $(a_i + k)/(a_j + k)$ must estimate the squared correlations r_{ij}^2, k is easily obtained as $(r_{ij}^2 a_j - a_i)/(1 - r_{ij}^2)$, where $a_j > a_i$. For n variables there are $n(n-1)/2$ estimates of this "additive constant" k, and the most stable estimate is obtained as the average of these various estimates. Then $a_i + k = \hat{v}_i^2$. For a perfect simplex the squared variation parameters will equal the squared coefficients of variation, and the additive constant is simply the mean squared coefficient of variation. Alternatively, the smallest variation parameter can be estimated directly from the inverse of the parametric covariance matrix. It can be shown that the reciprocal of the sum of all elements of the inverse matrix yields the smallest squared variation parameter. The difference between this inverse-based estimate and the smallest a_i provides the additive constant.

SCORING THE SUBJECTS

One of the most remarkable features of the absolute simplex is the implication it has for generating schemes for scoring the subjects that differ from the usual procedure of adding up the total number of items answered correctly. There are a number of possible methods for generating scoring methods for the absolute simplex; only one will be presented here.

The triangular factorization of the parametric covariance matrix and the unidimensional distance attributes of the absolute simplex suggest postmultiplying the data matrix by a score vector w of the form

$$v_1^2, v_2^2 - v_1^2, \ldots, v_j^2 - v_i^2, \ldots, v_n^2 - v_{n-1}^2 \qquad (3\text{-}24)$$

involving the estimated squared variation parameters. These weights represent distances along the linear continuum. Consequently, a particular subject's *simplex score* represents the sum of the entries in Eq. (3-24) for which he responded correctly. We may write the score for subject k as

$$s_k^2 = \Sigma(v_j^2 - v_i^2), \quad i = 0, 1, \ldots, n \quad v_i^2 < v_j^2, X_{kj} = 1 \quad (3\text{-}25)$$

when a correct response for the kth subject on the jth item in the data matrix X_{kj} is represented by a 1. Then for a perfect, error-free absolute simplex the total score for a subject is the squared variation parameter for the most complex item which the subject passes. This may be represented symbolically as

$$s_k^2 = v_j^2, \quad \max X_{kj} = 1 . \quad (3\text{-}26)$$

This scoring scheme has rather astounding implications for testing applications, for it can be noticed that transforming the scores s_k^2 according to the formula

$$P_k = \frac{s_k^2}{s_k^2 + 1} \quad (3\text{-}27)$$

yields direct information about the percent of subjects obtaining scores lower than that obtained by the kth subject. The transformation of scores (Eq. 3-25) using (Eq. 3-27) thus automatically creates a percentile scale. *No norms of any kind* (in the traditional sense of norms for total test scores) *are required to generate direct meaning for a person's score.* The remarkable absolute characteristic of the scoring technique here described appears to have no rivals in the entire psychometric literature.

In the case of an error contaminated data matrix, the scoring scheme suggested above works equally well, but now a particular subject's obtained position is projected to be slightly off his "true" position. Scores of two subjects with the same number of correct items will differ if they have a different pattern of responses.

ASSESSMENT OF COGNITIVE GROWTH

The traditional approach to measuring changes in learning or in other cognitive functions is to look at subjects' scores in particular situations across training trials. Table 3-1 might represent data from a typical study. The changes across trials are measured by the proportion of subjects passing or answering correctly on any given trial. The psychological problem posed by a study yielding data of the type described in Table 3-1 is how to relate the trial-by-trial changes in simplicity to some external variable, for example, reinforcement or training procedures. Usually changes are looked for directly at the level of the simplicity parameter. If the observed data represent a perfect absolute simplex, this procedure might be quite useful. However, the simplicity parameters themselves do not lie on a unidimensional scale. The simplicity parameters are transformations of possibly more significant parameters, the variation parameters, which for the absolute simplex do lie on a one dimensional continuum. Thus, rather than seek the effects of external variables on task simplicity, effects might more appropriately be looked for on the variation parameters or the squares of the variation parameters themselves. For example, let us assume that a constant increment occurs in learning or in complexity from trial i to trial j, as represented on the continuum of the squares of variation parameters. Such an assumption might look as follows:

$$v_j^2 = v_i^2 + \Delta \qquad (3\text{-}28)$$

Thus, there is a constant increment from trial to trial. The effect of this increment on the simplicity of the item may be seen in

$$p_j = \frac{v_i^2 + \Delta}{(v_i^2 + \Delta) + 1} \qquad (3\text{-}29)$$

Here we note that while an increment may be constant on the variation parameter scale, it may yield quite uneven effects on item simplicity. For example, suppose we were to start out on the first trial at $V_1^2 = 1$, and that the increment from trial to trial is 1 on the squared variation scale. The corresponding simplicity parameters then become .50, .67, .75, .80, .83, etc. Thus the increments on the simplicity scale become smaller and smaller in spite of the fact that linear increments in growth may occur on the variation parameter scale.

Another problem may arise even if the simplicity parameters themselves are seen to be good descriptors of cognitive growth. The item difficulties as represented by the observed proportion of people responding correctly to a given item may not be excellent representatives of the simplicity parameters. Because the simplex may be imperfect, the coefficient of variation may be a poor representative of the variation parameter; consequently, the transformation of the coefficients of variation leading to the observed difficulty may also be a poor representative of cognitive growth. Ideally, one would like to have an estimate of the variation parameter which most adequately represents not only the observed means but similarly represents all the interrelationships among the variables. Procedures for obtaining such estimates have been described earlier. Thus it may be that a transformation of these parameters by Eq. (3-2) will yield estimated simplicities which generate a much more meaningful pattern of cognitive growth. Such a conclusion would seem to be reasonable, since the effects of error and unsystematic bias have been removed from the item difficulties themselves by this procedure.

Comments on Bentler's Paper
by James D. Nivette
CTB/McGraw-Hill

Bentler's paper presents a new and interesting outline of one psychometric method for handling ordinal data. The need for developing a methodology or system for scaling ordinal data within the context of Piagetian tasks has already been pointed out by Elkind.

I should like to divide my comments into three areas of concern. First, I shall attempt to define some of the assumptions one makes when scaling Piagetian tasks; second, I would like to discuss some of the issues related to Bentler's approach to scaling data; and third, I would like to attempt to show some of the implications of the scaling methodology for research.

When considering the possibility of scaling Piagetian tasks, an inevitable question is whether the criteria for the tasks constitute a countable scale of scores which refer to some fundamental underlying scale of intelligence or cognition, or whether they lead only to nominal classifications of individuals into one of the postulated stages. It is obvious that there is a hierarchy in Piaget's stages; however, it is less clear that the tasks used to assign a person somewhere within this hierarchy are ordinal in nature, since it seems to be the quality and not necessarily the quantity of a student's responses which is important. The use of Bentler's method is based on the assumption that the items themselves are ordinal, measuring discrete increments in a scale which reflect differences between Piagetian stages. Piaget, on the other hand, does not necessarily talk about increments in the stages, although he makes it quite clear that the stages are developmental. He talks primarily about rearrangements or regroupings of previously acquired structures into more complex patterns which form a higher level of thought process. This seems most apparent when considering preoperational and concrete operational phases. In other words, the individual does not gain more of a particular trait and thus progress to another stage; rather, in order to pass from one stage to another, he reorganizes or synthesizes previously acquired skills. Although the individual acquires more knowledge, more skills, etc. as time passes, it is not the quantity of these that counts in determining the stage but the quality of the student's responses. This is true even though there is a simple invariant progression from stage to stage (for example, concrete operations always follow preoperations and preoperations never follow concrete operations). Inhelder also describes the process of moving from one stage to another as a matter of reordering information rather than one of acquiring new information. As Piaget himself has stated at this conference, the whole question of passage from one stage to another is currently under study.

In short, when studying the progress of an individual from one Piagetian stage to another, it seems clear that this is determined more by the restructuring and interrelating of concepts than by the degree of development of any one particular concept. Although the individual cannot get to one stage without having been in the previous stage, this still does not imply that more or less of any one trait at any one stage will be present. In fact, it is known that different types of traits derive as a result of attaining a particular stage. By implication, we may be discussing a latent hierarchical dimension which might be called "abstract reasoning" or "intellectual capability" which underlies all tasks and is indirectly measured by performance on these tasks. In that sense, while the dimension may be ordinal, the measurement of that dimension may not be. Thus, trying to make tasks, in the form of instrumentation, ordinal in nature in order to reflect the underlying ordinal dimension would seem to be in error (or at least unnecessary). Such instrumentation would not necessarily need to involve ordinal information but would only need to be able to categorize an individual, based on his abilities, into one of a set of particular hierarchical stages. One must not forget that there may not be a relationship between the ordinal nature of the latent dimension which is being measured by Piagetian tasks and any ordinal type of task itself. Therefore, the ordinal dimension of a task may be uncorrelated with the dimension it purports to measure.

Bentler's method results in or defines the scale based on correlations between tasks. Therefore, it is the relationship of one task to another which eventually produces some continuity in measurement and this scale. However, the scoring of Piagetian tasks is not necessarily quantitative, but rather is qualitative in nature. The judgment of the examiner as to response quality is what he will use to decide what level of classification within the Piagetian framework is being observed. Thus, the attempt of Piagetian tasks is to classify a person in a stage rather than to define his point of performance on a scale, equal interval or not, of comparison to other people. In other words, scaling implies at least ordinal measurement, but Piaget is more concerned about individual assessment and classification. Since the operations of measurement are different from those of assessment, there is some question in my mind whether Piagetian tasks are scalable at all. These tasks seem to aim at mere classification of individuals into stages on the basis of items not necessarily ordinal in nature. The stages themselves are hierarchical and sequential, but the measurement process does not seem to be. It is difficult to discuss the scaling of items or tasks within the Piagetian stages simply because the adding or development of one task over another does not necessarily mean that one will pass from one stage to another stage. Thus, it would seem almost improper to attempt to ordinally scale items in order to assess the passage of a student from one stage to the other.

Now that we have considered the possible independence of the underlying scale and the items designed to measure it, we can turn to the Bentler method specifically. Bentler has described clearly and thoroughly his method of scaling ordinal items both in the error-free case and in the case of error. In contrast to some other transformational methods of defining monotonicity coefficients which have been advocated, Bentler's absolute values (for example, proportions passing) do not require that an a priori rank order of items be specified, and thus the assignment of rankings to items is facilitated.

The drawback in using absolute measures for the purposes of establishing performance standards is that the validity of absolute measures derived from a sample of students is limited by the adequacy of the sample. This fact always limits the generalizability of the data generated in this manner. One of the problems in hypothesis seeking in the manner advocated by Piaget is that not much substantive evidence in terms of the stability of performance has been offered due to the small size of experimental groups. Thus, the referents to which the individuals subsequently assessed are compared are these limited groups to which their performance may not be related. In order for the use of absolute measures such as item difficulties to be meaningful in the establishment of any scaling of ordinal items, large quantities of data on varying samples of students would need to be collected. This would be necessary in order to ensure that the data gathered had enough stability to warrant the use of statistical techniques designed for the purposes of scaling the items in the performance of students.

It is interesting to speculate about the characteristics of the scale resulting from the use of this method. We have discussed the difficulty of determining whether the scale would be based on a hypothetical dimension which is truly ordinal or whether Piaget is actually proposing a nominal or classificatory scale, in which case it is assuming too much to talk about ordinal or rank-item responses. However, if ordinal measurement can be assumed, a question develops which relates to the use of test scores contained in the scale generated by Bentler's method. After developing a linear model for summarizing ordinal data, is the resultant scale of scores on individuals still ordinal in nature or does one now have data characteristic of a linear interval scale? The assertion of Bentler's paper is that, having applied his method, one has at least an interval scale of measurement. The author alludes to ratio and absolute scale powers for these values. This is based on the fact that absolute values or item difficulties have been used in deriving the estimates of the scale. While this concept is interesting and logical, the validity of the conclusions to which such data would point needs to be demonstrated empirically. The importance of this consideration cannot be overstressed since the implications for the use of the data are much stronger when higher-order measurement is involved. As Bentler points out in his paper, the validation of this concept will be difficult to achieve.

Bentler has done an outstanding job of showing how rank-order data may be eventually transformed into more meaningful scales composed of the latent dimensions underlying the data. If the Bentler method proves to be successful, it might provide researchers with a valuable tool for summarizing ordinal data. It seems to me that this method has implications for the determination of absolute scaling values for different varieties of tasks within the scale, such as conservation. Thus this technique seems to provide us with some preliminary method for developing hierarchies of tasks within groups of tasks. It will add a considerable amount of refinement to existing ordinal cognitive scales by enabling us, on a reliable basis, to put easier items or easier tasks first and more difficult items later. This issue, it seems to me, is central to any consideration of ordinal scaling and is of critical importance to the prediction and understanding of human behavior, as it provides us with a method of developing a hierarchy of operations within a particular psychological model that is dependent on ordinal data. Thus the improvement of psychological theory is facilitated through the use of a psychometric tool.

A central part of any consideration of ordinal data would be the scaling of that data. Scaling allows the psychologist the flexibility of making a judgment about a person based on objective results of performance. This obviates the need for "clinical" judgments relating to the skills of an individual. By implication the possession of more or less of some task or of some trait implies that the person has developed to a particular level of competency within a Piagetian series of stages. By far the two most interesting implications of Bentler's paper, to me, are (1) whether or not the method is appropriate to Piaget's tasks insofar as they may or may not be ordinal in nature, and (2) the practical applications of the model.

The first topic has been considered in a previous section. The last section of my discussion will focus on the second implication. The use of the model and the practical application of the model will depend to a great extent on what percentage of time psychologists spend dealing with ordinal data. Linear models such as factor analysis and other more traditional approaches are more useful in the study of certain psychological data. There are also data where rank-order models are more appropriate. In fact, one could logically argue that we don't really have interval data in the behavioral sciences, and therefore we should deal only with rank-order models. In any case, many psychologists are concerned with the implications and use of ordinal data information. Assuming Piagetian tasks are ordinal, and this is a fundamental assumption to the use of the Bentler method, the use of this particular model is especially interesting.

One question which has arisen is that of application. One can ask whether this model can be considered theoretical or practical. The answer to this question must depend somewhat on the use of the model in the future and the empirical results derived from that use. If the model is to be used practically in developing scales, the automating of such a procedure would be advantageous. In other words, the model should be programmed into some form of computer application. At present, one can only imagine that the detailed arithmetic operations involved would be cumbersome and time-consuming.

Obviously the issue relating to deriving and summarizing meaningful data from Piagetian tasks—or tasks dealing with any ordinal-type data—is open. The issues of use of non-error-free data and multicategory items are problematic. Bentler has developed an interesting and relevant approach to this topic. Studies of cognitive development might benefit from the use of such a model for studying results by offering a scale which is equal interval. The advantages of such a scale are great considering the assumptions of most parametric methods of studying research data.

Open Discussion

Most of the discussion period was devoted to obtaining clarification of the implications of the model offered by Bentler. Bentler began with some comments on the issue raised by Nivette of the practical applications of his model.

BENTLER

I see monotonicity analysis to be of immense practical value to the investigator working with binary data of the type one encounters frequently in developmental and educational settings. There simply are not many alternatives to this technique for the analysis of such data. It won't be as useful for rating scale data, or other continuous data, where the linear models of factor analysis can do quite well.

The output from a monotonicity analysis enables one to conclude that a particular set of variables is highly monotonically related, and that these variables can be placed into a scale for the purpose of measurement. It then becomes a strategic question for the investigator as to whether he's interested in scaling these data to obtain estimates of various simplex parameters. I can envision situations in which the investigator would have no particular reason to find these parameters. For example, if the variables are going to form a test which is to be scored by the number of correct answers, and if scores are going to be referred to norms, I wouldn't bother to find the parameters; they are not used in this situation anyway. On the other hand, if the "spacing" of the variables were of some importance, as in learning trials, or as in the study of sequences or stages of development, I would think it essential that absolute simplex scaling be undertaken. When Goldschmid and I constructed our conservation scales, for example, we didn't have simplex scaling procedures available. Thus we weren't able to determine the relative spacing (stages) between conservation tasks. For purposes other than simply finding out how well a child conserves, it would be desirable to know the spacing. Another practical illustration: suppose that the question of sequence is of interest to an investigator but that the means of several variables don't differ greatly one from another, so that he can't draw any good conclusions about the nature of growth. It may well be that error confuses his picture, so that the estimated simplicity parameters could clarify what's going on. Thus I can see my simplex scaling as a very practical procedure in some instances, but irrelevant in others.

The question of computer programs is of course an important one. I cannot imagine performing any of the analyses I have mentioned without the help of the computer. I have just finished writing programs to perform monotonicity analysis and absolute simplex scaling. Anyone who writes to me is welcome to a copy of these programs.

Carson McGuire suggested that the discrimination model he and Fruchter devised also had relevance to the developmental process. Bentler was then asked about the nature of the unit of complexity in his model. He explained that the unit of measurement is absolute, even though the variation parameters depend on the sample of subjects. Thus, with both old and young subject groups, one might obtain a scalable hierarchy, yet the variation parameters involved could be different for the two groups. So proper care in sampling and all normal statistical precautions need to be observed.

Kresh pointed out that the Bentler model does not say anything about timing along the scale, even if one has an absolute simplex. Bentler agreed, noting that the parameters are usually obtained from a cross-sectional sample, which may enable one to specify the sequence of complexity but cannot determine longitudinal rate. That is, you may be able to predict what will happen next in the sequence but not *when* it will happen. Also, longitudinal data, in contrast to cross-sectional data, can determine order of complexity; the formal model has the same problem of reversibility one observes in children (the sequence small-bigger-bigger is as good as big-smaller-smaller).

EVANS

I wonder if you have not presented us with a tautology. What you led us through by way of derivation took us back to where we were at the beginning: if you start with a Guttman scale with a particular set of scale types, you finally get a score indicating the proportion of people of that scale type or below it. But I think your main point is that life is not like a Guttman scale, and we're going to have a great deal of décalage within a given scale type. There will be confusion in the data matrix. The strength of your argument has to rest, I think, on the fact that you can handle the décalage—the variation within stages—better than other models can. It's not clear to me how you've shown us that your model does handle this question of variability within stages—this difficulty of creating an ordinal scale where it seems an ordinal scale does not, in fact, exist.

BENTLER

Well, my answer as to the existence of the ordinal scale must first go back to the Monotonicity Analysis paper (see Appendix). In order to be able to find any type of dimension which indicates that items do relate monotonically one to another, there must be sufficient internal consistency to the data. In the perfect Guttman scale you have perfect transitivities—everybody passes items up to a certain point and fails thereafter. The degree of perfection or closeness to a scale will be summarized by a homogeneity coefficient, just as it could have been summarized by Guttman's old reproducibility coefficient. Obviously if you have a large amount of error—low homogeneity—you can't do as well in defining the stages as you could when you have less error. That's the nature of the world, it seems to me. The absolute simplex, however, allows you to go a step beyond simply saying that you have a certain degree of homogeneity. Even with error you have some hope for being able to order your variables, if an order exists. The simplicity parameters may well yield an ordering which was at first unrecognizable, and you can determine how to order subjects who do *not* conform to particular scale types. The old unsolved problem of scalogram analysis, or ordering nonscale types, is completely solved using the absolute simplex. The person's simplex score embodies this information; it takes into account the pattern of errors.

BURKET

We were talking about achieving a ratio scale or even an absolute scale. If you apply this scaling procedure to items based on height or weight, the parameters you obtain would depend on the distribution of height or weight in your sample and on how your item categories were defined. You probably wouldn't recover parameters which correspond to height and weight in general. I wonder if there isn't some way you could get at such an absolute scale by assuming a specific distribution of heights or weights in a population and then sampling from that population.

BENTLER

I view my procedure as useful mainly because it's assumption-free. You need assume no particular type of distribution. People seem to believe in normal distributions, but I don't find them particularly attractive—certainly the Goldschmid-Bentler conservation scale scores are not normally distributed. But life might become very interesting if you could realistically assume certain distributions, as you suggest. In that case you could think of ways of transforming your parameters so that they would yield simplex scores showing the cumulative distribution to correspond in shape to that you would obtain from, say, the normal distribution. The exact nature of the transformation would depend on the data you had. It's an interesting suggestion, and certainly a possibility.

Burket wondered if one would then retain the ability to generate norms; Bentler thought it possible with an additional transformation. McGuire asserted that norms were unnecessary because determination of developmental level was sufficient. Kaiser disagreed, noting that if one knows something about differences in scale values, stronger practical suggestions can be made. Bentler added that the usefulness of the simplex scale transformation is that it takes you back to a probability distribution.

BEILIN

The model is based on at least one assumption—namely, an additivity assumption with regard to the relationship between item 1, let's say, and item 2. Now, what if the relationship between item 1 and item 2 is really not additive but is something else? For example, in some theories there is a reorganization of elements which gives rise to a different kind of quality. In effect, that kind of theoretical assumption—whatever the theoretical assumption is, whatever the theory is—can be violated by the use of this kind of psychometric model

BENTLER

I think there are two separate answers to what you say. One of them is that you can look at the absolute simplex as a model for fitting the data with a minimum number of parameters. For this kind of data, the model which fits all the data with fewest assumptions and with the fewest parameters is the absolute simplex. Now one can generate an even simpler model for certain data—obviously all data aren't going to be appropriate—if you say that variation parameters increase in a specified manner from one item to the next. Then you need a starting parameter and an increment and you can generate everything! Whether or not this type of model fits the data, who knows? I'm very interested in the problem of classical conditioning, for example. Here one can very likely describe the learning involved in classical conditioning by a very simple model, like the one I have described. In fact, Theios' model for classical conditioning, which is a stochastic process type of model, really amounts to an absolute simplex of the type I've described. There is a very close relationship between simplices and stochastic processes and, by and large, this fact is not recognized.

A second kind of answer to your question is the following. It can be shown, although I haven't demonstrated it here, that this model is even more interesting than it seems at first because you don't really need to assume additivity. It turns out that a multiplicative function of parameters will do just as well as an additive one. There's always a certain amount of indeterminacy here, if you prefer that way of looking at it.

STEPHENS

Have you compared your procedures with Guttman's simplex analysis?

BENTLER

Guttman talked about parameters for variables, the ratios of which generate correlations. But he didn't realize that the parameters had to be very exclusive. He said, for example, that if you multiply the parameters by any constant you can still generate the correlation matrix. The correlation between variables one and two is given by the ratio of the two variables' parameters. It certainly is true that if we multiply both parameters by some constant k that the correlation stays the same. The problem is, if you take any other metric, given by multiplying your variation parameters by a constant, you cannot recover the variables' means. These averages represent another fundamental aspect of the data matrix. Guttman only talked about correlation matrices. He had no intuition, as far as I know, about the fact that data matrices generate these parameters in certain special ways, and that the parameters themselves are extremely restricted—that one doesn't have the kind of freedom he conceived of to choose values. This is why, in fact, I call these matrices absolute simplexes. I don't think Guttman or anybody else realized that the correlation matrix parameters actually have some relationship to the basic data matrix from which one starts. This is a fundamental feature of simplices which eluded people for a long time. Guttman called his correlation matrix a "simplex," and I call my matrix an "absolute simplex" to try to indicate there are restrictions on parameters and that these have something to do with the data matrix.

Theoretical Regularities and Individual Idiosyncrasies

READ D. TUDDENHAM
University of California, Berkeley

In this paper I shall report on a research program which brashly attempts to synthesize Piagetian theory with methods derived from mental tests. This program is as yet unpublished, but it was initiated in 1963 at the University of California and is still being developed by my students.

Of course, we are by no means the first to adopt a more or less psychometric approach to appraising cognitive development. Vinh Bang, Helmick, Almy, Laurendeau and Pinard, and Nassefat have all made quantitative investigations of parts of the developmental sequence. Additionally, Dodwell, Elkind, Smedslund, Lovell and many others have elaborated one or more of Piaget's experiments in order to test his conclusions. We take our place in a long and rapidly growing list of other investigators, most of whom have stayed a good deal closer to Piaget than we have. Our program, in contrast, departs in very major ways, both in goal and in method, from the extraordinarily fruitful line of attack initiated by Piaget—so much so that while acknowledging my general debt to Piaget, I hereby absolve him from all personal responsibility for what, judged in terms of his goals and objectives, must be called a veritable "syllabus of errors."

A brief bit of personal history may help explain my heresy. To paraphrase David Wechsler's self-description, I am a reformed but essentially unchastened differential psychologist, who enjoyed the privilege of spending academic 1961-62 in Geneva with Piaget and a part of the year with Inhelder. Though not centrally concerned with epistemology or with normative developmental theory, I was fascinated to observe at first hand the work of the Geneva group. Agreeing wholeheartedly with Piaget's belief that learning is founded on action, I decided when I returned to the University of California that the students in my laboratory course should learn by doing. In order to teach them some of the subtleties of test construction, I assigned a project: to convert Piagetian experiments into test items meeting strictly psychometric criteria, while conserving, insofar as we could, the essence of the original problems. Marcel Goldschmid was my excellent teaching assistant during that first year. Our efforts together may account in part for a degree of resemblance between his subsequent activities and mine.

Though the original objective of this continuing project was pedagogic, I soon came to see that it might have value for research as well as for teaching. Our goal was not to produce a new Stanford-Binet. Of regular mental tests we have already more than enough, and their value is itself under sharp reexamination. However, there are other purposes to be served by psychometric instruments with content drawn from the Geneva experiments.

In the first place, it would be hard to exaggerate the importance of Piaget's influence upon teaching methods and curriculum. A major current emphasis is upon accelerating cognitive development. Though I share Piaget's skepticism about acceleration programs, I feel there will soon be needed appropriate psychometric instruments for making independent evaluations of such attempts.

A second utility for such an instrument might lie in assessing the readiness of particular children for specific educational experiences, especially those founded upon Piagetian theory. This is a task for which traditional mental tests are not well adapted.

A third goal is to serve the traditional interest of differential psychologists in the relationships between such variables as age, sex, and social class on the one hand and cognitive level on the other, by providing more extensive and more reproducible data on these problems, with content presumably much freer from cultural bias than are the Stanford-Binet and WISC.

Fourth, the psychometric approach might possibly serve theory. I do *not* mean that it might verify or refute Piaget's major formulations concerning epistemogenesis or the stages of cognitive development, which are well established at least in broad outline. However, the theoretical foundations of mental testing are in need of reconstruction. In 1904, Spearman proposed an elegant theory of intelligence to account for individual differences on psychometric tests, and his doctrine of the "indifference of the indicator" rationalized the adventitious collections of items which constitute general intelligence tests to this day. Unfortunately, the theory was fatally damaged by discordant empirical findings. Recurrent refurbishings of the factorial position, usually by postulating more factors, derive not from a really new and basic synthesis, but from the need to explain the relationships among newer and more diverse kinds of tests. Yet the dilapidation of factor theory has not destroyed the possibility that a structural theory of an entirely different sort, for example that of Piaget, might succeed where factor analysis has faltered. This possibility is very attractive even to me, a sampling theorist in the tradition of Thomson and Tryon.

Moreover, as a sampling theorist, I have always been distressed by the absence of a rational theory to govern the sampling of item content for inclusion in standardized tests. While experience over 60 years had demonstrated the empirical worth of certain types of items (e.g., comprehension, vocabulary, etc.) for predictive purposes, the best current tests consist of items chosen with more regard for their statistical properties than for their content.

At the very least, Piaget's demonstration of the logical identity of superficially dissimilar cognitive problems suggested that the logical formulation of items might provide a more definable and systematic basis for item selection than the almost haphazard item compilations which comprise the Binet and its derivatives. At the best, Piaget's contributions might provide a basis for constructing a measure of general ability founded not upon empirical curves of percents passing, but upon a genuine theory of cognitive development. Such a measure, if successful, might diagnose a child's cognitive status more precisely than MA or IQ, and imply the instructional approach best suited to his needs.

If one grants the legitimacy of the goals I have outlined, one might still ask "Why abandon the méthode clinique?" To be sure, the flexibility of the méthode clinique, which enables one to shape the dialogue to the responses of the particular child, is ideally suited, at least in Piaget's hands, to learning how the child thinks. Yet when one's purpose is not to formulate or substantiate a theory, but rather to compare different children under identical conditions, the method of inquiry must not itself risk introducing variability into the results. Moreover, the interrogation required to elicit the qualitative subtleties of a child's thinking takes too long for the psychologist to be able to cover any substantial variety of tasks. In short, the nature of our problem places constraints upon our method, and the method must be judged in relation to the problem we have chosen.

Psychometric considerations must necessarily alter considerably the format of cognitive problems originally approached by the méthode clinique. What then, were our objectives in item design?

The goal where we have had most success is in developing methods of test administration and scoring which rival Stanford-Binet or WISC items in explicitness and reproducibility, and in respect to the practical constraints of brevity and interest to children. We hope we have not lost the essential content in the process. Our items are intended to take no more than 5 minutes each on the average. The materials are attractively colored and children uniformly have enjoyed working with them. They are portable, but bulkier than WISC kits. Our particular concern just now is to make them lighter and more compact.

A crucial aspect of reproducibility is control of verbalization. Most investigators have followed Piaget in utilizing interrogation, even though the questions were sometimes read from a standard list. This approach standardizes the examiner's questions but not the subject's answers. Scoring entails a degree of subjectivity in classifying responses, and almost forces resumption of the méthode clinique to clarify obscure or incomplete explanations by the subject. In order to obviate ambiguities in interpreting children's language, we have tried, not always successfully, to create situations in which the child's reasoning may be inferred from what he does rather than from what he says. An example of what we seek is Smedslund's version of the transitivity problem, where the child's choice between sticks reveals either the perceptual or the logical basis of his thought. The water-level, reversal of perspective, and locus problems can easily be cast in nonverbal, multiple-choice format, where the child merely points to the correct alternative. Seriation, hierarchical classification, displacement, probability, and some others can be made to depend upon scorable manipulations of the material by the subject.

On some items where our ingenuity thus far has failed, the scoring still depends upon a verbal response. The correct response on conservation items, for example, is often "the same," and time pressure precludes asking children to justify their responses. Lest they learn to say "the same" merely because it appears to satisfy the examiner, we are now developing items measuring conservation of inequalities, where "the same" is not the correct response.

A related goal has been to build into our items checks upon children's understanding of the directions, especially their knowledge of relational terms—"more," "less," "the same," "longer," "shorter" etc. Such precautions are necessary to avoid imputing to reasoning level, errors which may reflect only children's uncertainty about how the examiner is using words.

We have also built into some of the items measured amounts of demonstration and practice, both to insure further against misunderstanding, and to see whether or not the child's level can be raised in the course of the testing. Generally speaking, this has not significantly improved performance. A few children seem to be helped, though it is not always clear whether they are genuinely in a transitional stage, or whether we have merely clarified the task for them.

Scoring is a difficult problem. Different items have entailed different approaches. Most of our items have several parts, but often the successive parts are merely replications of each other, included to minimize the likelihood of chance success, as, for example, indicating the water level in a wrapped bottle held successively in different positions. In such instances, no more than a simple sum score is justifiable. In actual fact almost all subjects score either zero or the maximum, and it would do little violence to the data to treat such items dichotomously.

In other instances, the successive parts of an item increase in difficulty, and sometimes in the logical complexity of the task. If the sequence of parts constituted a Guttman scale for everyone, equal weighting of the parts would order the subjects by merit as well as do more complex schemes. However, ubiquitous errors and accidents interfere. At this preliminary stage of our work it seemed desirable to weight the parts in such a way that the total score not only reflected the merit of the subject's performance, but also identified his pattern of performance across the several parts. A record of such patterns is essential to testing empirically the intra-item consistency of the subjects, at the same time that a total score is required to correlate one item with the rest. Other workers have "classified" patterns but have not attempted to reduce such classifications to a linear scale. It can be done by scoring the successive parts one or zero in the successive columns of a binary number which represents performance on the item as a whole. Such numbers however are cumbersome, and tend not to correspond very well to what seems intuitively to be the relative merit of different performances.

We have utilized a sort of compromise which works well when an item has only three or four parts. In a typical item, there may be two attempts allowed on each of two levels of difficulty. Initial success on the easier of two tasks is scored 2; success on a second trial after practice or further demonstration is scored 1. Success on the more difficult subitem is scored 4, and the second attempt scored 2. This provides scores from 0 through 6, each of which denotes a particular pattern, thus:

Part	A_1	A_2	B_1	B_2	
Weight	(2)	(1)	(4)	(2)	Score
Pattern	−	−	−	−	0
	−	+	−	−	1
	+	(+)	−	−	2
	−	+	−	+	3
	+	(+)	−	+	4
	−	+	+	(+)	5
	+	(+)	+	(+)	6

Two additional patterns are:

−	−	−	+	2
−	−	+	−	4

These are extremely rare if B is actually more difficult than A, and can be eliminated by the rule of giving B only to subjects earning a score on A.

Regardless of method of scoring, our items of all kinds show a decided empirical tendency toward bimodality. In such a case it is simple to trichotomize the item into those who have the idea, those who don't, and the small handful who earn partial scores and who may be in a transitional stage. Our tables by item on grade, sex, and race differences have been prepared on this basis. In instances where the parts are of equal difficulty and the probability of chance success on each is high, as in lateral reversal, the intermediate scores reflect little more than luck.

What, if anything, have we found out to date? At this stage, results are provisional and some analyses are incomplete. Here are a few highlights, but first a word about our sample and our testing procedure.

Our subjects over the last 5 years have been roughly 400 children in kindergarten and the first four grades drawn from schools in three cities of the California Bay Area. The schools were deliberately selected to cover a wide range of socioeconomic levels. Approximately 20 percent were black, somewhat over 10 percent were Oriental. Data were collected in a school by a team of examiners, usually five, who set up five tables in a lunchroom or auditorium, each table equipped with materials for two of the items under development. Children were brought in in groups of five, one for each table. Every 10 minutes each child moved to the next table in the circle, completing our quasi-musical chairs game in the 50-minute period between recesses. This procedure imposed stringent constraints on the length of each item—probably good discipline for experimenters confronted with an almost infinite array of attractive possibilities. On the whole, it worked very well, systematically eliminating order effects as between items and providing a good deal of social facilitation to the children being tested.

While we have experimented with more than 40 items, many proposed by my students, we have fairly extensive data on about 20, which cover a considerable range of content. Most of these have been aimed at the transition from the preoperational stage to the stage of concrete operations.

Here are brief descriptions of them. The conservation of quantity is measured by adaptations of the experiments on lumps of clay deformed in shape, and water poured into shallow versus deep containers. Conservation of area is tested with grouped versus dispersed barns in fields of equal size; conservation of volume by apartments built in islands of various shapes and sizes. Two items involve spatial reversals. In one, a child must correctly place a small car painted red on one side, blue on the other, at various places on a spiral track. In the other, he must select from among several small photographs the one which shows how a small farm would look from various vantage points. Also presented in multiple choice format is the well-known problem on the horizontality of water levels. The task of placing small sticks in serial order is presented at various levels of difficulty, as are some of the geometric problems formulated by Piaget. We have collected data on the transitivity-of-length problem studied by Smedslund, and are developing items on hierarchical classification and on conservation of length and of number. For work with fourth graders, we have developed items dealing with probability, with the conservation of weight, and with the relationships of weight and volume to displacement of a liquid. We think that some of our items now embody the essential idea of the corresponding Piagetian experiments in a much more objective and quantifiable format. Other items, despite numerous revisions, are not as satisfactory. Some we have abandoned altogether, and others are being revised yet again.

Ten of our earliest items were given to a single sample of 200 children. Owing to lack of time, I shall show you results for only one of the ten.

Figure 4-1 (*Clay*) presents data for an adaptation of Piaget's famous experiment on the invariance of a mass of clay under shape transformations. Our procedure provides a demonstration for the child who initially lacks the conservation. However, as others have noted, there are few instances where demonstration is helpful to the child who doesn't have the concept, and few fall into the transitional category.

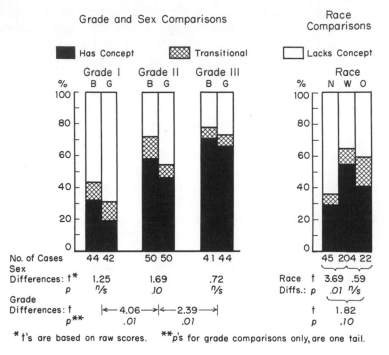

FIGURE 4-1   CONSERVATION OF QUALITY (CLAY).

Grade differences are marked here and on certain other items, especially the most complicated ones like *Seriation* and *Islands*, but are slight on some of the others presumably measuring the same stage of cognitive development. This was not anticipated. Boys do slightly better than girls. This was a general finding on all items, and the converse of findings with verbal tests like the Stanford-Binet.

Although we had no direct measures of socioeconomic status, it was possible to analyze the data by race, and in this sample, race and socioeconomic status were strongly correlated. Race differences tend to be larger than sex differences. Blacks do less well than whites on every test, and on *Clay, Seriation, Perspectives*, and *Water Level*, the difference is significant at the 1 percent point. What may be more surprising is that the Oriental children are superior to the whites on at least half the items, though the number of Orientals is too few to establish the significance of the result.

The data I have cited are based on total scores. What about inconsistencies within items where, as in the case of clay, some scalar property might be expected? An empirical score distribution is not enough to demonstrate the existence of a scale. There must be a priori grounds for the ordering (as for example when one subitem was designed to be harder than another) for as in tossing unbiased pennies, we may expect a distribution of scores even when all items are equal in difficulty and subjects are behaving randomly. In this latter case only two patterns can properly be considered to fall on a scale—either all correct or none correct, with intermediate scores assignable to unreliability.

Smedslund's transitivity is of this sort. Essentially the same comparison is repeated four times, and the items are equal in difficulty. The score here is a simple summation which does not permit us to specify the frequency of each pattern.

Our data show that a percentage of children ranging from 12 percent in Grade 1 to 61 percent in Grade IV managed transitivity so consistently that the result cannot be imputed to chance. Reciprocally, the number who were fooled by the Müller-Lyer illusion declined from 47 percent in Grade 1 to none in Grade IV. The 40 percent in the middle score range behaved inconsistently or unreliably, but cannot properly be regarded as fitting an intermediate point on a cognitive scale.

Seriation presents a different case. Here, Task A_1 requires the child to fill in eight sticks of varying lengths after E has placed sticks 1 and 10. In Task A_2, for those needing help, E places sticks 2 and 9. Tasks B_1 and B_2 follow the same pattern as A_1 and A_2 except that all the sticks are of equal length and differ only in the proportion of each painted red. Maximum score is 6 and B is not given if subject fails A_2. Here there is reason to make an a priori ordering from easy to hard of $A_2 > A_1 > B_2 > B_1$, though there is some arbitrariness in placing A_1 below B_2.

The scores, scalar patterns, and percentage frequencies for 319 subjects in Grades I through IV are as follows:

Order of presentation	2d	1st	4th	3d		
Subitem	A_2	A_1	B_2	B_1		Percent
Weight	(1)	(2)	(2)	(4)	Score	frequency
	(+)	+	(+)	+	6	37
	(+)	+	I	−	4	17
	(+)	+	−	−	2	17
	+	−	−	−	1	9
	−	−	(not given)		0	15
				Total =		95%

Off-scale patterns are infrequent:

A_2	A_1	B_2	B_1	Score	
+	−	(+)	+	5	1%
+	−	+	−	3	4%

In such instances, the apparent existence of a scale, coupled with the rarity of off-scale responses, implies that a simple sum across equally weighted subitems would not seriously alter the ordering of subjects. For this reason we are more and more inclined to abandon weighting schemes in favor of simple sums or dichotomies depending upon whether the item is scalar or nonscalar.

Let us move next to a consideration of consistency and inconsistency as between items. One way of approaching the question is by intercorrelation. We have calculated correlations from both continuous and dichotomized variates, with very similar results. For the original ten items, the intercorrelations of the items with each other and with age, sex and father's occupation are given in Table 4-1.

TABLE 4-1   INTERCORRELATIONS OF PIAGET DERIVED TEST ITEMS

Based on Approx. 200 Public School Children of Oakland and Richmond, California[*]

	1	2	3	4	5	6	7	8	9	10
	Clay	Water Pour	Sheep and Fields	Islands	Persp.	Tracks	Seria- tion	Trans.	Geom. Forms	Water Level
1. Clay	—	65	36	23	30	01	35	22	13	19
2. Water pouring	65	—	41	27	24	09	37	31	12	20
3. Sheep and fields	36	41	—	15	17	08	25	07	17	20
4. Islands	23	27	15	—	15	13	22	13	12	21
5. Perspectives	30	24	17	15	—	07	30	26	11	29
6. Tracks	01	09	08	13	07	—	13	14	03	24
7. Seriation	35	37	25	22	30	13	—	28	12	27
8. Transitivity	22	31	07	13	26	14	28	—	06	24
9. Geometric forms	13	12	17	12	11	03	12	06	—	09
10. Water level	19	20	20	21	29	24	27	24	09	—
Age	23	18	01	32	12	06	20	03	-03	20
F's occupation	26	32	19	06	11	01	32	22	15	14
Sex (m/f)	14	16	10	04	04	-08	03	19	04	10

[*]N = 100_c 2nd graders, 50_c 1st graders, and 50_c 3rd graders, drawn from five Oakland and five Richmond schools chosen to be representative of the entire school populations concerned.

Let us digress for a moment to look at the bottom three rows of the table.

It is not surprising that correlations with age are virtually all positive. Nevertheless, the correlations were lower than expected, even allowing for the relative unreliability of items as brief as these.

Correlations with father's occupation are also all positive, and higher than the correlations with age, although these items tend to involve reasoning about matters universally available to observation, e.g., the horizontality of water levels. It is hard to see how social advantage could be a very large factor in success on some of these items. The genetic selection implicit in occupational level may well have more to do with it, but on this point we have no data.

Boys do slightly better than girls, but most correlations with sex are insignificant.

In the table proper, the most surprising outcome, considering that all items were intended to measure the transition from preoperations to concrete operations, is the rather low level of interitem correlations. What accounts for so much apparent specificity? Certainly unreliability plays a role. With items only 5 minutes long, we could hardly expect really high values, although the maximum intercorrelation of a Stanford-Binet item with all other items in its testing range has a median value of .66, according to McNemar, with 90 percent between .45 and .85. Among our items, only *Clay* and *Water Pouring* have maximum inter-correlations as high. Yet the low correlation of these relatively reliable items with the remaining eight implies that specificity rather than error is the more important factor. Dodwell, Lovell and Ogilvie, and others have also reported findings suggesting noncorrespondence of cognitive stage across different content levels.

Contingency tables tell the same story as the correlations. Although they are more affected by discrepancies in the difficulty levels of the items compared, they are more easily grasped by those of us at the level of concrete operations. Here is one (data for all grades combined) where difficulty discrepancies are minimally disturbing:

		Water pouring			
		— (0—1)	Transitional (2 7)	+ (8—9)	Totals
Clay	+ (4)	11*	13	84	108
	Trans. (2—3)	8	9	10	27
	— (0—1)	72	14	9*	95
	Totals	91	36	103	230

*Major discrepancies (+— and —+) = 20/230 or 9 percent

Here is clay vs. perspectives (r = .30):

		Perspectives		
		— (0—3)	Transitional (4—5)	+ (6—8)
Clay	+ (4)	45	29	50	124
	Trans. (2—3)	9	10	6	25
	— (0—1)	65	22	17	104
		119	61	73	253

Clay is apparently the easier item. Hence the only sharp discrepancy is success on perspectives coupled with failure on clay—17/253 or around 7 percent. These discrepancies would be much more numerous if we included those of one step as well as those of two steps. It is worth remembering that these are all reasoning items, and reasoning has long been considered a factorially complex domain in which specificity is the rule, not the exception. Moreover, these items have deliberately minimized the role of verbal skill. It is an interesting speculation that the greater item correlations found in traditional intelligence tests, and indeed the apparently better correspondence across Piagetian experiments when conducted by the méthode clinique, may be to some degree a function of the dependence of both things correlated upon verbal facility. In any event, we have begun to ask ourselves whether or not it is legitimate to combine into a single scale items which appear to have so little in common.

How close have we come to meeting our own objectives? We have contrived, in most instances with some success, to convert 20 odd of the experiments described by Piaget into a standardized format which is relatively objective, which minimizes examiner variance, and which meets ordinary test criteria of brevity, interest, portability, and the like. By minimizing dependence upon children's verbalizations we have sacrificed concern with qualitative aspects of their thought. There is compensation, however, in reducing the dependence of success upon verbal facility. The fact that children's behavior in our test situations so closely approximates what Piaget has reported is perhaps helpful refutation of the old charge that children were confused or led by the méthode clinique, or that theoretical inferences are overinterpretations of children's imprecise speech.

A crucial consideration is whether or not our items assess the cognitive structures which the original experiments were intended to demonstrate. On the whole, I think that they do. Obviously the process of thought which underlies success or failure with one of our items must be inferred from behavior rather than demonstrated by a searching verbal inquiry. Our approach would never have provided the insights which have led Piaget, Inhelder, and their coworkers to their theoretical formulations—but the theory now exists. Its experimental verification is a different problem from ours.

The approach I have described is better suited to survey testing of large numbers of children over a few problems relevant to some special curriculum, or to assessment of a child in a reasonably short space of time with respect to a variety of problems. The relationships of cognitive development to age, sex, social class, or school history can be more readily determined by our approach than by the more time-consuming experimental methods. I look for our methods to aid, also, in cross-cultural and cross-language research, where deemphasis of children's verbal explanations is an advantage. Work has already been done using some of our tests among Ga people in Ghana, and in Ethiopia.

On the other hand, our items are limited in content to matters concerning physical events and relationships, where logical or spatial reasoning is required. I am sure that educational achievement tests and even conventional IQ measures will be better predictors of success in certain school subjects, especially in language and social studies, which are far from our area of concern.

We have been rather surprised to find considerable inconsistency, or at least independence, both within items and between them. Within items which have scalar properties, the number of children who fall off-scale seems to be no more than 10 or 15 percent, but our analyses are not complete. Between items, independence seems to be the rule, even though the items are of appropriate difficulty levels to make discriminations among the children tested, and even though they were all intended to involve the same major stage. Error is certainly a factor here, and improving item reliability is a high priority. Nevertheless, the evidence thus far obtained has about extinguished whatever hope we might once have held that we could place each child on a single developmental continuum equivalent to mental age, and from his score predict his performance on content of whatever kind.

As a differential psychologist, I must confess that I am pleased, rather than dismayed, that the intractable individuality of human beings, which has plagued normative psychologists since before Wundt tried to eliminate individual differences in reaction time, continues to assert itself, even in the face of Piaget's elegant normative theory.

Comments on Tuddenham's Paper
by J. Douglas Ayers
University of Victoria

Tuddenham has reported on a most comprehensive attempt to develop an ordinal scale of intelligence for the period from preoperational thought through to concrete operations. Both the research and the test development associated with it represent a distinct contribution because they provide a basis for evaluating the possibilities of developing a functional set of ordinal scales based on Piaget's model. Another distinctive feature of his paper is the specification of criteria that are required for developing standard measures to test individual differences. In this respect, he is much more aware than most researchers in child development of the importance of adequate testing procedures in the conduct of research studies.

Tuddenham has also pointed out that Piagetian measurement procedures are not appropriate for developing a scale of intelligence. Piaget has undoubtedly added more knowledge of conceptual development than any other single investigator. Despite this, many of his observations have been questioned due to dissatisfaction with approximate dates for each stage, the tendency to ignore individual variation, and particularly with incomplete reporting of results. Undoubtedly the méthode clinique was suited to Piaget because of its great flexibility in probing for thought patterns and structures, and without it, it is doubtful that Piaget would have developed the theory for which we are so indebted. But I believe Tuddenham's research and that of many others in cognitive development clearly indicate that Piaget's role has been essentially that of an innovator. His clinical method and heuristic procedures provide us with few positive answers, but rather with an almost limitless number of suggestions for the further study of cognitive growth, as evidenced by the increasing number of studies based on his model. Piaget's measurement procedures are not only less rigorous and less standardized than those of most psychologists today, but they are unsuitable for the development of scales of intelligence which will reveal individual differences among children.

There are several crucial tasks confronting researchers in cognitive development today. It is necessary to develop both sound research procedures and reliable measuring instruments. What is disappointing about most of the research that has been conducted using Piaget's theory as a model is that it has simply replicated the Piaget and Inhelder studies, usually under more controlled and standardized conditions, or it has attempted to accelerate the acquisition of cognitive structures by intervention. The amount of new knowledge that has been added is limited and very little progress has been made in resolving the methodological issues or measurement problems, as evidenced by the reviews of Wallace (1963) and Sigel (1968). It could be argued that further improvement in experimental methodology will not result in much significant research unless there is a concomitant improvement in testing procedures. Thus, Tuddenham's work is significant in that he has studied the acquisition of concepts, operations, and structures using more adequate testing procedures. He has proposed four criteria for developing satisfactory test items to measure cognitive development: (1) standardized administration and scoring procedures, (2) control of verbalization with nonverbal responding wherever possible, (3) checks on the understanding of directions, and (4) measured amounts of assistance either in the form of demonstration or practice.

It is interesting to note that Tuddenham found that measured amounts of demonstration and practice did not significantly improve performance. "A few children seemed to be helped though it is not always clear whether they are genuinely in a transition stage or whether we have merely clarified the task for them." This finding is in general agreement with most intervention experiments. For example, acquisition of conservations has not been accelerated when training has been based on demonstrations of the conservation or when practice has been provided with the task itself.

Notwithstanding the careful standardization of procedures reported by Tuddenham and his use of large representative samples, he found, as did Dodwell (1961), Lovell (1961b), and others, that there is a wider age range for children's attainment of various levels of conceptualization and that the sequence may not be as invariant as Piaget indicates. There seem to be several possible explanations for not finding neat ordinal scales: the theory needs revision, the research methodologies are inadequate, or the measurement procedures are inaccurate. While either theory or methodology may have set limits on the advancement of knowledge, it is proposed that traditional psychometric practices and beliefs have actually thwarted the development of adequate measures.

Let me clarify this position. Traditional measures of abilities sample maximum performance, as, for example, in a vocabulary test. To measure cognitive processes in children, one must determine optimal performance at a point in time along some scale of development. Chittenden (1969) has recently made a similar proposal. He has suggested that new techniques for assessing cognitive development should take the typical/maximal distinction into account and should try to focus on "characteristic" responses rather than "best" responses. In any case, adaptation of traditional techniques is not apt to be effective in developing an ordinal scale of intelligence as Tuddenham's research shows. What is likely required is a completely new approach that is not hampered by traditional psychometric practices and beliefs. Both Chittenden (1969) and Ayers (1969) have suggested some of the criteria that might be used in measuring cognitive development in children.

The traditional Piagetian scoring categories of conserver, nonconserver, and transitional may also be placing restrictions on the development of new procedures. Dr. Tuddenham studied extensively various methods of scoring, but found that complicated schemes apparently were no more effective than the tripartite scheme. Also, there are generally relatively few children in the transitional category. As a consequence, he has proposed that transitional scores represent chance scores in lateral-reversal tasks. Perhaps this can be used as a more general explanation, for the transitional-scoring category. With many of the Piagetian tasks, chance success is large. And when this is not a sufficient explanation perhaps there is a wide variation in content (as between seriation tasks, say with three sticks and ten sticks) or there may be a real difference in task complexity (as for example, between continuous and discontinuous substance). It is proposed that the resolution of the adequacy of the traditional Piagetian scoring categories will not be answered completely by determining the effect of the chance factor. It is also important to determine the effect of variation in content and task complexity by administering series of graded subtests. Another, and closely related, measurement problem that has not been considered sufficiently is the effect of the order of presentation of tasks. Tuddenham reports that where there was a series of related tasks of increasing difficulty, the most difficult was presented first on the basis that scores would be weighted inversely with difficulty. However, the data show, for example, for seriation effects, that 95 percent of the subjects fall on a perfect Guttman scale. This suggests that the easier tasks should be presented first. Taking the children through the subtests in sequence may have resulted in improved performance. Also, if simpler content, say five sticks for the seriation task, had been presented before the ten sticks, perhaps an even larger proportion of the students would have performed at a higher level of competence.

On the basis of the above arguments and evidence, it is proposed that the measurement of cognitive processes in children requires the development of procedures that will assist in determining optimal performance at a point in time along some scale of development. It is unlikely that providing graded subtests will be sufficient. In order to ensure optimal performance, it will likely be necessary to administer sequences of questions related to the prerequisite skills for each concept, operation, or structure. The problem is to match the questioning with the cognitive capabilities of the individual child and not just the typical child.

It was difficult for this reviewer to do justice to Tuddenham's comprehensive paper in the time available, and the selection of items for discussion undoubtedly reflects the biases of the reviewer. It should be noted that there are many suggestions regarding testing procedures and several intriguing hypotheses about the findings that would provide valuable guidance for anyone attempting to standardize Piagetian tasks. In fact, the reviewer believes that the publication of Tuddenham's carefully standardized tests would serve a number of functions. But probably the most important function would be to ensure comparability of testing procedures among studies of the same Piagetian tasks.

Open Discussion

The low intertask correlations reported by Tuddenham aroused great interest, and the entire discussion focused on the various ramifications and possible interpretations of these data.

Inhelder began by pointing out that the several tasks used by Tuddenham are not all solved completely at the same age, i.e., the age at which the task is solved varies from task to task. Thus, mastery of the island problem—buildings of the same area on islands of different sizes—comes only at age 11 or 12, while conservation of quantity comes much earlier, and so on. Therefore she wondered just how Tuddenham used them to evaluate and classify the children.

Tuddenham replied that ". . . although our items borrowed the names and the materials of some of the Genevan experiments, we really dealt with only part of what was contained in the Genevan experiments." He described his procedure with the island problem and added, "Now this is by no means coextensive with the work that was done in Geneva using these materials, so we didn't really cover the range that you people were concerned with."

Flavell asked if in fact he did not get any systematic invariant relations between tasks, and if he found any children who could not do the seriation task but who did succeed on the island problem.

TUDDENHAM

Those correlations are awfully bad, and I've got some contingency tables which are really what you would expect for those correlations. There is a great amount of specificity or independence between different items. Of course error rears its ugly head. There is a lot of unreliability involved. There is more evidence of consistency within the item than there is between one item and another item, both intended to be appropriate for 6- to 7-year-olds. The tasks are not all equal in difficulty, but, hopefully, all of them are pitched at roughly the same broad stage. Of those who can do the hardest of our items, a substantial number, but not all, are able to do the easier ones. But there are people who break the correspondence. It is very confusing.

LOVELL

In your Table 4-1, I take it that these intercorrelations are based on a mixed bag of 100 second graders, 50 first graders, and 50 third graders, and you didn't calculate the correlation matrix within grades. I would like to point out that we have done this in our longitudinal studies with formal thinking and we find there that the coefficient of concordance increases as the child gets older. Had you calculated the intercorrelation matrix for age within grade in addition to grades alone, perhaps a more stable picture would have been presented.

TUDDENHAM

Maybe these things are unstable right at the point they are being acquired and that is why they don't show more correspondence across content areas.

However, something else should be pointed out. By taking children by grade rather than by age, we've restricted the age variability quite a bit, because the very brightest 7-year-olds were not in the second grade, they were in the third grade, and the very dullest 6-year-olds were not in the first grade but were probably still at some pre-first grade level. So the somewhat restricted variability of this group is another factor to consider. But I think we should go back and do them by age; that is an interesting suggestion.

Elkind noted that Burt and others have reported age changes in intercorrelations contrary to those suggested by Lovell. Lovell replied that Burt's results were obtained with measures of general ability and the Piagetian experiments fall into a rather different universe of discourse; he felt the Piagetian system requires rising correlations as the child gets older because the level of thinking becomes increasingly consistent across tasks.

TUDDENHAM

I think what our data may show is that before they become consistent across tasks, the task that a particular child is able to master doesn't give you much notion of whether or not he will be able to master other ones. In the stage where they're just getting these things, it seems to be very much a matter of chance which ones they get first. And then later, presumably, they have them all.

LOVELL

But there is another point that's been neglected in the Piagetian studies. We have consistently found that in bright children, once the operational schema is available in some areas, it goes rapidly across the field, whereas in the dull child, it sort of pokes its head in this area, and then occasionally here, and there's literally no transfer. As Bruner said years ago, the mentally retarded child has to learn everything afresh, as it were.

FLAVELL

It seems to me that Tuddenham's failure to find invariant sequences may be a function of the fact that the items picked had never been suggested as items which are linked by any kind of invariant sequences. For instance, the general view is that the child ought to know something about simple seriation before he can deal with, say, transitivity, but there is no real reason to expect relationships among unrelated tasks.

The session closed after Inhelder noted that in Geneva they had found relationships and ordering much more stable among some sets of tasks than among others.

Some Problems Associated with Formal Thought and Its Assessment

CHAPTER
FIVE

KENNETH LOVELL
University of Leeds

At the outset I wish to pay my tribute to the work of Professor Piaget and Dr. Inhelder for the insights into the growth of the human intellect which they have provided. I wish to pay tribute, in particular, for their identification of that type of thinking which they have termed "formal operational."

This paper is divided into four main sections which deal with, respectively: some characteristics of formal thought; the extent to which subsequent experimental findings have confirmed the views of the Geneva School; remaining difficulties associated with the growth of formal thought; and the assessment of formal thought in the new British Intelligence Scale. It will be appreciated that throughout, my treatment of the various topics must be brief, and that in the first section I have to rely heavily upon the views of Inhelder and Piaget since we are dealing with a phase of intellectual growth which they claim to have identified and subsequently described.

As the child moves up through the age range of 7 to 12 years he is increasingly able to structure a number of qualitatively similar factors such as linear length, weight, area, speed, time, and the like, all of which may be subsumed under the general heading of "first-order relations." But there comes a day when he encounters problems in which he realizes that a particular effect may be brought about by several concomitant influences. To solve these more complex problems, new thinking skills are required, for interfering variables sometimes give rise to inconsistent or even contradictory results. Thus he may find that most light objects float but that at times the rule is transgressed, as when he finds that some heavy objects float and some light objects sink.

At the level of concrete operational thought the isolation of a variable is via inversion or negation, in the sense that the variable whose role has to be assessed is seen by the child to be present in some instances but not in others, or it is introduced by him on some occasions but not on others—as when he pushes or does not push the pendulum. But he cannot negate the length or weight of an object. This shows at once the limitations of his thinking. On the other hand, the adolescent can neutralize the effects of these variables by carrying out reversibility by reciprocity. Again, at the level of concrete operational thought the child can only introduce or eliminate a variable in order to see its role. But at the level of formal thought a young person can eliminate a variable not only to control its own effect, but also to find the effects of changes in a second variable without changes in itself. Thus with the onset of formal thought, variables can be separated by neutralization as well as by exclusion; a variable can be eliminated not only to establish its own influence but, far more important, as a means of studying the influence of other variables.

Reverting again to the stage of concrete operational thought, it is noted that the child carries out a direct organization of perceptible or imageable data. It is true that there is some extension of the actual in the direction of the possible, but it is only the simple potential extension of actions or operations with respect to some specific content. He does not elaborate hypotheses. Rather, through the coordination of his actions he structures only the reality on which he acts. But in formal thought he enunciates a series of hypotheses and deduces the consequences for each particular condition. Then after experimentation or reflection, he selects those hypotheses which are compatible with his evidence. Put rather differently, we can say that the young person looks upon the facts in front of him as that subset of a set of possible transformations that have actually come to pass. Moreover, the facts are not regarded as such until he has obtained experimental verification using procedures that pertain to the complete set of hypothetical relations for the given problem. It is here that we come to what Inhelder and Piaget regard as the heart of formal thought, namely the reversal of direction between reality and possibility. Further, since it proceeds from what is possible to what is empirically real, formal operational thought is essentially hypothetical-deductive in nature.

Having stated the fundamental characteristic of formal thought, we can proceed to look at it in other ways. In formal thought, when verbal statements take the place of objects, a new variety of thinking—propositional logic—is imposed on the logic of classes and relations. Herein lies another fundamental property of formal thought, namely the quality to operate with propositions. Moreover, propositional logic opens up a whole new range of operational possibilities that are far greater than simple groupings of classes and relations. So, faced with certain situations, the adolescent can invoke dysjunction, implication, etc., since formal thought begins with possibilities rather than with the organization of perceived data. Now while Inhelder and Piaget admit that propositional logic needs some inner verbal support, since it deals with more than the mere registration of perceived data, they do not accept that the power of propositional logic is fundamentally due to this inner support. Rather, such power is due to the combinatorial ability which makes it possible to analyze reality into a set of possible hypotheses, this combinatorial power in turn being secondary to the still more fundamental property of formal thought, namely the subordination of reality to possibility.

Formal thought can also be characterized as "second degree operations." This is sometimes a very helpful way of looking at formal thought in education. At the level of first-order operations the child is able to monitor his thought processes and distinguish between reality and the order he imposes on it. Using the criteria of classification and seriation he can organize events, whether actual or potential. These first-order operations result from the coordination of his actions upon objects. But in formal thought the adolescent is able to structure relations between relations. Inhelder and Piaget point out that propositional logic certainly demands second-degree operations since between—or interpropositional—operations are performed on statements whose within—or intrapropositional—content consists of class and relation operations. Lunzer (1968) likewise points out that the pupil cannot really appreciate the necessity of holding constant the variables not being considered at the moment, unless while he is testing one hypothesis he is also aware of alternative hypotheses and their consequences. In other words, the subject must be aware of the hypothesis in question and the implications which follow, and at the same time be aware of the second-order relations between the various hypotheses. The schema of proportion, or the recognition of the equivalence of two ratios, is a good example of a second-degree operation.

Looking at formal thought as second-degree operations certainly helps us to understand why certain concepts are not available, except in an intuitive sense, until adolescence. Whereas the basic concepts of mathematics and science, such as number, length, mass, weight, time, temperature, etc., can be elaborated at the level of concrete operational thought, concepts such as commutative group, heat, momentum, and photosynthesis require formal thought for their grasp.

In their book *The Growth of Logical Thinking* Inhelder and Piaget indicate two broad groups of problems, the solutions to which require formal thought. In the first group, exemplified by the pendulum experiment, pupils have to provide proofs of hypotheses by the experimental manipulation of variables. In the second group, pupils have to discover relationships involving direct and inverse proportion, and solve problems necessitating an understanding of reciprocity in physical systems. The difficulty has been to see the relationships that exist between the thinking skills involved in these two groups of problems. Inhelder and Piaget argue that there is a psychological relationship through the combinatorial reasoning instanced in both groups by saying that the processes involved in the two groups of experiments operate in terms that can be represented by the same logical system of relations, namely the four group. I am not in a position to argue this, but I agree with Lunzer's previously cited study (1968) that it may well have been necessary for Piaget to use a logical notation to unravel the inferences a child can make at successive levels of intellectual growth. However, it requires a logician to argue with Piaget over the latter's efforts to construct "logics" corresponding to levels of thought; it is not the task of a mere educator to attempt this. My approach to the problem of whether these two groups of experiments are linked by a common intellectual complexity will be through empirically obtained evidence.

In the second part of my paper I want to address myself to three questions. First, have more recent studies confirmed, in situations other than those covered by the experiments of Inhelder and Piaget, that the adolescent's thinking does show the characteristics posited by the Geneva School? Second, does the adolescent specifically show evidence in more recent studies of second-order operations? Third, do the two groups of experiments outlined by Inhelder and Piaget show evidence of some common intellectual complexity or common thinking skills?

To answer the first question I will briefly mention a few of our findings with respect to thinking in history. Details of part of the earlier work in this area can be found in a paper by Hallam (1967). Pupils of varying ages from 11 to 16 years were given short passages to read on various historical topics such as The Norman Conquest, Cromwell and Ireland, and the Queen—Mary Tudor. After subjects had read the passages and had any word explained which they did not understand, they were asked a number of questions. The passages remained in front of them and they could refer to them as often as they wished. In this kind of study it has repeatedly been shown that pupils' answers can be classified as preoperational, concrete operational, and formal operational, with other replies at intermediate points between these stages.

At the level specified as concrete operational, answers clearly show: (1) ability to use the information provided but limited to what is immediately apparent in the text; (2) ability to forecast a result from the evidence but unable to form a mature hypothesis; and (3) movement from one point of view to another but no attempt to coordinate the two or more points of view. On the other hand, at the level specified as formal operational thought we do find evidence that the pupil goes beyond the given, tries out his thinking in a systematic manner, reasons by implication at an abstract level, attempts to relate different variables, and realizes a multiplicity of possible links. For example, to the question relating to the passage on Queen Mary Tudor, "Do you think it sensible to have conformity in religion in a country?" a pupil aged 14 years 8 months replied:

This is a very difficult question to answer because there are basically two ideas in the present day. On the one hand you have the idea that all should be subservient to the state, and, on the other hand, you have the idea that choice is a good thing. There's a lot to be said for both sides. But religion, being essentially a private thing between man and God, should be divorced from politics whenever possible. However, where a situation arises where there are two conflicting religions or ideologies, I think that in such a case it is probably permissible to attempt to enforce a uniform front to hold together the country in time of stress. Two bitterly opposed religious parties is a thing that should be discouraged because neither thinks anything of the other and is prepared to go to any lengths because religious fanaticism, when entering into politics, is often a more evil thing and more dangerous than politics, although politics in its own way is often both.

Levels of thinking remain fairly steady across historical passages. In one study, a measure of the level of logical thought in three stories yielded a figure of .87 using Kendall's Coefficient of Concordance. However, our data do suggest that formal thought in history comes late; a mental age of 16 to $16\frac{1}{2}$ years seems to be necessary. Studies at Leeds in other subject areas have likewise shown that pupils' answers can be assessed as being at the stages of pre-, concrete, or formal operational thought.

The second question asks if more recent studies have shown a move in adolescence or preadolescence from first-order to second-order operations. A number of studies which I shall briefly mention do indeed suggest that such is the case.

Lunzer (1965) constructed a number of verbal analogies, numerical analogies, and numerical series. These exercises were worked by pupils between 9 and 17+ years of age. The difficulty of the verbal analogies and of the numerical analogies involving proportional functions over that of numerical series demanding addition or doubling and halving led him to write, "The main conclusion seemed to be that both verbal and numerical analogies required the application of formal reasoning in the sense that the subject needed to establish second-order relations."

A study at Leeds (Lovell & Butterworth, 1966) involving the growth of the schema of proportion clearly showed that a central intellective ability underpins all the tasks used involving proportion. The first component of the Principal Components Analysis correlated highly, +.79 or more, with performance on the following tasks: the proportion function as in numerical analogies, Rings and Shadows experiment (Inhelder & Piaget, 1958), Equilibrium in the Balance experiment (Inhelder & Piaget, 1958), relations between the size of the external angle of a regular polygon and the number of sides, ratio of the areas of similar triangles given the dimensions of one pair of corresponding sides, and verbal analogies. Over 60 percent of the variance on these tasks which involve relations between relations is accounted for by the first principal component. On the other hand, performance on tasks involving easy numerical series and the calculation of the volume of cuboids from given dimensions correlated less than +.5 with the first principal component. The latter tasks involve skills which are, of course, available to older elementary school pupils since their solution depends upon first-order relations. But even at 15 years of age only some 45 to 50 percent of the answers which involved relations between relations were answered correctly.

A third relevant study has been carried out in the United States. Steffe and Parr (1968) investigated the ability of fourth, fifth, and sixth grade pupils to solve proportionalities presented in pictorial and symbolic form. They conclude that many children can solve proportionality problems presented in pictorial form if the solution is available through visual inspection. But when the pictorial data do not permit solution through visual inspection, proportionalities become extremely difficult for these pupils, with the exception of high-ability sixth graders. Only those who had IQs higher than 110 and perhaps a mental age of around $13\frac{1}{2}$ to $14\frac{1}{2}$ years had the ability to solve $\frac{6}{15} = \frac{3}{X}$ when the problem was presented pictorially.

Taking the evidence together, there is strong support for the view that formal operational thought can be characterized as second-degree operations, whereas the thinking of elementary school children cannot.

Our third question asked if the two groups of experiments used by Inhelder and Piaget involve some common intellectual skills. A number of studies carried out at Leeds by my students or at Manchester by Dr. Lunzer's can make some suggestions by way of answer. The results are best summarized as follows.

Lovell (1961a) used five combinations of ten of the experiments used by Inhelder and Piaget. These were given to different groups of subjects between 8 and 18 years of age (192 subjects in all). Kendall's Coefficient of Concordance (W) was taken as an index of the stability of the level of pupils' thinking across the various tasks. The value of W varied from .89 to .52 depending upon the age and ability range of the pupils concerned. Jackson (1965) investigated the level of logical thinking in 48 elementary and high school pupils of average ability. The stages of logical thinking employed were six, namely, 1A, 1B, 2A, 2B, 3A, and 3B, while the experiments used were Conservation of Motion, Oscillation of Pendulum, Communicating Vessels, Falling Bodies on an Inclined Plane, Equilibrium in the Balance, and the Law of Floating. The responses of 10 subjects were all at the same substage, and a further 29 had answers included within two substages. Thus just over 70 percent of the subjects had their replies included within two or less substages.

Hughes (1965) carried out a longitudinal study of a group of 40 pupils over a 4-year period. Pupils of average and below-average ability were first tested at 11+ years and tested yearly until they were 14+ years old. The tasks used were Equilibrium in the Balance, Colorless Chemicals, Oscillation of Pendulum, and Flexibility of Rods. Kendall's W was again taken as a measure of the stability of the level of thinking. It was found that W varied from .39 on the first testing to

.57 on the fourth, suggesting that as the move to formal thought takes place with respect to these tasks the level of thinking becomes steadier. This evidence also implies that those who are slow to move towards formal thought in one of the tasks tend to be slow to move in the other tasks. The logical thinking scores on these tasks obtained on the fourth testing were also intercorrelated with scores on other tasks such as tests of nonverbal intelligence and numerical analogies. All the intercorrelations were positive. A principal components analysis (true, a hazardous undertaking with only 40 cases) yielded a first component which showed substantial correlations with all the tests, the lowest being .57 with the Oscillation of Pendulum and the highest .81 with Colorless Chemicals.

Another study by Lovell and Shields (1967) involved 50 children 8 to 10 years old who had verbal IQs on WISC of 140 or higher. One purpose of this study was to see if the characteristics of formal operational thought could be found in the thinking of these children. A wide battery of tests was given and it was found that there were positive intercorrelation coefficients between the scores on all the tests. Further, a principal components analysis and a rotation of factors to the Varimax criterion yielded a factor which correlated .83 with Equilibrium in the Balance, .72 with Colorless Liquids, and .60 with Oscillation of the Pendulum. Incidentally, only the older children gave responses at the level of formal operational thought and even then such responses were comparatively few.

If now we look at the scattered and varied evidence which has been briefly mentioned here, it can be suggested that the test scores obtained on the two groups of tasks do show some tendency to cluster together, that is, there is some tendency for the pupils' thinking to remain steady across the tasks. But the size of the coefficient of concordance depends upon the homogeneity of the group and on other influences that we shall discuss later. It seems, then, that there is evidence that the two groups of experiments do demand some common intellectual skills for their successful performance. Furthermore, looking over all the evidence given in this section of the paper, it can also be suggested that Piaget was correct in positing two successive levels of logical thought.

In the third part of this paper I will mention a few of the many difficulties which remain with respect to our understanding of the growth of formal operational thought. Inhelder and Piaget do not say much about the content of a task, as distinct from the intellectual structures demanded to find a solution to it. To be fair, however, the Geneva School does agree that a person need not be at the same operational level in all fields of thinking. For example, Inhelder states: "both adolescent and adult are far from reasoning formally all the time. The attainment of a cognitive stage merely means that the individual becomes capable of behaving in a certain way which was impossible before" (Tanner & Inhelder, 1960). In the same work Piaget emphasizes that an adult operates at varying levels during the course of a day; when his car engine went wrong he operated at "empirical trial and error on a very low level . . . . At other times I go even lower and almost give way to magical behaviour" (p. 126).

It does appear, then, that there are a number of other issues which influence the appearance or nonappearance of formal operational thought when the solution to the task demands it. Familiarity with the content of a task seems likely to facilitate the use of formal thought in its solution. Again, credibility seems to be an important influence. Lunzer (1965) points out that in the experiment involving falling bodies on an inclined plane, logical necessity and initial belief go together, whereas in the experiment involving the oscillation of a pendulum, they do not, since initial belief suggests that weight must be a relevant factor. In a study at Leeds involving female college students 18 to 19 years of age, many maintained that weight must be a relevant factor in the time of oscillation of the pendulum, in spite of their own evidence to the contrary. This initial belief seemed to arise from the fact that there is always a weight attached to a grandfather's clock to give energy to the system.

Other ongoing work at Leeds shows that in some studies there is a positive relationship between attitudes to subject matter and level of logical thought obtained in that subject area. We cannot, of course, be sure whether pupils who do well in a school subject have good attitudes toward it, or whether good attitudes toward a subject facilitate the growth of logical thought in that area. Again, as I indicated earlier, both concrete and formal operational thought come later in history than in many other school subjects. In a way this is not surprising, for not only is the pupil faced with action far removed from his immediate world but he is confronted with situations which envelop the inner motives of adults living in earlier centuries and even in other geographical areas. Current studies at Leeds involving tasks from *The Growth of Logical Thinking* and tasks involving logical thinking in history—all given to the same subjects— suggest that formal thought tends to show itself first in Colorless Liquids, then in Equilibrium in the Balance, and then in history. Nevertheless, I estimate that the value of W will not exceed .5.

Formal thought, then, does not seem to be available evenly across all areas of experience. In our present state of knowledge it is not possible to say for certain whether the operational schemata of formal thought are just not available in certain situations or under certain conditions, or whether it is necessary to posit some kind of analytic set, proposed by Beilin (1968) in connection with conservation, which activates the individual's cognitive apparatus and permits him to analyze the data inherent in the situation. Nevertheless, it does appear from the work of Hughes (1965) that the abler the child and the earlier the first signs of formal operational thought appear, the more rapidly and consistently does this kind of thought spread to other areas of experience.

Another problem is that of the nature of the influences which determine the transition from the stage of concrete to that of formal operational thought.

Inhelder and Piaget consider that beyond some minimum age due to neuro-physiological development, it is social attitudes and exchanges, cultural conditions, and the effects of schooling which determine the age of the onset of formal thought. There have been few published results of cross-cultural studies which might throw light on this problem. Peluffo's (1967) work in southern Europe led him to the view that combinatorial and anticipatory thinking were strongly interfered with by an underdeveloped milieu and by lack of schooling. Again, Goodnow and Bethon (1966) showed the very poor performance of unschooled 11-year-old Chinese boys on a task involving combinatorial reasoning. Although they did as well as American pupils of average ability on tasks involving conservation of weight and area, they did rather less well than dull American subjects on the combinatorial reasoning task. Indeed, the proportion of correct responses to this task, both in the dull American pupils and in the unschooled Chinese pupils, was less than .20.

Particularly interesting is the work of Kimball (1968) among children in Malawi. He tested, individually, 36 boys and 36 girls at each grade from 1 to 8 inclusive, or 576 pupils in all. Twenty-three tasks were given; these involved the making of shapes from wooden blocks, conservation of area through paper cutting, conservation of continuous quantity using tumbler and bowl, questions concerning an electric circuit, "cause and effect" via a story, and equilibrium of a balance arm. Three of the tasks were of outstanding difficulty for these subjects. The first, involving the making of shapes from blocks, does not concern us. The second and third of these tasks do, as they indicate how slow is the movement in these pupils towards formal operational thought, especially when one realizes that the average age of the pupils in grade 8 was 15.2 years.

In the second task a story was given: "Aliki and Safira go to the market. Aliki steals some bananas when the seller is not looking. When the children return to their home, Aliki's mother asks him to cut some firewood with an axe. While he was working the axe misses the wood and cuts his foot." Each subject was then asked: Why did Aliki cut his foot? Would he cut his foot if he did not steal? Did the axe know that Aliki stole the bananas?

The third question was answered correctly by many grade 1 pupils and by most grade 2 pupils. But not until grade 7 was the second question "Would he cut his foot if he did not steal?" answered correctly by 50 percent of the boys. In neither grade 7 nor 8 did 50 percent of the girls answer this question correctly. Clearly the notion of chance is coming late.

The third task involved equilibrium in the balance. To the question "What will happen if I take my hands away?" with respect to the situation given by Figure 5-1, most grade 1 pupils gave correct answers. But to the same question asked with respect to the situation depicted in Figure 5-2, it was not until grade 8 that 50 percent of the boys answered correctly. Even so, fewer than 50 percent of the girls at grade 8 gave correct responses.

FIGURE 5-1   FIGURE 5-2

The performances on the two tasks show how late is the growth towards formal thought in these pupils, and they had been carefully selected to represent pupils in all regions of the country. It is interesting to note that the total score obtained on all the tasks correlated .65 with chronological age and .83 with school standard, but not significantly with the years of school science which they had had. The last finding is not surprising when one recalls that so much learning of science and other subjects in African schools is by rote.

The findings of Peluffo, Goodnow and Bethon, and Kimball are clearly consonant with the view of the Geneva school that culture pattern and schooling affect the age of the onset of formal operational thought. Unfortunately, we do not know the precise features of culture or schooling which accelerate or retard the growth of formal operational thought. Elsewhere (Lovell, 1969) I have raised, but not answered, the question as to whether or not traditional African cosmology tends to retard the onset of formal operational thinking in African pupils.

Educators are naturally concerned with the growth of formal thought in their pupils and they would like to know how to facilitate its growth. Suchman's (1966) work in this country is not unconnected with this issue. However, few controlled studies have yet been made in which an attempt has been made to aid the development of formal thought. In one study now nearly completed in England, pupils aged 7, 9, 11, and 13 years were tested on the Oscillation of the Pendulum, Bending Rods, and Colorless Liquids experiments. A very careful record was made of the number of variables isolated. Subjects in the experimental group were then trained, by the heuristic method and for one session only, on the apparatus with which they were originally presented. Three months later both the experimental and control groups were presented with the same experiment again, but with modified apparatus, together with a new experiment which involved a modified and rather more complicated form of the Balance. On retesting, the experimental group isolated more variables than the control group in the case of the three experiments in which training had been given. But in the Balance experiment the control group isolated as many variables as the experimental group at 7, 9, and 11 years of age. It was only among the 13-year-olds that the experimental group isolated more variables than the control group; in other words, only at 13 years of age was there any transfer of training.

A study at Leeds just completed involved the level of logical thinking in Religious Education, an elective subject in the General Certificate of Education examinations. At the beginning of a school year two groups of pupils, aged 14 and

16 years respectively, were questioned on passages relating to the Crossing of the Red Sea, Hosea, the Temptations, and the Prodigal Son. Some of these topics were taught by a good teacher during the school year, others were not taught at all. In the following July—10 months later—all the pupils were tested again on the same passages. The results show that for both groups of pupils the mean stage of logical thought attained increased significantly on the second testing, but the rise in the case of the taught topics was only marginally more than in the case of the untaught topics. We also had two control groups tested on the same topics and matched with the above two groups for age, IQ, and school attainment, but not taking Religious Education as an elective subject. In both these control groups there was also a rise in the mean level of logical thought between the September and July testings. However, both in September and July the mean levels of logical thinking actually attained were lower than the corresponding ones for the two groups taking Religious Education. Other work at Leeds is currently studying the effect of teaching history for a school year using two contrasting methods.

Mention has already been made of the work of Hughes (1965) carried out at Leeds in which pupils were tested on the same tasks once a year for 4 years. While it was possible to trace the changes in intellectual growth in the pupils involved, it was quite impossible to arrive at any judgments concerning the influences which were responsible for considerable growth in some pupils but little or none in others. The work of Neimark and Lewis (1968) is also interesting in this respect. In this study, children between 9 years 5 months and 11 years 6 months (mental age 9.07 to 13.77 years) were tested on problems said to demand formal thought for their solution and retested 1 year later. Their data indicate (Table 1, p. 531) that on three measures of performance, almost one-third showed no improvement between one testing and the next. However, we remain in the dark as to why this is.

What scattered and fragmentary evidence is available is consonant with the view that training on tasks involving formal thought has little transfer value for the majority of pupils before 13 years of age. Our evidence also supports the view I expressed earlier; namely, that knowledge of and attitude toward the subject matter are likely to facilitate formal thought. At the same time it remains true that we have a long way to go before we shall be able to say with confidence and precision which patterns of child rearing, methods of teaching, or types of culture are most conducive to the development of formal operational thought.

The fourth part of the paper says a little about some of the kinds of tasks used to evoke formal operational thought that have been included in the new British Intelligence Scale now under construction. In spite of the good service that has been rendered by the Stanford and Terman-Merrill revisions of the Binet scale, and by WISC, the British Psychological Society has argued strongly that there is a need for a new scale. It will be appreciated that it is possible here to discuss only such details as have been made generally available by Warburton, Fitzpatrick or Ward (see Warburton, 1966).

It is hoped that the scale will yield 12 subscales, thus giving scores for specialized abilities as indicated: V (Verbal), from the Vocabulary Information and Comprehension subscales; R (Reasoning), from the Matrices, Induction, and Operational Thinking subscales; N (Number), from the number subscale; S (Spatial), from Koh's Blocks and Visual Spatial Subscales; M (Memory), from the Visual Memory and Auditory Memory subscales; and F (Fluency), from the Creativity subscale. The combined scores on the 12 subscales will yield an index of general mental ability. Moreover it is expected that the scale will cover the age range 2 to 18 inclusive. At the moment, a statistical analysis is being made of the data obtained from the tryout sample which was drawn up according to a design of the type used in analysis of variance. Four main sources of variation were taken into account: sex, urban versus rural location, three socioeconomic levels, and three levels of ability. Within each age group there were thus 36 categories of children.

In the Comprehension subscale of the Verbal test, items of the type devised by Peel in his study of children's thinking are used. They are designed to bring out the changes that occur in the move from concrete and formal operational thought around 9 to 15 years of age. The first sentence of the item contains a leading statement which is quite irrelevant to the judgment required of the subject. This is followed by a description of events related to the problem but which, taken by itself, is insufficient to form the basis of a judgment. Limiting circumstances are also given. For example: "Roads over the Canadian Rocky Mountains are often very steep and have many sharp bends. One night a bus, driven by a man called Jack, left the road and crashed down the side of a railway cutting on to a coach of a stationary train. Many of the passengers in the bus were killed, while the injured in both bus and train had to wait until light before they were rescued." Was Jack a careful driver? Why do you say that? Three levels of response are postulated: prelogical, in which the replies show irrelevance or tautology; concrete, in which the replies are dominated by the content; and propositional, in which a hypothetical response is set up and examined in light of all the evidence.

The Induction subscale of the Reasoning tests involves the use of colored counters in the early part of the subscale, while in the later part, cards representing various problems are placed underneath a transparent pegboard. Subjects are required to observe, analyze, and elaborate simple rules regarding the change in position of the colored pegs. To do this they must be able to grasp relationships of alternation, constancy, randomness, reciprocity, and rotation.

The Operational Thinking subscale is naturally designed to investigate qualitative levels of thinking. The items range from ones requiring sensorimotor coordination to those demanding formal thought. For the younger pupils there are items concerned mainly with the logic of classes comprising simple sorting tasks. Older and more able pupils undertake a series of problems involving inference. A simple type of problem involving inference might be: "Mary, Joan, and Susan went swimming. When they returned they were questioned as to who swam the furthest and who the least distance. They replied that Susan did not swim as far as Joan although Susan swam further than Mary." Who swam furthest?

A more advanced problem may be woven around a story involving, say, cowboys and Indians and the burning of a farmhouse. Admission or denial by the cowboys of being present at the incident can be symbolized by p or $\bar{p}$ respectively, while admission or denial by the Indians of being present at the event can be symbolized by q and $\bar{q}$ respectively. The four basic possibilities, pq, $p\bar{q}$, $\bar{p}q$, and $\bar{p}\bar{q}$, can be combined to yield the 16 binary combinations which can be stated in the form of rules. So in essence the problem consists of the examiner stating the rules one at a time, as in the example "The Indians deny that they were present," and the subjects examining each of the four basic possibilities and deciding which conforms to the rule. The problem can, of course, be made more difficult. This kind of exercise may, incidentally, also help us to unravel the relationship between psychological and logical difficulty.

Taking the new scale as a whole, it will be possible to provide a profile of a subject's scores on the six abilities—V (Verbal), R (Reasoning), N (Number), S (Spatial), M (Memory), and F (Fluency)—and at the same time give a final score which will provide an index of general mental ability. Moreover, in those subscales which contain items based on the ideas of Piaget and others, it will be possible to show the qualitative level of thinking; namely, preoperational, concrete, or formal operational.

It seems likely that the construction of the new British Intelligence Scale will throw considerable light on the relationship between the development of formal thought and variables such as sex, socioeconomic background, urban-rural environment, and others.

Comments on Kenneth Lovell's Paper
by Thomas G. Sticht
Human Resources Research Organization

Does Learning Recapitulate Ontogeny?

Lovell has presented us with a brief summary of the main characteristics of Piaget's construct of formal thought, as distinguished from preoperational and concrete operational thought. He has also presented evidence to suggest that, working within the framework of Piaget's theory and methodology, logical thought *can* be classified into successive concrete and formal levels. In so doing, he isolated three problems which limit our understanding of the growth of formal operational thought:

1. That there is much intraindividual variability in the kinds of content which can be dealt with by formal thought;
2. That there are individual differences in the age of appearance of formal thought with respect to a given content; and
3. That there is little understanding of the nature of the influences which determine the transition from the stage of concrete to that of formal thought.

The first two problems, those concerned with intra- and interindividual differences, are of special interest because they pose one of the perennial problems in psychometric measurement, namely, the problem of making idiographic use of nomothetically based scales.

This problem is particularly acute when one recognized major source of variability is the content with which the individual will deal. It seems to me that if there is a desire to accurately characterize people with regard to their position in Piaget's developmental sequence of thought, Lovell's review would suggest that some sort of test battery approach, wherein for different age groups and/or other defined subgroups, various content areas might be represented.

Historically, one tactic for handling the problem of the influence of content upon test performance has been to avoid direct confrontation with subject matter content and to, if I may, divide and assimilate content into higher-order mental abilities believed common to a number of content areas and then describe an individual with respect to the degree to which he possesses or lacks these abilities, usually in reference to the performance of others. Based upon my understanding of Lovell's descriptions, this approach appears to be that underlying the development of the new British Intelligence Scale. That is, rather than describing performance restricted to some particular subject matter, tasks presumably representative of the abstract mental abilities of number, reasoning, etc. are presented. As I understand it, in certain instances, as in reasoning, performance would be scored both quantitatively with respect to answers correct, and qualitatively with respect to where the individual is located in Piaget's system of logical thought development. What we have here, then, is the determination of one's cognitive thought structure relative to different abstract mental processes called reasoning, number, etc. It would seem, then, that, with respect to determining where an individual stands in regard to his thought structure in a given content area, this estimate made by the British Intelligence Scale will be no more accurate than the relationships between the various mental abilities and performance in the content areas, and will most assuredly be less accurate than a direct evaluation of thought structure with a sample of the content in question. Without belaboring the point, I will add that, since it is almost certain that the British Intelligence Scale omits important mental abilities, Guilford (1967) himself having proposed some 120 candidates, the Scale is likely to be even less accurate in estimating in what stage of thought a person will operate with respect to a particular subject matter.

I would like to leave the psychometric problems in midstream at this time to address a few remarks to the third problem detailed by Lovell, namely, the problem of understanding the influences which determine the transition from one stage of thought to the next. In particular I want to comment upon the teaching practices which have typically been used by Lovell and other followers of Piaget to attempt to accelerate the development of succeeding stages of thought. In general, these practices have involved what is variously referred to as the "discovery," "heuristic," or "induction" method. Lovell mentions several studies which lead him to suggest that ". . . training on tasks involving formal thought has little transfer value for the majority of pupils before 13 years of age." I will add that in most studies related to this problem which I have read, attempts to move children or adolescents from one stage of development to the next have used heuristic or discovery methods, and have shown very little success. In view of this fact, I would like to suggest that it *not* be concluded, as has sometimes occurred, that the development of stages cannot be accelerated, but rather that the discovery method may not be an appropriate method—even with so-called "reinforcement" as used by Smedslund (1961a).

As an alternative to the discovery method, I would like to suggest that more didactic approaches should be evaluated for their effectiveness in promoting the movement through the various stages of development. In particular, I would like to recommend the investigation of teaching methods based upon the systems principles of task analysis and synthesis—principles developed over the past two decades primarily by military and industrial training specialists and currently receiving considerable interest as the *modus operandi* of a branch of education called "instructional technology."

Task analysis and synthesis emphasize the clear and distinct statement, in behavioral terms, of the instructional goal to be obtained and the instructional steps required to attain terminal performance. One outcome of applying a task analysis approach to the problem of accelerating the development of formal thought in history, a problem discussed by Lovell, is that didactic training of the suboperation of "formal thinking" per se, in addition to training on tasks *involving* formal thinking, would be accomplished. Such an approach, i.e., a didactic teaching of the operations and suboperations involved in the quantification of inclusion relations, was used with great success by Kohnstamm (1963) with children averaging 5.7 years of age. This amounts to an acceleration of approximately 2 years for the appearance of this phase of concrete logical operations. Perhaps such a didactic approach might also prove useful in accelerating the appearance of formal thought in some content areas. Perhaps it would not. But in this regard I would like to say that I agree with Lovell that we do not know which methods of teaching are *most* conducive for the development of formal thought. The available evidence, however, tempts me to suggest that the discovery method may likely be the *least* conducive to this development.

My final point is concerned with Lovell's observations concerning certain student variables which seem to "influence the appearance or nonappearance of formal operational thought when the solution to the task demands it" (p. 88). Lovell points out that the factors of familiarity, credibility, and attitude to subject matter may influence the appearance or nonappearance of formal operational thought. In general, it appears that the more familiar or credible the subject matter and the more favorable the student's attitude towards the subject matter, the more likely it is that formal operational thought will be available to solve the problem at hand. Now I would like to assume for the time being that in some manner, as yet not known, the factors of familiarity, credibility, and student attitudes are all interrelated and that they act in some unified way to permit the adolescent to deal at a formal operational thought level with a given subject matter. Since I am assuming that these factors work in a unified manner, I would like to use the term "familiarity" as an inclusive term and discuss tasks in terms of their familiarity or unfamiliarity for a given student. With this in mind, it appears to me that Lovell's review suggests the hypothesis that whenever a person capable of formal thought encounters an unfamiliar task, the probability of instances of formal thought operations decreases. With respect to problem solving, this means that fewer solutions to related problems will be found, and attempts to solve the problems will reflect considerable use of concrete operations. In general, these are the results which Lovell's review presented.

If we now consider a little generalizing of the *converse* of the foregoing hypothesis we arrive at what I think is a theoretically and heuristically significant hypothesis, namely: at any stage of development above the sensorimotor, tasks of such unfamiliarity can be found that the person is unable to completely apply the operations of his highest attained developmental stage, and in such cases the probability of operations characteristic of earlier stages of development will increase. If the probability of operations at lower stages of thought is directly related to the unfamiliarity of a task, then this hypothesis contains the notion of a regression of thought structure such that the greater the strangeness or unfamiliarity of the task or task situation, the lower the level of thought to which a person would regress to cope with the situation. What this hypothesis suggests, then, is that there may be both ontogenetic development of thought structure which follows Piaget's stages and subject-matter development of thought structure which follows the same stages of development. Ontogenetic development sets limits beyond which children of given ages cannot function; for instance, 4-year-olds cannot perform operational thought. Subject matter development permits the possibility that a given individual may not perform at his highest ontogenetic level of development with unfamiliar task situations.

In support of the hypothesis that subject-matter thought development may follow Piaget's developmental scheme I can offer only indirect evidence—one anecdote which I believe is particularly apt—and the results of training research from our laboratory studies and instructional design experience. First for the anecdote. At the American Educational Research Association meeting February 7, 1969, I attended the highly successful symposium on Teaching Piagetian Theory à la Piaget. At this symposium the chairman, Greta Morine, reported that her graduate students had a great deal of difficulty in learning Piaget's principles, concepts, and procedures by the lecture, reading, and discussion method of instruction which typifies so much of higher education. To overcome this difficulty, Morine decided to use Piagetian pedagogical principles; principles most people would regard as appropriate for children perhaps, but not for sophisticated, educated, intelligent, graduate students. The following quotation from Flavell (1963) summarizes some of Piaget's educational principles. Although outlined with respect to children, it was these same principles which Morine followed in teaching Piaget to graduate students.

> In trying to teach a child some general principle or rule, one should so far as is feasible parallel the developmental process of internalization of actions. That is, the child should first work with the principle in the most concrete and action-oriented context possible; he should be allowed to manipulate objects himself and "see" the principle operate in his own actions. Then it should become progressively more internalized and schematic by reducing perceptual and motor supports, e.g., moving from objects to symbols of objects, from motor actions to speech, etc.

I would submit that Morine's success in teaching Piaget à la Piaget is evidence for the hypothesis that when students are faced with highly unfamiliar tasks, like learning Piaget's methods and theory, subject-matter thought development tends to recapitulate ontogenetic thought development. For this reason learning is best when guided according to principles which parallel the ontogenetic development of thought.

Additional indirect evidence in support of the above hypothesis is provided by the results of training research performed by the Human Resources Research Organization (HumRRO) of the George Washington University over the past decade or so. The task has been to determine effective strategies and methods for training men whose academic and intellectual and, presumably, genetic backgrounds have produced a virtual *aurora borealis* in the spectrum of mental aptitudes. These men are adults, somewhat beyond the age range discussed by Lovell, being primarily between 17 and 25 years old. In many years of designing training programs for these men, HumRRO has developed a method which works especially well with lower-aptitude men, whose Wechsler IQs might range from near 70 to around 90 or 95. This strategy has formalized to the point of having a name: the Functional Context method of training (Shoemaker, 1967). This method of training is characterized by three instructional prescriptions:

1. Instruction should be sequenced to proceed from the concrete to the abstract. "Hands on" experience with objects of instruction should precede the presentation of abstractions about these objects.
2. Where machines and equipment are concerned, instruction should be from "whole to parts." For instance, in teaching about radios, a complete radio ought to be examined first, and then analyzed into components such that the student can always relate the "part" to the previously experienced "whole." Thus instruction should proceed through analysis and synthesis as outlined by Silvern (1965) in formulating his concept of *anasynthesis*.
3. At all times, instruction should be programmed so that the student is able to understand the functional significance of each topic to the next in terms of his prior experience, whether that be preinstructional experience or experience accumulated in the training program.

It seems clear to me that the Functional Context method of instruction expounded by HumRRO is quite consistent with Piaget's pedagogical prescriptions mentioned earlier. Both approaches suggest the desirability of progressing from concrete, action-oriented contexts to more theoretical, abstract situations. Using these ideas, many low-, average-, and high-aptitude men have effectively learned abstract electronics and physics concepts in training programs designed by HumRRO.

Recent research conducted in our laboratories (Taylor & Fox, 1967) lends additional support to the notion that thought structure in a given subject matter may be developed by use of an instructional system which parallels, to a degree, Piaget's developmental process of internalization of action. In this work, low-aptitude men were required to learn to apply the concepts of range and bearing in a coordinated plotting task. The men were unable to learn the task when instruction was exclusively verbal and presented in lecture format. However, when the task was presented in a concrete, action-oriented manner, with individualized practice in plotting, using simplified language and pictorial examples, and with prompt knowledge of results and correction provided, the low-aptitude men were able to learn the task.

Again, the foregoing research by HumRRO, as with Morine's experiences in teaching Piaget to her graduate students, appears to me to justify the hypothesis that the development of thought in unfamiliar subject matter involves something of a retracing of ontogenetic thought development. Perhaps the further development and evaluation of this hypothesis may improve our understanding of the influences which determine the transition from one ontogenetic stage of thought to the next, a problem so clearly illuminated by Dr. Lovell in his presentation.

Open Discussion

The comments ranged rather randomly over a variety of questions during the discussion period; the topics discussed were sex differences, the nature of "the structure," and instruction. The last of these, instructional procedures, drew the most comment.

Flavell suggested that Werner's notion of spiral development could be considered an ancestor of Sticht's hypothesis (". . . subject-matter thought development tends to recapitulate ontogenetic thought development"). He also felt that the idea might be related to Werner's microgenesis concept, which he described as the notion that in a perceptual situation, at the first instant of the perceptual act you have something global which then becomes differentiated. Lovell said that from the teaching point of view one should encourage the early concrete and intuitive introduction to abstract second-order concepts to build familiarity and positive attitudes and to speed the process of transition to formal thought. However, he also noted that in his work the issue of heuristic versus didactic procedures is treated as an empirical one and is currently under study.

ELKIND

It seems to me that Sticht dismissed the discovery method, but also said one must go back and teach the Piagetian ideas at the level of concrete operations, which in a sense, is saying that they have to discover it. I would hate to think that when someone has achieved formal operational thought, we still have to go back each time and teach him in very elementary ways. If every person has to discover right from the beginning, then perhaps we don't teach in the right way or explain it well. I believe we can teach at the formal operational level without having to make students go back and discover the whole themselves.

STICHT

All I can say is that Lovell's review of the literature indicates they had no great success using the discovery method in transitions from one stage to the next. This is quite different from applying concrete thought within a stage. I would suspect that the discovery method might be a more efficacious method of teaching within a stage level. But what everybody who teaches statistics at the college level says is: "The first thing to do is to have students get in there and bang away on the equipment, because if you start out with theory, you're lost; nobody understands that stuff from the theoretical point of view first."

In our work, which has been involved in training people of middle aptitudes, going from about lowest of around 70 on the Wechsler to maybe as high as around 150, we find that nobody who's exceptionally bright ever fails to learn by a hands-on, action-oriented method. In fact, they learn faster than by a formal lecture. But the person who really benefits is the lower-aptitude person. The hands-on, the action-oriented, from the practical to the theoretical, the whole-to-parts—these methods work. An interesting question raised here is: if you diagnose people with respect to developmental stage, should you do this on the basis of their problem solving and thinking or in terms of the instructional methods that will work for them?

BYERS

That is interesting, because Lovell pointed out earlier that it was important to teach content prior to the advent of the ability to deal with the content on a formal level. Now if that's done, it may help answer Elkind's question about not having to go all the way back to the basic discovery operations at the concrete level. In other words, if the person has learned certain material, perhaps he is not able to operate with it at the fully formal level at the time it was originally given in instruction. But as he grows, he develops the ability to deal with it formally. At that point, instruction does not have to go all the way back to the concrete level.

BEILIN

I find it difficult to accept the observation that was made about learning in colleges. If it were really true, then nobody would really be passing any courses in mathematics and history, or, in fact, *most* college courses, because they're not carried out at the level of concrete operations. They're carried out quite abstractly, for the most part. You may facetiously consider the possibility that nobody really is learning in colleges. But I think that, seriously, it's very hard to accept that general note. It may be true in the particular case that learning some of the Piagetian notions may be a little difficult, but I don't think that many people need pictures to be able to learn these kinds of accomplishments—certainly not those who are at least normal college students.

LANGER

I just want to comment on the familiarity of material and the didactics of structure. I made some recent observations, which are really anecdotal at this point, on four college students at the University of California who had had courses in physics and in correlation in statistics. I gave them two of the Inhelder and Piaget problems. To the one, on the oscillation of the pendulum, the students would invariably answer: "Oh, I had that problem in physics, and I know the weight doesn't play a role. Now, how do I know that sort of thing?" And they would begin to play with the pendulum. Invariably they'd be nonsystematic, using very simple variables one at a time, and I think one could readily assert that they were operating somewhere like stage 2a on the Inhelder and Piaget scale. What one sees there, it seems to me, is an accommodation—a memory of something they had been taught in physics. But one isn't quite sure that the structures are really being assimilated.

The same thing was true of these students with respect to the correlations problem—they would immediately recognize it as being a correlational problem that they had had in their courses in statistics, and invariably they only compared two variables when there were four variables to be dealt with. Again, the operations were rather low-level for what you might expect from college students.

I do not think the issue is the didactics involved in teaching students specific problems and techniques for solving them. Rather the question is, can they transfer to other problems? The question is what are they transferring and what is the operation of transfer? If one asks Gagné, for example, "What is the operation of transfer?", it is very difficult to find an answer to that kind of a question. As a matter of fact, Gagné will admit that, on many problems, he is not successful in teaching his students to transfer. He claims it is an empirical problem. It may be an empirical problem, but until one can state something about the theory of transfer, one cannot teach the students anything that is generalizable. And this is really the issue with those attempts that are being made from Gagné's theory. It is conceivable that one may obtain some specific kind of success, but at this moment it seems highly unlikely that one will have any success when he's really looking for transfer, which is one of the major criteria.

Interspersed with this discussion on instruction were some questions about sex differences in language and formal thought. Some had found such differences and others had not. Agreement about the critical variables was not achieved.

Also considered was the issue raised by Evans.

EVANS

I have a theoretical difficulty. Lovell has given us ample evidence at the formal level and Tuddenham before him at the changeover to the concrete level, that there is a good deal of décalage—that, indeed, the coefficient of concordance between tasks (the formal operational kinds of tasks) is about .57. When that is compared with the average correlation between pairs of tasks, it comes down to about .4 something. This is a fairly low correlation and means that there is a good deal of disparity. Also, Sticht has talked about the ontological development of the structure and this repeating itself in the subject-matter development.

Now, my difficulty in comprehending this is that I do not understand what the structure is apart from its manifestations in particular tasks. I wonder if either of the speakers or Dr. Inhelder would provide some clarification on this theoretical point. What is meant by "the structure," apart from its similar emergence in a variety of similar tasks? And, possibly, could they relate their answer to the transfer paradigm if that happens to be appropriate?

STICHT

By positing a subject-matter development and ontogenetic development, I was trying to avoid the problem. I was thinking rather in terms of Gagné's cumulative learning hypothesis, which is somewhat like learning subject matter. As you know, he says there is no such thing as a developmental stage. Other people say there are, obviously. But I would like to say that it seems to me that one might concede that there is a usefulness to this dichotomy, in that the ontogenetic development could set an upper limit to what could be learned at a given age. In other words, as I mentioned, for certain maturational levels, perhaps formal operational thought cannot exist—say 4 years old, or push it down, 2 years old. There has to be a limit someplace, biologically. Maybe there is some way that the ontogenetic developmental scheme can restrict the peak level at a given point. Whereas to account for the décalage, you might posit this other thing, which is more like the cumulative learning idea of Gagné.

Evans was asked to clarify his question. Evans repeated that he could not think of the structure apart from its manifestation in a particular task and so wondered what "the structure" was. He wanted to know if it was a series of explanatory devices a person has or if the idea was more of a model for discussing performances. Inhelder pointed out that her paper the next day would deal with the issue more adequately, but said that the term "the structure" was inappropriate. Instead, one should speak of "substructures" of which there are all kinds. She felt that in spite of all the problems involved in the notion, people probably really have to think in these kinds of terms.

The Role of Experience in the Rate and Sequence of Cognitive Development

CHAPTER SIX

MARCEL L. GOLDSCHMID
McGill University

While Piaget has defined intelligence in part as "adaptation to the environment," he has not concentrated much on the role experience plays in shaping a child's cognition, nor has he said much about other aspects of the child's development, such as social and emotional factors and their relative influence on intellectual development. He has, by and large, disregarded individual differences, and has, instead, attempted to uncover universal sequences and laws governing the acquisition of knowledge. Subsequent studies have only begun to deal with experiential variables. In fact, reflecting upon a number of experimental investigations in the area of preoperations and concrete operations, Sigel (1968) has stated that: "perhaps the most poorly defined set of variables influencing the course of cognitive development can be broadly subsumed within the context of experience" (p. 508).

The purpose of this paper is to briefly review some of the theoretical and experimental work on the role of experience in cognitive development, as viewed by Piaget. I shall begin with an analysis of training studies, moving on to a consideration of emotional, social, and cultural factors, and conclude with a discussion of the rate and sequence in the development of cognition.

TRAINING STUDIES

In the late '50s and early '60s a number of investigators tried to induce Piagetian concepts in the laboratory (e.g., Morf, 1959; Smedslund, 1961a; Wohlwill and Lowe, 1962). These attempts were largely unsuccessful. Flavell (1963) has reviewed these early efforts and concluded that "Piagetian concepts have so far proved inordinately difficult to stamp in, whatever the training procedure used" (p. 378). He challenged other investigators to provoke the acquisition of Piagetian concepts with more appropriate methods. This challenge has been taken up by several researchers and learning studies have, in fact, continued to this day.

In contrast to the early experiments, however, the second phase in this area of research has seen the introduction of training procedures which are based primarily on Piaget's notions of how logical operations develop. The use of such concepts as reversibility, compensation, and the emphasis on relevant perceptual cues (or disregarding misleading perceptual cues) have led to significant improvements in cognitive functioning in trained subjects (e.g., Brison and Sullivan, 1967; Fournier, 1967; Gellman, 1967; Goldschmid, 1968a; Goldschmid, Kasimer, Cayne, Burck, 1968; Kohnstamm, 1968; Lasry, 1968; Sigel, Roeper and Hooper, 1966; Wallach, Wall, and Anderson, 1967).

Piaget (1964a) has discussed three criteria he deems important in deciding whether an investigator has succeeded in teaching operational structures. The first is concerned with the durability of learning. The studies reported most recently (e.g., Fournier, 1967; Gellman, 1967; Goldschmid, 1968a) have demonstrated that provoked conservation was maintained 3 weeks to 6 months after training. In my present longitudinal study, control and experimental subjects will be assessed repeatedly over a period of two years.[1] The two most recent posttests, the third and the fourth, which were administered 26 weeks and 12 months after the training, indicated that the trained subjects are still performing at a significantly higher level than the untrained subjects. Thus, we can conclude that it is indeed possible to accelerate the long-lasting acquisition of certain Piagetian concepts.

A second criterion proposed by Piaget has to do with transfer or generalization. Again those three studies mentioned above were successful in inducing conservation behavior which generalized from trained to untrained tasks of

---

[1] The purpose of this study is to assess the role of experience in the development of conservation. A group of 110 normal 5-year olds who demonstrated comprehension of relational terms but a lack of conservation were randomly assigned to six experimental groups (N=15 each) and a control group (N=20). Half of the subjects were trained on conservation of discontinuous quantity, two-dimensional space, and substance; the other half on continuous quantity, number, and weight. Each half was further divided into three groups which were trained on reversibility, compensation, and a combination of reversibility and compensation, respectively. This study is supported by NRC-grant 281-20.

conservation. In my own study I have used two types of transfer tests. Scales A and B of our test (Goldschmid and Bentler, 1968a, 1968b) included six tasks which are intercorrelated and homogeneous. The training involved three of these tasks. Posttests indicated that performance improved significantly not only on the trained tasks but on all six tasks of the scales. A more remote transfer also occurred to another dimension of conservation as measured by scale C.

The third criterion suggested by Piaget is vague and therefore more difficult to evaluate. He asks, "in the case of each learning experience what was the operational level of the subject before the experience and what complex structures has this learning succeeded in achieving?" (p. 18). If one takes into account not only the behavior of trained children in the posttest but also their explanation, it is evident that their reasoning has indeed improved. Their responses are not only significantly better than those of the control subjects, but include the kind of logical explanations typically given by the "spontaneous" conserver, explanations which of course were not given during the pretest by either group. If one thinks, however, of other improvements, say for example generalizations from conservation to transitivity, seriation, or classification, Piaget's last question is very difficult to answer. In the first place, one would have to demonstrate *empirically* before training that these schemas are indeed related and form a general "structure." In one of our studies (Goldschmid and MacFarlane, 1968) with slightly older children we found, for example, that the intercorrelations among six tasks—probability, classification, seriation, transitivity, perspective, and conservation—were of a very low order and in some instances nonexistent.[2] Thus, on the basis of these data one could hardly expect a transfer from conservation to these particular tasks to represent a valid criterion as to whether "more complex structures" have been learned (cf. Kohnstamm, 1966).

Another criterion which was first used by Smedslund (1961b) is that of resistance to extinction. In an experiment designed to induce conservation of weight, he found that children who had been successfully trained on conservation tended to extinguish their conservation behavior when the examiner surreptitiously removed some clay from one of the two objects, whereas another group of children, who had acquired conservation spontaneously, tended to resist extinction. This criterion has been widely accepted and given prominence without a careful evaluation of its adequacy. I doubt very much whether this is an appropriate criterion, at least in the way Smedslund used it. On a theoretical basis, could it not be argued that differences in personality and experience between these groups of children may have accounted for the different responses to the "cheating" of the experimenter? Kohnstamm (1966) has suggested that if he would apply this criterion of extinction he would only do so after:

---

[2] See also Tuddenham's paper in this volume.

having accustomed the young child to the idea that the stranger (E) some-times systematically tries to mislead him, otherwise the timid child may fall back on the old answer which E definitely suggests to be correct, while the self-confident child may resist. Variables of personality or child-adult inter-action should not interfere with the testing for quality of cognitive growth (p. 63).

Now let us consider some empirical evidence. In my present longitudinal study, we used the same extinction test as Smedslund for weight and a similar one for discontinuous quantity (which also included an external referent), but instead of using two different age groups (i.e., older, "spontaneous" and youn-ger, "provoked" conservers), children who came from the same "subject pool" and had been randomly assigned to the control and experimental groups were compared. The results indicated that trained subjects resisted extinction signifi-cantly more often than the control subjects.

To conclude, I believe that there is now a fair amount of evidence (at least with respect to the preoperational and concrete operational stages) which suggests that it is indeed possible to accelerate cognitive growth in a Piagetian sense, i.e., to induce a genuine schema which heretofore was not present in the child. It appears, furthermore, that training is particularly successful when children are exposed to cognitive elements which Piaget has defined as logical prerequisites of a given concept (cf. Kohlberg, 1968).

But the question remains as to whether the establishment of a concept, as genuine as it may be, indicates the acceleration of a child's *general* intellectual growth. Is there an amelioration of the child's cognitive structure ("structure d'ensemble"), or is it specific to a particular schema? It may be possible to deal with this problem by experimenting with other transfer tests after training has occurred. Indeed, I am planning to administer other Piagetian tasks, which are appropriate for this age group, to both my control and experimental subjects, in order to determine whether the significant advances the trained children made in conservation generalize to other schemas. As mentioned earlier, such an evalua-tion must be coupled with an empirical assessment of the interrelationship (and scaling) of several concepts in the same children. Unfortunately most of Piaget's results were derived from cross-sectional studies rather than from the same group and/or longitudinal studies.

We obviously can go much further not only with respect to tests of generali-zations, but, given ingenuity and patience on the part of the experimenter, we may also undertake a more massive acceleration simultaneously or successively in many different areas of cognitive functioning. Some of the newly suggested Piaget-based curricula for preschool, kindergarten, and elementary school (e.g., Sonquist and Kamii, 1968; Stendler-Lavatelli, 1968) propose to do just that. A more continuous school experience, in contrast to laboratory experimentation, would afford the opportunity (albeit perhaps in a less well-controlled manner) to expose the child to a significant number of logical operations before he acquires them spontaneously. Only if more massive training is undertaken, I believe, will we have any clear ideas as to whether the cognitive structures of the child have been accelerated in general or whether there is simply improvement in one area or one schema.

Piaget himself has not seemed very interested in training studies and has referred to the question of acceleration with some amusement as the "American question." Yet the overwhelming majority of these studies were not carried out with the primary purpose of acceleration per se, but rather to pinpoint the specific experiential prerequisites for acquiring a given schema. Some of Piaget's closest collaborators in Geneva and Montreal and other investigators have given this question serious consideration. Should one be primarily concerned with pedagogical implications of acceleration studies, even though many of the procedures used in the laboratory to isolate experiential variables are not necessarily the most efficient ones (Kohnstamm, 1966)?

Finally, even if we prefer the child to discover new relationships and act upon objects on his own, as opposed to having to follow a tightly structured curriculum or receiving particular training, we still need to know what *specific* kinds of environment, materials, and stimulation the child should be exposed to in order to enhance (not necessarily accelerate) his cognitive development.

PERSONALITY VARIABLES

While Piaget has been concerned almost exclusively with cognitive structures, he has acknowledged the importance of affective factors in the child's intellectual development. He and others (Anthony, 1956b, 1957; Mehrabian, 1968; Odier, 1956; Piaget, 1953; Sigel, 1968; Wolff, 1960) have attempted to relate his theory of cognitive development to theories of personality development, particularly to psychoanalytic theory. Piaget's point of view is that affective and cognitive development are not only parallel, but influence each other. There is, however, little empirical evidence on the interrelationship between emotional and cognitive development. In previous studies (Goldschmid, 1967, 1968b) I found that children with a high level of conservation were (1) more objective in their self-evaluation, (2) described more favorably by their teachers, (3) preferred by their peers, and (4) less dominated by their mother than children with a low level of conservation. In addition, I found that the personality makeup of high conservers and low conservers was quite different. For example, a group of high conservers, which was matched with a group of low conservers on sex, age, and IQ, was described by their teachers as clever, cute, good-looking, handsome, lazy, quiet, and worrying. The low conservers were described as afraid, big, bossy, cruel, healthy, noisy, quick, restless, rough, silly, and tall. These preliminary data suggest the existence of a meaningful relationship between cognitive, emotional, and social factors of development.

I believe the time has come to relate Piagetian concepts to psychosocial and personality characteristics on a larger scale. Such relationships may explain the individual differences that many studies have demonstrated, not only within groups, but also between different groups of subjects of the same age. As a next step, instead of training on cognitive schemas, we may be able to experiment with manipulations of *noncognitive* (or nonPiagetian) variables and assess their effects upon the acquisition of Piagetian concepts. Only if we take account of the interactions among different facets of a child's development will we be able to arrive at a theory of *psychological* development rather than merely a cognitive or a social or emotional theory of development.

CULTURAL VARIABLES

Cross-cultural research, which has only begun, has indicated so far that the sequence of development postulated by Piaget may indeed be universal, but that significant between-group differences of age levels for a particular concept may exist (Goodnow, 1962; Greenfield, 1966; Hyde, 1959; Piaget, 1964a; Price-Williams, 1961, 1962).

Within-culture differences have also been found with respect to socioeconomic class, although the situation is far from clear or consistent (cf. Goldschmid, 1967; Kohlberg, 1968; Mermelstein and Shulman, 1967; Sigel and Mermelstein, 1965; Stendler-Lavatelli, 1968). Some experimenters have suggested that Piagetian tasks, besides having the advantage of being based on a developmental theory, may be less culture-bound than the traditional IQ tests and may therefore better serve in intelligence assessments of children from a wide spectrum of cultural backgrounds.

Sigel (1968) has further considered the potential influence of linguistic variables and the role of play in cognitive development. Few empirical data are available as to the relationship between these variables and Piagetian tasks, but it would be surprising if differences in linguistic background and/or play experience did not have a significant effect on the child's acquisition of cognitive schemas.

RATE VERSUS SEQUENCE OF COGNITIVE DEVELOPMENT

While it may be extremely difficult if not impossible to construct Guttman scales of cognitive concepts (cf. Goldschmid and Bentler, 1968a; Kofsky, 1966; Wohlwill, 1960), available empirical evidence suggests that the "sequence," as postulated by Piaget, may indeed exist. As has been stressed throughout this paper, the *rate* of cognitive development, on the other hand, may vary considerably from group to group and between individuals within a group.

One exception to the studies generally supporting the sequence of cognitive stages as postulated by Piaget was reported by Mehler and Bever (1967, 1968) and Bever, Mehler and Epstein (1968).[3] They claimed that young children between the ages of 2 years and 6 months and 3 years and 2 months were able to conserve number, whereas children between 3 years and 2 months and 4 years and 6 months were not. Older children again demonstrated conservation behavior. The authors suggested that

> the child does not gradually acquire quantity conservation during his fourth year; rather he reacquires it . . . The temporary inability to solve the conservation problem reflects a period of overdependence on perceptual strategies . . . Thus nonconservation is a temporary exception to human cognition, not a basic characteristic of man's native endowment (Mehler and Bever, 1967, p. 142).

Their interpretations were challenged by Piaget (1968a) and Beilin (1968). We (Goldschmid and Buxton-Payne, 1968) have also replicated Mehler and Bever's study, but controlled some variables that they seemingly had ignored, such as the understanding of relational terms, phrasing of questions, explanations, etc. Our results indicated no reversal or U-shaped curve; instead, an age-related curve emerged for conservation of number, just as you would predict for Piaget's theory, i.e., older children performed progressively better than younger ones. To conclude, while a considerable amount of data has accumulated which suggests that experimental factors may enhance or delay cognitive development, there is little evidence which would indicate a reversal of the sequence of cognitive stages as proposed by Piaget.

IMPLICATIONS FOR EDUCATION

Obviously, when one considers the role of experience, one thinks of the relevance of educational procedures and curricula for cognitive development. A detailed discussion of this topic would go beyond the scope of this paper. Fortunately, there are a number of reviews which deal with this subject (e.g., Flavell, 1963; Goldschmid, in press; Hooper, 1968; Kohlberg, 1968; Sigel, 1969; Sullivan, 1967). Suffice it to say that there is considerable controversy as to whether Piaget's theory is useful to educators and, if so, in what way. Piaget himself has been rather reluctant to enter into this debate except to give a few hints and suggestions here and there.

---

[3] Bandura and McDonald (Bandura & Walters, 1963) have reported a reversal of stages in moral judgment as a result of an experimental manipulation.

CONCLUSION

In order to derive a theory of psychological development, I suggest that we relate Piaget's theory and research to social, emotional, and environmental variables, not only on a theoretical, but also on an empirical level. Experience undoubtedly plays a significant role in the acquisition of cognitive concepts and accounts at least in part for the differences found within and between groups on practically every Piagetian variable studied. While it has been demonstrated that specific training will elicit or produce schemas or cognitive concepts in a genuine way, these results do not necessarily imply an acceleration of general cognitive growth. If one does not view the learning of a schema as implying a change in cognitive structure ("structure d'ensemble"), one is then faced with the difficult task of first empirically determining the relationship of different concepts which form a structure and thereupon training subjects, not only on one schema, but on a great many, and then reassessing the child's standing on the *structure d'ensemble.* Such massive acceleration in the acquisition of Piagetian variables is probably more feasible outside the laboratory, in kindergarten, preschool, or enrichment programs. These attempts must be evaluated with all the criteria mentioned in order that we may gain a still better understanding of the role experience plays in the child's cognitive development.

Comments on Goldschmid's Paper
by Kenneth Lovell
University of Leeds

Professor Goldschmid's paper was a thoughtful and balanced presentation of a somewhat thorny topic.

My first point is that while Goldschmid is correct in saying that Piaget has not concentrated much, at least explicitly, on the role of experience in shaping intellectual growth, I do think it's necessary to point out that he has stated on more than one occasion that experience is important in this connection. In *Language and Thought*, published in the late 1920s, he is clearly of the view that social intercourse with peers forces a child to reexamine his own thoughts, so that he can satisfy his need to communicate his thoughts to other children and his need to understand what they are saying to him. Again, in *The Growth of Logical Thinking*, Inhelder and Piaget are emphatic that the onset of formal operational thought is—over and above some minimum chronological age and degree of physiological maturation—greatly dependent upon schooling, culture, and social attitude.

In general terms, it now seems that the Geneva school posits that the onset of operative thinking is, apart from maturation and autoregulation, dependent upon: (1) social interaction, discussions, arguments, etc., which are prevalent in all cultures to a greater or lesser extent, and (2) upon the general features of the culture and schooling which vary greatly between subcultural groups, and so on.

The second point I'd like to make is that looking now at the overall evidence, it does appear that training in reversibility and compensation, with emphasis upon relevant perceptual cues, does lead to changes in cognitive functioning. Although at the same time I would point out that in at least one of the studies that he mentions—the Sigel-Hooper study—pupils involved had IQs of 130+, and they may very well have been at or near the transitional stage anyway.

However, it is important, when thinking of the criteria used by Piaget, to bear in mind that Piaget is talking about the teaching of "operational structures," that is, an integrated system of actions. With this in mind, let us follow Goldschmid as he quickly goes to the heart of the problem. The evidence, he says, as to whether training on conservation leads to improvement in performance with respect to seriation, classification, etc., is only meaningful if the relevant schemas are related in a general structure. If they are not, then these involve independently learned skills, and, from the point of view of this conference, Piagetian test items would have no more and no less rationale than those employed in the Binet scales, namely, they are tasks which children at certain ages can perform. While, then, there is evidence that training can induce a cognitive schema which has durability and at least limited transfer, the evidence is still not at all clear as to whether there is a change in the operational structure in a strictly Piagetian sense. It seems, from the observation of young children— quite apart from the training experiments—that while the independent schemas develop first (showing the characteristics of first-order operations, although over a very limited area) later, more elaborate schemas are available which are more flexible and more usable over greater and greater areas of experience. Training which generates these rather narrow schemas at first may well be advantageous to the child. Operative thought may be extended to other areas earlier, but we really don't know.

I do agree with Goldschmid that we need longitudinal studies of children who have experienced training. Since Goldschmid and Bentler have themselves shown that many of the conservation tasks cluster together—they lie on a single dimension—one might expect improvements on a number of the conservation tasks in the training group. But, for my own part, I would like to see these children followed up to see how they develop with respect to, say, the concept of time, the concept of temperature, spatial concepts, and whether later on there is any evidence that the concept of volume is coming earlier. All these are important questions. We don't know, for example, if children who have not had these particular training experiences catch up later on. We've seen so much evidence with respect to, say, reading, that children who go through particular programs and improve are later caught up with by other children who did not have these particular experiences and training programs. Again, we have much evidence in England that concrete, operational thinking is not in evidence in, say, historical thinking, before a mental age of around 12 years. Will it come any earlier in pupils who have experienced training on conservation tasks?

Studies of very bright children show us that once concrete operational thought is in evidence in one area, it becomes rapidly available in many areas. On the other hand, when concrete operational thought is evident in educable retarded children, it seems to be almost in isolated areas, with little transfer from one area to another. What are the differential effects of training on the very able and on the very dull? How much transfer takes place in very bright and in very dull pupils? These are some of the questions that we need to have answered.

My third point brings me to the question of personality—personality and performance on the conservation tasks. I feel that there might be a little of the chicken/egg problem here with respect to the Goldschmid study. Children who are concerned about school are likely to be doing better in school work and are likely to be regarded by their teachers as better all around than pupils who are not. I agree, of course, wholeheartedly that social and emotional factors are extremely important relative to cognitive development. But I would also like to see a longitudinal study, from about the age of 3 or 4 years upwards, showing what kinds of personalities show early and late conservation, instead of assessing the personality at the conservation stage.

My fourth point is that I would like to say how much I agree with Goldschmid's conclusion that there appears to be no good evidence to indicate a reversal of sequence of the cognitive stages proposed by Piaget. Without understanding a term such as "more," it's difficult to see the validity of the Mehler and Bever data. A recent study in our country by Margaret Donaldson at Edinburgh has given clear evidence that children at 3 years of age do not understand the word "more."

Finally, let me say that I also concur with the author that general cognitive growth is most likely to be stimulated by long term effects—by home, by preschool experiences, and by school experiences more generally. That is not to imply that I disapprove of training procedures or that they are useless. It could be that even if they do no more than produce rather specific schemas—which may or may not be valuable on occasion—training in a variety of areas may actually facilitate the development of what Piaget calls "operative structures."

Open Discussion

Goldschmid's paper elicited a long reply from Inhelder covering several points and a set of somewhat shorter, but still far from brief, comments by Elkind and Beilin. Goldschmid's rebuttals, first to Inhelder and then to Elkind and Beilin, also went into some detail. Along with Lovell's comments, these exchanges added considerable substance to the topics being discussed.

INHELDER

If there is time I shall talk about cognitive learning studies. I have a lot of comments to make. The first point is that we have observed that cognitive learning very much depends upon the child's initial level, and this is what few researchers have studied in sufficient detail. For instance, in one of our conservation experiments in cognitive learning, we found that when children were initially completely preoperational and were then given at least three sessions of operative training, without any external reinforcement, the great majority (87½ percent) did not make any real progress, while a minority (12½ percent) attained an intermediate level.

But the situation is rather different for those children who start at the intermediate stage. Of the latter group, only 25 percent made no progress at all and 75 percent benefited, to varying degrees, from the learning procedures. For half of the latter group, the acquisition of the conservation concept was no more than an extension of the structuration that had already begun at the time of the pretest. But for the other half, true progressive development took place, of which it is easy to follow the successive moments of integration during the learning sessions. So it's not that children learn nothing, but that what they learn depends on their developmental level. That's my first point.

For the second point, I should say something to Goldschmid about his control groups. As I understand it, you used the same control group before the pretest as after the first (and even a second) posttest and you then said that the children who went through the learning sessions are more advanced than those in the control group. But you did not compare the children after the learning sessions with a control group that had already acquired the relevant concept spontaneously. (Goldschmid: No.) That makes some difference. We have done this, and there are always some slight differences in the integrated processes when they are acquired relatively rapidly through training sessions. But we were not just trying to determine whether acceleration is or isn't possible, but to distinguish between the various cognitive processes.

Now, my third point. Some authors have tried to dissociate reversibility, compensation, and identity for experimental purposes. However, in studying their reports, we very often notice some distortions in the reasoning processes of their subjects in tests taken some weeks later. This is because it is an artificial dissociation. The understanding of conservation as a whole requires the development of various interrelated processes, so if you accentuate (deliberately or accidentally) one aspect at the expense of others, you sometimes have distortions and later on there may even be a kind of breakdown.

Now, let me come back to Kohnstamm's experiments, since several of you have referred to him and his class-inclusion experiments.

The important thing is to know what kind of criteria you are applying when you say that a child acquired, or didn't acquire, inclusion, or attained only an intermediate level. Here the importance of exploring in detail all aspects of the concept as spontaneously acquired by the control group becomes clear. In fact, in one of our pilot studies we demonstrated that a control group was able to give operational answers to several related problems, and, also, that they had certain ways of explaining their answers. Kohnstamm's criterion for deciding that the concept had been acquired was only one of our criteria based on the behavior of the control group. A Guttman-type scale could be established, and 9 out of our 11 subjects satisfied the Kohnstamm criterion, but only 3 subjects acquired all aspects of the concept and succeeded in exactly the same way as our control group.

GOLDSCHMID

One point with respect to Lovell's comments: I think it's justified to raise the question of how much one should expect in terms of transfer. If you train children on conservation, I think it is reasonable to expect generalization of conservation from trained to untrained tasks, if authentic learning has occurred. But could you really expect changes to occur in any number of other tasks? I think there has to be a limit as to how much you could expect from a simple training on one task. Besides, I mentioned in the paper that to use transfer to other areas requires, in my mind, the establishment or the demonstration that empirically there is a relationship between these tasks before you use that kind of transfer as a learning criterion.

Now, to Inhelder's comments. The first point had to do with the possibility that my experimental subjects were at an intermediate level of conservation behavior. Let me emphasize that we first selected subjects (5-year-olds) who demonstrated a lack of conservation on our pretest. Then the subjects were randomly assigned to the experimental groups and the control group. So I do not feel that the successful learning of the experimental groups can be attributed to a prior intermediate level of conservation.

On the second point, about a second control group, we actually do have another control group, namely the 560 children in the norm group for our test (Goldschmid & Bentler, 1968b). And I will be able to compare both the experimental and control groups with these norms. As of now, 1 year after the training, I find that the experimental group is still way ahead of the control group. Both groups continue to make slight progress, but the absolute difference between the two is still as great now as it was a year ago. It will be very interesting to see in a year from now—when one would expect conservation to have occurred spontaneously—whether the control group has caught up with the experimental group.

The third point had to do with distortions later on—sometime after the training. Now, in our case, we have not found a deterioration in the explanation of conservation in any of the four posttests.

The fourth point referred to Kohnstamm's study. He has dealt with the issues you raise here in his book (Kohnstamm, 1968). All I would like to say here is that, in contrast to most of the studies that I mentioned, he was not primarily interested in isolating experiental factors which lead to the acceleration of a concept (in this case, inclusion), but was trying to find the most efficient pedagogical device to train children. And as I mentioned, I do not think that the particular methods we have used are necessarily the most efficient ones in accelerating cognitive growth, but they may serve to isolate some crucial prerequisites in the acquisition of these concepts.

ELKIND

I would like to comment on the training of the personality. I have always had trouble understanding the rationale of the training studies within the Piagetian framework, and the reason I have difficulty is that, especially with respect to general intelligence tests, we know that these are processes which take a long time to develop. It seems to me that most of our training is based upon a learning theory which is concerned with relatively short term and primarily accommodative learning and that we have tried to leap into experimental psychology without taking the proper intervening step. There is another kind of learning, spontaneous learning, which we ought to take the time to examine. Children do acquire these things spontaneously; now how do they do that? Is it the same way they do it in school situations? Is what they acquire through a few days' training the same kind of thing that they acquire spontaneously? I don't think so, and I think that we need to look at how children proceed and perhaps make some theoretical guesses. There is theoretical work to be done. We cannot simply assume that learning theory is going to solve our problem with training or with learning in the Piagetian sense. It is another kind of learning.

I feel the same way with respect to personality. You cannot simply take Freud's theory and Piaget's theory and say, "Here's egocentrism, here is conservation, and here are personality variables, and we find a parallel between them and that explains personality." That's nonsense. What you have to do is make some hypotheses about what a cognitive structure means with respect to personality and then test them out. Because as long as you find correlations, all you can say of the brighter child is that there is something else that explains the personality. That is, you cannot simply take your existing theories and try to parallel them and hope that this is going to solve all your problems. What we have to do—Piaget has had the courage to do this—is make some guesses as to what goes on between learning and spontaneous development—what goes on between cognitive structure and personality, and then begin to test out these hypotheses and not hope that correlations are going to solve all our problems.

BEILIN

I'd like to say something that is somewhat consistent with that point. Take the studies that Goldschmid cites, and consider the explanations that are given in some of those studies for the processes that are involved in the acquisition. If you were to take the explanations seriously, they would contradict one another. If you accept, for example, the Gellman study and its rationale, it says something very different from what Goldschmid says. Both of them cannot be correct logically, at least with regard to the explanation of what occurred in the studies. I happen to have one of those successful conservation studies, too, and if my explanation is correct, neither Goldschmid *nor* Gellman is correct.

I'm rather surprised that Goldschmid in his presentation made a great issue of the fact that the real interest in these studies was in the processes, and yet he hasn't been explicit about what is actually learned in these studies and the processes that are involved in them. If they are really that crucial, what, in effect, have these learning studies been able to demonstrate with regard to processes? The fact is that even if these learning studies are correct in being able to say that learning can be achieved in this way, you still do not know if that means that all children can be affected by these learning procedures. Remember that Bruner made the same kind of general assertion about the effects of learning, and yet when you look at his study, the effects are demonstrable for 6-year-olds and 5-year-olds but not 4-year-olds. So in spite of the great claims that he made with regard to his training study and effect of identity training, his procedures didn't work for 4-year-olds. Now why don't they work for 4-year-olds?

One thing that Goldschmid also leaves out in his discussion is, why do the great mass of training studies provide negative results? What's the explanation for why they don't succeed? Similarly, why, in the rather selective group of studies that do have positive outcomes, do you achieve these results? An adequate explanation of what's going on here has to encompass both the studies that succeeded and those that did not succeed, and it has to take into account all the processes that are ostensibly involved with it. There has been very little real discussion about this.

GOLDSCHMID

Let me first respond to Elkind. It seems to me that the main purpose of the training experiments was exactly to study the processes involved in learning these concepts. It's a telescoping of this process into a relatively short time sequence in the laboratory. To be sure, it would be lovely to use an ecological approach and to follow the child everyday from morning till night and find out exactly what he is doing and what he is learning. This approach has been followed by Dr. Barker and his associates, but it is obviously very time-consuming.

As far as personality studies are concerned, I myself am not particularly interested in relating different theories. I am more interested in empirical links. I'm interested in seeing whether personality characteristics would explain, in part, individual differences that occur within a group on every Piagetian task. Ultimately, I hope that such demonstrated links of different facets of development will help us construct a psychological theory of development.

Now, to turn to Beilin's comments. There were differences in the procedures which were successful, this is true. I don't think that's so unusual—there are many concepts and many things a child can learn via different routes. For example, in my own study, we used three different procedures: reversibility, compensation, and a combination of these two. All experimental groups learned significantly better than the control group, although the training involved very different elements. Now, if I had had the stamina and a great many more research assistants, I could have had still more experimental groups, incorporating still other experimental procedures, and compared them with the six that I did use. The fact is that conservation can be learned via different routes invoking different principles. Piaget himself has referred to many elements involved in conservation. And then you ask, how do you explain the studies that were successful and those that were not? This question deserves much more time than we have now and really offers enough scope for another paper. Grossly oversimplifying matters, it appears that some of the earlier studies involved a relatively simple presentation and transformation of the material within the context of a reinforcement model. More recent studies did not attempt to teach conservation directly but provided training on logical prerequisites of conservation, involving, for example, compensation, reversibility, and so on. Piaget's task analysis of conservation has been very helpful in this effort. I am confident that the same approach will be successful in the training of other Piagetian concepts.

CHAPTER SEVEN

Does the Piagetian Approach Imply Instruction?

SIEGFRIED E. ENGELMANN
University of Illinois

The key issue associated with Piaget's theory of development and learning has to do with the mechanism by which a child progresses from one stage of development to the next. The Piagetian observations about what children can and cannot normally do at different ages are generally accurate. But what do they mean? How are they explained? Does the explanation imply instruction, and does it account for the facts that can be observed not only under what we might call "normal circumstances," but also under exceptional circumstances?

It is always possible to find a number of tasks that children at different ages typically fail. And it is possible to order these tasks so that we are provided with a typical "developmental profile" of children on the selected tasks. But for this type of endeavor, we do not need a theory. A theory must tell us how and why. It must specify the ways in which these tasks are related. Studies, such as those by Tuddenham (see Chap. 4), cast serious doubt on whether the various Piagetian tasks are linked together in the manner suggested by the Piagetian theory, or whether they simply represent a collection of tasks that children typically fail before the age of 6. Tuddenham obtained low intercorrelations on pass-fail performance for a variety of concrete-operational tasks. *Décalage* phenomena are inexplicable in the Piagetian scheme. Yet these phenomena cannot be shrugged off very easily. The Piagetian theory is supposed to be more than an account of normative data. It is supposed to tell us about necessary conditions, not statistical tendencies. If a child passes the conservation-of-substance test with plasticine balls and fails the conservation-of-substance test with liquids, his performance is not consistent with the Piagetian theory. Each of these problems supposedly requires the same cognitive "structure" for its solution. Does the child have the structure or not?

One of the problems associated with trying to either substantiate or discredit the Piagetian interpretation of development is that there are often alternative ways of explaining behavior within the Piagetian scheme. It is quite easy to find conservation tasks that sophisticated adults generally fail. In other words, the cognitive processes of these adults do not seem to operate within a structured whole. (One problem that usually stumps adults is this: We have a glass of oil and a glass of water. Both are identical; both are filled to the same level. We remove precisely one spoonful of water from the water glass. We put the spoonful of water into the oil glass, and mix the contents thoroughly. Now we remove precisely one spoonful of the oil-water mixture from the second glass and return it to the water glass. The questions: Is there more oil in the water glass than there is water in the oil glass? Is there more water in the oil glass than there is oil in the water glass? Or are the amounts the same? Answer: They are the same.)

The problem of the mechanism by which changes in behavior are induced, however, remains critical to the Piagetian theory. We can observe in many ways that a 14-year-old child is different from a 5-year-old child. The older child uses more sophisticated language. He knows more words and understands more about the properties of different types of objects. He exhibits gross differences in the type of arithmetic problems he can handle, in the types of inferences he can draw from statements that are presented to him, in his general knowledge, and so forth. But what is the mechanism that has changed the older child? To say that he has matured is to beg the question. We base our judgment of maturity upon his behavior, upon the things that he is able to do. It is very difficult to judge whether or not a child who is sitting in a chair with his hands folded is mature or immature. We base judgment on performance. If he performs well on a number of problems, if he measures up to specified criteria, we conclude that he is mature. If not, we judge that he is immature.

When dealing with "developmental theories," there seems to be a temptation to treat every difference between a 6-year-old and a 14-year-old as a critical difference. There is a tendency to note that "older children generally respond in such and such a way." The response, however, may simply be different, not more accurate or appropriate for the task. The response may be no more revealing about the presence of a cognitive structure than the response of the younger child. If we treat such differences as a critical difference, simply because older children who are more sophisticated in other ways tend to respond in this way, any difference becomes "proof" of our theory, regardless of how preposterous it is. For example, we could postulate a radiational theory of growth. Invisible, undetectable rays are being projected from outer space. The longer one is exposed to these rays, the more he learns. We would predict that older children would know more than younger children because of the increased exposure to the "learning-producing" ray. We could produce a number of tests that happily substantiate our theory.

The argument that a child's maturation or development can be inferred from his improved performance over the years is to beg the question. We are using the words *maturation* or *development* as catchalls that are synonymous with our observations. What do we mean by development? We mean that the child has progressed in A, B, C, etc. What do we mean when we say that he has progressed in A, B, C, etc.? We mean that he has developed or matured. We still have not identified the mechanism by which the change has been induced. We have merely constructed something of a circular definition.

Although there are other mechanisms suggested by the Piagetian theory, there seem to be five primary principles that describe development:

1. "Learning is subordinated to development and not vice versa" (Piaget, 1964a, p. 17).

2. Learning is associated with developmental stages, and these stages occur in an invariant succession. Stage B must *always* follow Stage A.

3. Only one type of learning can be accelerated through the use of "external reinforcement." "The logical structure is not the result of physical experience. It cannot be obtained by external reinforcement. The logical structure is reached only through internal equilibration, by self-regulation" (Piaget, 1964a, p. 16).

4. It follows that the only way to "teach" logical structures is through the process of internal equilibration and self-regulation. Conversely, if we observe a child who has acquired "logical structure" in connection with a specific test, we could conclude that the child had acquired his skills through an internal process of self-regulation.

5. The structures that are induced through equilibration last a lifetime.

We could certainly add to the list above, but for the sake of this paper, let's limit ourselves to these five points. If they represent valid principles, a great deal is implied both for assessment of a child's "development" and for curricular development. (We could not introduce tasks into a curriculum if it is impossible for the children to learn to handle these tasks.) If the Piagetian principles are not valid, however, then they are of questionable value for either assessment or curricular development. If, for example, operational learning (or logical structures) can be induced through the use of external reinforcement, the implications both for assessment and curricular development would be drastically altered.

I have conducted several experiments that question the Piagetian theory. In one (Engelmann, 1967a, pp. 25-51), I taught a group of kindergarten children the principles of compensation. During the instruction, the children never observed water transfer and never saw even a diagram of water transfer. They had no opportunity to "equilibrate" or observe what happens when water is transferred. On the test of conservation after 54 minutes of instruction, distributed over a 5-day period, 10 of the 15 experimental subjects conserved, according to the criteria established for the experiment. None of the comparison subjects, who were nearly a year older than the experimental subjects, conserved on the posttest.

In another experiment (Engelmann, 1967b, pp. 193-207), I taught a small group of disadvantaged and another small group of advantaged 4- and 5-year-old children how to handle different applications of a particular formal operation. I then tested them on a new application that had not been presented during instruction. Four of the five advantaged children and three of the five disadvantaged children successfully solved the new problem. Yet all but one of the children who solved the problem failed a test of conservation of substance (liquid transfer).

When I was invited to this conference, I decided to perform another, more elaborate experiment. The object of the experiment was to accelerate children's operational knowledge or "logical structures" without seriously accelerating their experiential learning. The objective, in other words, was to accelerate *only* that aspect of development that the Piagetian theory assumes cannot be accelerated.

Before describing the experiment, I would like to make two points:

1. I would not normally teach the skills in the way I did if I were interested in teaching the children in the most interesting, most reinforcing manner. The method of presentation I used was not designed for most efficient learning; it was designed to provide maximum inferences about the five principles above. Also, because of time limitations, I did not check out the children at each step of the program before proceeding to the next.
2. I discovered that there was some "coaching" of the children in the experiment by one of the assistants in our program. The coaching was minimal and had no real effect on the outcome.

I worked with seven kindergarten children on the logical structure of conservation problems, including specific gravity problems. The instruction was designed so that the children had no opportunity to handle physical objects, to observe transformation, to equilibrate. At only two points in the program did the children observe demonstrations other than static diagrams. One time was when I introduced two cups that were identical in size and shape. One was filled with cotton, the other with a rock covered by cotton. I had the children hold both of the objects and note whether one of the objects was bigger than the other and whether one of the objects was heavier than the other.

The other time that they had an experience with real objects was when I demonstrated with two pieces of chalk that objects could move at different speeds during a specified duration of time. I abandoned the demonstration when it became apparent that I could not teach conservation of speed without using real objects.

Aside from these two instances, the children worked on the logic of conservation. The training was designed to prepare them for a range of possible tests, not for any given specific test. The total instructional time was about 3 hours, distributed over a 2-week period. I did not bring the children to specific criteria of performance. If I had had more time, I would have.

Four of the children were then tested primarily on conservation of substance, weight, volume, specific gravity, and speed. (These were not the four best performers in the instruction sessions.) By chance all of these children were 6.0 or 6.1 in age. Since the children were taught only certain logical operations, they would not be expected to perform any differently than other children their age on problems other than those for which instruction prepared them. In other words, the 3 hours of instruction were not designed to change these children into older children. Their verbal behavior, their spontaneity, their ability to extract the meaning from complex statements, and their general knowledge about things—all would remain unchanged. As noted earlier, we can find many differences between these and older children, but if we allow these to form the basis for our conclusions about development, then any test that will allow us to discriminate between younger and older children becomes a critical test.

One child, a disadvantaged black girl (Ann)* did not conserve on problems of liquid amount. However, her performance was generally very good on problems of conservation of weight, volume, and specific gravity. There was some question about her performance on several items, but she was quite consistent both on the problems that involved transitivity and problems involving transformation of identical objects. Her performance on the problem of specific gravity was quite interesting. Before putting the objects in the water, she classified them in a typical preoperational way. Again, no assumption should be made about how the children will perform in this type of situation, because they were taught nothing about the behavior of specific objects. They were not taught, for example, that wood floats and iron sinks. They were taught only the logical structure or the rules about floating or sinking. They weren't even taught that if an object sinks one time, it will sink the next (which I realized later was a rather obvious oversight on my part). After the child had placed the objects in the water and observed their behavior, her explanations were anything but preoperational; they were formal and correct. She seemed to use the information yielded by her experiment quite well. Throughout the test, however, there was some problem of phrasing questions so that she could respond to them.

The critical issue associated with this child's performance was the discrepancy between her ability to handle the specific gravity problem (a formal operational problem) and her inability to conserve on the test of liquid amount. Although she failed the test of conservation of substance with water, she passed the conservation test with plasticine balls.

The second child (Dan) was a bright kindergarten-age boy, the son of a mathematician. He did very well on the tests of conservation of substance, weight, volume, and specific gravity. His answers were spontaneous and given with certainty. To test his ability to generalize his "logical structure" of floating or sinking, he was presented with a container filled with mercury and two steel balls, one large and one small. The boy indicated, "Both of those balls will float in the mercury."

*The fictitious children's names have been inserted here to correspond to those in Kamii's paper which follows.

When asked whether the mercury is heavier than the water or vice versa, the child indicated that the mercury is heavier.

This child failed the test of class inclusion, again implying something of a contradiction about the invariant succession of stages.

There was some doubt about whether the children in the experiment understood that objects made of the same material were actually made of the same material. A test was introduced in which the investigator asked whether or not a candle would float. The investigator then proceeded to cut the candle into a large piece and a small piece—a more obvious instance in which the objects to be tested were made of the same material. The children were asked whether the large piece would float and whether the small piece would float. Any inconsistency in responses to this test would clearly be taken as evidence that the child did not have the concept of ratio as it relates to floating and sinking of objects. When the black girl was presented with the test, she suddenly changed her mind, indicating that the candle would float and that either part of the candle would float. When asked why she had changed her mind, she pointed to a flake of the candle that had dropped into the water. She said something to the effect, "That piece is floating, so the whole candle will float."

A third boy (Bill), who did relatively poorly on a number of the substance, volume, and weight problems, did surprisingly well on the test of specific gravity. He generally accounted for the behavior of the objects tested (although his remarks were not spontaneous, and additional questions were often required to clarify his response). When he was presented with the problem of the steel balls and the mercury, he correctly concluded that if the small ball floated, the other ball would float. When asked which of the media, water or mercury, was heavier, he studied the problem for perhaps 10 seconds. He then asserted that the mercury was heavier.

A fourth kindergarten-age boy (Carl, a fraternal twin) performed solidly on all tests, including the test of class inclusion. However, he (and all of the other children) missed items in the conservation-of-speed test.

These children did exhibit the ability to generalize. For example, they had never seen during the instruction that a plasticine ball could be transformed into a ring. They hadn't seen transformations with any three-dimensional objects. The children handled these problems very well. The black girl indicated at one point that the object could be returned to its original shape. She even reached for the object, saying, "Here, let me show you." The fraternal twin drew a series of imaginary lines from the center to the perimeter of the ring and indicated, "It's longer this way." He then held his hand palm down, making a downward pushing motion and said, "But it's shorter this way."

The children generally did well on the test of specific gravity. They used the information they received from the experience of floating an object to classify it. They understood that if the whole object sinks, any part of the object will sink. They could indicate why the objects floated or sank, and they could generalize to another medium which they had not seen before, mercury.

Before returning to the Piagetian assumptions about development and learning, let me make several points quite clear. I selected the examples above because they relate to the question of mechanism. Not all of the children performed with 100 percent accuracy on all tests. One of the children actually did rather poorly on some. However, I have no doubt that this child could be brought to the desired criterion of performance with additional training, using only external reinforcement and not physical experiences. And remember, these changes in behavior noted above were the product of about 3 hours of instruction. If it is desirable for children to perform well on these and similar tests, 6 or even 10 hours of instruction would represent a modest investment. Children normally require years to learn what the children in the experiment mastered in a few hours.

Let's take a look at the Piagetian assumptions about learning in relationship to the performance of the children in the experiment.

1. Is learning subordinated to development? These children seemed to have learned, and learned a great deal. Furthermore, they learned from presentations that did not allow for internal self-regulation. They learned very little about things and about how they would behave. They did not perform differently than other children their age on classifying objects before putting them in water. What they had learned was the logical structure that would allow them to handle a variety of floating and sinking problems, a variety of displacement and substance problems, not merely those presented in the test. Generally, they would have been able to draw conclusions about the relative weight of any two media—helium and neon for example—given the facts that a particular object "sinks" in neon and "floats" in helium. Generally, they would have been able to work a variety of conservation-of-volume problems. For example, they would have been able to indicate how one goes about getting a volume of water equal to a volume of clay. They had learned the logical structure, and it is not at all obvious how this learning was subordinated to their "development."

2. Does development of learning occur in an invariant succession of stages? If so, how do we explain the performance of some of our experimental children? The black girl did not seem to be building structures on existing structures. She seemed to have a very solid fix on weight, volume, and substance as it relates to plasticine balls. Yet she failed the water transfer test. The second boy, the most solid and spontaneous performer, failed the test of class inclusion (as did all but the fraternal twin). All of the children failed the conservation-of-speed test. Some of these children "developed" in a rather unusual fashion, according to Piagetian principles.

3. Can learning of logical structures be induced through the use of external reinforcement? I think the answer is clearly yes. The children in the

experiment were not taught items. They were taught rules. In general they used these rules appropriately in response to presentations they had not observed during instruction.

4. Can we clearly infer from the child's performance whether or not he has gone through the equilibration process? I think not. We can certainly find "differences" in performance, but for these differences to be relevant they must be related to the child's demonstrable ability to handle "logical-structure" problems.

5. Do the structures that are induced through equilibration last a lifetime, and do they differ generally from structures induced through "external reinforcement"? I doubt whether they are different. This is not to say that "externally reinforced behavior" will not extinguish if it is not continually reinforced. It is to say that there is probably no difference between this behavior and "self-regulated behavior." This is strictly my opinion, but I find nothing in the literature to contradict it (including the extinction experiments in which the important variable of duration since time of acquisition is not controlled). Certainly, we can write off the experiment I have described by saying that the learning will not last. And I certainly cannot present data that it will last a lifetime. However, I believe that these children will retain what they have learned. I'll find out next year.

In many respects, the experiment I have described is as sloppy as my description. There was no control group. The children were not given pretests. (However, it was apparent from the children's responses during instruction that initially none of them could conserve substance, weight, or volume; nor could they perform on tests of specific gravity.) However, the experiment is useful and worth reporting, I believe, because it gives some insight into the mechanism by which children are transported to higher stages of development. Changes occurred, and these changes were a function of specific experiences that these children had. The experiences were not "normal" for most 6-year-old children, and the resulting performance was not "normal."

The main point of confusion associated with Piagetian theory has to do with the relationship between the observations of what children normally do and the theoretical principles that account for these observations. It is quite possible for one to acknowledge that the Piagetian observations are generally quite accurate and for one to totally reject the theory. This is the position that I take. Children at a given age cannot generally handle conservation of weight problems. But if you want them to be able to handle such problems, you can teach them. If you want them to be able to handle a class of similar problems (or deal with a class of objects or events that have the same characteristics as conservation of weight problems), you can teach them. The mechanism is actually quite simple. Children are taught. They may be taught through physical experiences. They may be taught through other types of experiences.

It is possible to teach children a wide variety of discriminations, including those that involve logical structure. All red objects share a certain characteristic. This characteristic can be taught. It can be demonstrated in such a way that a child can generalize it. So it is with other rules, and to learn "red" is to learn a rule. All instances of compensating changes share a set of characteristics. These characteristics can be taught in quite the same way red is taught. The child is presented with instances of the concept and is taught the relationship between the characteristics and the language used to describe these. Unfortunately, I cannot go into great detail on the nature of concept analysis and the procedures by which generalization is induced, but I would like to stress that the most efficient way to teach is rarely the way suggested by the Piagetian model. Although a child must be exposed to instances of a particular concept before he can learn the concept, the physical experience often represents a noisy instance, one that is not well designed to teach what the salient characteristics of the concept are, or which aspects of the objects or events should be attended to. Many more instances of the noisy physical experience may have to be presented before the child learns the rule.

So far as I am able to determine, the Piagetian theory provides us with nothing more than a set of accurate descriptions about the performance of children at different ages. It does not provide us with the theory that clearly implies instruction, lack of instruction, or evaluation of instruction. An ordinal scale of developmental stages would, I'm sure, provide a great deal of interesting data that is not easily extracted from present IQ tests or other developmental instruments. But of what particular value would it be? Would it actually tell us what we can or cannot teach a given child? Would it actually imply the procedure that we should use to teach? Would it help describe that mechanism that transports a child from one stage of development to another? Or would it tend to give stature and credence to a theoretical framework that is not only highly suspect but equally irrelevant to instruction? If the Piagetian theory specified the mechanism that causes change, the children in the experiment I have described would not have been able to learn the logical structure they learned. They would not have been able to violate the supposed invariant succession of stages. They would not have responded to a presentation that did not allow for equilibration. And if the Piagetian model did provide a tight, theoretical framework, we would have been able to specify, for example, why the black girl failed to conserve on the liquid-amount test. The reason is appallingly simple, but it is not to be found in the Piagetian theory. The girl was not taught the rules needed to handle liquid-transfer problems. She was absent during 2 days of instruction that focused upon the compensating changes of rectangular objects.

Comments on Engelmann's Paper
by Constance Kamii and Louise Derman
Ypsilanti Public Schools
The Engelmann Approach to Teaching Logical Thinking:
Findings from the Administration of Some Piagetian Tasks[1]

We would like, first of all, to express our appreciation to CTB/McGraw-Hill for the opportunity it provided to engage in first-hand observations of the results of a particular method of instruction. In early childhood education, empirical evidence of the effects of teaching according to different schools of thought have been limited to standardized test scores, which are known to be inadequate for the evaluation of preschool instruction (Deal and Wood, 1968; Kamii, in press; Kohlberg, 1968; Zimiles, 1968). Very little is yet known about how young children learn.

We were intrigued by the position Engelmann intended to discuss at the Invitational Conference on Ordinal Scales of Cognitive Development. His position was that Piaget's theory has no potential application to education except that it points out some of the skills that children are not normally taught. He had further stated that any of the deficiencies articulated by Piaget could be taught, such as the child's normal deficiency in understanding specific gravity. We were particularly curious about how specific gravity could be taught to young children because they usually do not achieve formal operations until they are in their teens.

Having accepted the invitation of CTB/McGraw-Hill to be the discussant of Engelmann's paper, we learned he planned to teach specific gravity, conservation, and the judgment of speed to young children as evidence of his viewpoint. We suggested to him that we administer a posttest to the children he was going to teach. He agreed, and we would like to note that we appreciated his willingness to let outside researchers evaluate an aspect of his work. The posttest was given on January 28 and 29, 1969. In order to agree on the fairness and appropriateness of the questions, we went over all the items the day before the testing began. The tests dealt with the areas that Engelmann had selected to

[1] This investigation was conducted as part of the Ypsilanti Early Education Program, which is supported by Title III of the Elementary and Secondary Education Act of 1965 (No. 67-042490). The opinions expressed herein, however, do not necessarily reflect the position or policy of the funding agency, and no official endorsement by the Office of Education should be inferred. One of the objectives of the Ypsilanti Early Education Program is the development of a preschool curriculum based on Piaget's theory. Constance Kamii is the Curriculum Director of the Program, and Louise Derman is its Curriculum Supervisor. The authors are grateful to Norma Radin, Research Associate, for originally suggesting that we personally test the children taught by Engelmann, and for contributing many ideas to the paper itself.

teach, namely the child's judgment of speed (Piaget 1964b), specific gravity (Inhelder & Piaget, 1958, Chap. 2), and the conservation of volume, weight, substance (Piaget & Inhelder, 1962), liquid, and number (Piaget, 1965). The class-inclusion task (Piaget, 1965) was also given for theoretical reasons, although this was an area that had not been taught. Whenever Engelmann felt that the children might not understand our question, the agreement was that we would ask a different question in addition to the one we wanted to ask. We took turns in questioning the children, and detailed protocols were taken. The sessions were also tape recorded.

There were seven subjects in the teaching experiment, but only four could be tested as the others were absent due to illness. The children were in kindergarten in a University of Illinois lab school and had had their sixth birthday. Of the four, one (a girl) was from a lower-lower-SES home, and the others (all boys) were professors' children. They will be referred to in this paper by fictitious names: Ann, Bill, Carl, and Dan. All four belonged to the purple group of their kindergarten class, a color designating the more advanced children in the class.

The test was given in a small testing room in the basement of the children's school, where the offices of many researchers are also housed. Engelmann and his assistants could observe and participate in the testing wherever they wished. The four children quickly became absorbed in the task and forgot their initial apprehension about "the two ladies who came to see if they could fool you." At times, there were as many as four or five observers in addition to the two testers, but the children were at ease and communicative even in front of an audience.

The findings to be reported below will be limited to the specific-gravity and conservation experiments.[2] The implications of these findings will then be discussed with regard to early childhood education.

SPECIFIC GRAVITY

Procedure
The procedure for the specific-gravity experiment is discussed in Inhelder and Piaget (1958, chap. 2). In this experiment, the child is given a number of objects and asked to dichotomize them into "things that you think will sink in water" and "things that you think will float." When the classification is completed, the child is asked to explain, with respect to each object, why he thinks it will sink (or float). He then verifies his predictions and is asked to summarize his observations. The objects we used were, among others, the following.[3]

[2] In the judgment-of-speed experiment, none of the children showed evidence of mastery.

[3] There were also a ping-pong ball and red, green, and yellow wooden beads on the first day. These objects were eliminated on the second day because they were yielding insignificant information in view of the limited amount of time available.

Plastic boat

Pieces of aluminum foil

Black, rubber ball ($\frac{3}{4}$ inch in diameter, and referred to below as "tiny")

Red rubber ball (2 inches in diameter, and referred to below as "big")

Big white candle (9 inches long)

Little white candle (2 inches long, the size intended for birthday cakes)

Big needle

Little needle

Penny

Paper clips (2 sizes)

Ball bearings (in various sizes from $\frac{3}{16}$ inch to $1\frac{3}{4}$ inches in diameter)

Toy metal plate ($3\frac{1}{2}$ inches in diameter)

Block ($5\frac{1}{2}$ inches x $2\frac{3}{4}$ inches x $1\frac{1}{4}$ inches)

Spice bottle (empty and covered)

Big piece of green soap

Big piece of Ivory soap

Two little pieces of soap (both white)

Big Montessori cylinder

Little Montessori cylinder

Theoretical Purpose of the Experiment

Our view and that of Engelmann differ with respect to the theoretical interpretations of the purpose of this experiment. For him, the significance lies in whether or not children can apply rules that have been taught verbally. If they can learn rules which Piaget says children cannot normally formulate until they are capable of combinatorial thinking, then, Engelmann argues, kindergarten children can be said to be able to do formal operations without waiting until "the period of formal operations." For us, the importance of the experiment lies in the children's process of thinking. In our view, formal operations refer not to the rules or their application (i.e., the final product) but to the process of hypothetico-deductive thinking. Specific gravity is only one context in which it is possible to explore (1) how the child starts to discard his hypotheses when he becomes aware of the contradictions among them, (2) how he goes about constructing a new hypothesis, and (3) how he goes about verifying it. The same processes can be seen just as well with the bending of metal rods (Inhelder & Piaget, 1958, chap. 3) as with specific gravity.

The Children's Application of the Rules

The rules that appeared to have been taught the children were the following:

1. If an object floats on water, it floats because it is lighter than a piece of water the same size. Conversely, if an object sinks in water, it sinks because it is heavier than a piece of water the same size.

2.   By substitution, if an object floats on another medium, such as mercury, it floats because it is lighter than a piece of that medium the same size. Conversely, if an object sinks, it sinks because it is heavier than a piece of that medium the same size.

3.   If an object sinks or floats, any part of that object will also sink or float regardless of its size.

As far as the application of the above rules was concerned, the children used them very well in the test situation to explain many phenomena. When asked why they thought an object had sunk or floated, the children gave the first rule correctly. When they were surprised to see that a large, heavy ball bearing floated on mercury, they could explain this phenomenon by referring to the second rule. (Because it's lighter than a piece of mercury the same size). When we took out a knife and a large candle that the children thought would sink, and asked where we should cut it so that the tip would be small enough to float, the third rule was correctly applied. One child noticed a tiny piece of wax floating on water, and concluded from this observation that the whole candle had to float.

While the children could apply the rules correctly, one of the things that concerned us as we talked with them was their comprehension of their own statements. For example, when asked "What does 'float' mean?" one child answered, "It's lighter than a piece of water the same size." When we then asked her to explain why she had put particular objects in the floating category, her statement changed to "Because it is light." Another child used rule No. 1 to explain his initial classification, but when faced with the reactions of specific objects, he exclaimed, "How come everything in the sinking pile floats?"

The children's vacillation between the rule and other types of explanation intrigued us. For example, Carl talked in the following manner about the objects he thought would float:

Examiner: (Picking up a block) Why do you think this will float?
Child: Because it is wood.
Examiner: But it is heavy. Did you feel it?
Child: (Receives block from examiner and feels its weight in one hand. He seems to be bothered.)
Examiner: Do you want to change your mind?
Child: Yes. (Puts block in the group of objects that will sink.)
Examiner: (Picking up boat) Why will this float?
Child: Because it's lighter than a piece of water the same size. (Later, while verifying his predictions, he said of the same boat,) "It floats like this (upright position), but it sinks like that (lying down)."

Examiner: How come it floats like that and sinks like that?
Child: Because the air goes out.

Thus, while it can be said that this child had learned the rule about specific gravity, he applied it only to certain objects.

Because we thus had serious reservations about the children's comprehension of the rules they were using, we later decided to probe into the rules with two pieces of soap. One of them was little and sank. The other piece was a large cake of Ivory soap that floated. The children were all puzzled by the fact that although the two pieces looked exactly the same except for size, the large one floated and the little one sank. They quickly explained, however, that the little cake was "heavier than a piece of water the same size." When asked, "Isn't it funny that the big one floated and the little one didn't?" Dan replied, "I have seen them (little pieces of soap) sink, but I don't know why they sink."

The Children's Classification of Objects
Our purpose in asking children to classify the objects into things that float and things that sink was not to test them on the accuracy of each prediction. Our interest was in the *logical consistency* involved in the children's notion of specific gravity—not in their *physical knowledge* of whether or not each object floated. For example, if a candle was believed to sink, what mattered to us was whether or not two candles of grossly different sizes were thought to sink regardless of their absolute weight.

According to Inhelder and Piaget (1958, p. 23), the classification of objects into things that float and things that sink is hard for preoperational children because, for them, each event is an isolated incident without any necessary logical consistency among the events. Therefore, for preoperational children (1) the same object does not have to have the same physical nature over time, (2) two identical objects can have opposite properties, and (3) similar items of different sizes can have different properties. Although the first two of these phenomena were not common, all three were observed.

All the children seemed to believe that the same object maintains its physical properties over time. However, when they were faced with the metal plate which floated at times and sank at other times, this belief was no longer solid. For example, Bill accidentally placed the metal plate on the water in such a way that it floated. At the examiner's suggestion, he took the plate out and put it on the water again. This time, however, the plate sank because he happened to slide it into the water at an angle. When he was asked what he thought the plate would do on the third trial, he said, "It'll probably float" (basing his prediction on random phenomena). To the question "What makes you think it will float?" he replied, "It floated the other time." To the question, "It sank, too. Why will it float this time?" he answered, "I don't know."

To cite an example of the second type of difficulty described by Inhelder and Piaget, Ann attributed opposite properties to two identical small cakes of soap. She put one of the pieces with the things that would float, and the other piece among the things that would sink. After all the objects had been dichotomized, the examiner picked up the two pieces, and the following conversation took place:

Examiner: How come this one is going to float (piece from the category of "float")?
Child: Because it is lighter.
Examiner: And this one (from the other category)?
Child: Because it is heavier.
Examiner: Is this one (the one judged "heavier") bigger or smaller?
Child: They are both small. (She did not show any sign of any awareness that her statements were contradictory.)

The above questions were again asked by Engelmann later in the session, and again, without any awareness of the contradictions, the child gave the same response. ("This will float (pointing to one piece), and this will sink (pointing to the other piece).")

Chart 7-1   The Classification of Objects[a]

	Will float	Will sink
Ann	Plastic boat	Small Montessori cylinder
	Toy metal plate	Big piece Ivory soap
	Big piece aluminum foil	Red wooden bead
	Little piece soap (white)	Big needle
	Little ball bearing	Penny
	Ping-pong ball	Small paper clip
	Tiny ball bearing	Block
	Small needle	Small paper clips
	Big paper clip	Big Montessori cylinder
	2 small pieces aluminum foil	Big ball bearing
	Small needle	Spice bottle (empty and covered)
	Small candle	Big piece green soap
		Small piece aluminum foil
		Little piece soap (white)
		Tiny black rubber ball
		Green wooden bead
		Big candle

[a]The objects are listed in the order in which the children placed them in each group. All the children classified all the objects that were given to them, without leaving any as being unclassifiable. See Footnote 3.

Bill		
	Plastic boat	Small ball bearing
	Big piece aluminum foil	Toy metal plate
	Tiny black rubber ball	Big red rubber ball
	Little candle	Block
	Big needle	Spice bottle (empty and covered)
	Penny	Big piece green soap
	Big candle	Big piece Ivory soap
	Little needle	Big Montessori cylinder
		Little Montessori cylinder
		2 little pieces soap (white)
		Small paper clip

Carl		
	Green wooden bead	Big piece green soap
	Yellow wooden bead	Spice bottle (empty and covered)
	Tiny black rubber ball	Toy metal plate
	Block	Big piece Ivory soap
	Penny	Big candle
	Plastic boat	Big ball bearing
	Big piece aluminum foil	Large Montessori cylinder
	Ping-pong ball	
	Little candle	
	Small Montessori cylinder	
	Big red rubber ball	
	2 little pieces soap (white)	
	Large paper clip	
	Small paper clip	
	Small ball bearing	
	Tiny piece aluminum foil	
	Large needle	
	Small needle	

Dan		
	Large Montessori cylinder	Penny
	Block	2 little pieces soap (white)
	Toy metal plate	Big piece green soap
	Big piece aluminum foil	Big piece Ivory soap
	Little candle	Big red rubber ball
	Big candle	Big paper clip
	Spice bottle (empty and covered)	Small paper clip
	Ping-pong ball	Needles
	Small Montessori cylinder	
	Green wooden bead	
	Yellow wooden bead	
	Tiny black rubber ball	

The third type of difficulty was extensive. All the children showed some evidence of believing that the same thing would sink if it is big, and float if it is small. As can be seen in Chart 7-1, Bill and Dan thought the big ball would sink and the tiny one would float. Ann predicted that the big candle, big ball bearing, and big needle would sink ("because they are heavy"), and that the little candle, little ball bearings, and little needle would float ("because they are lighter"). (She also predicted that the larger paper clip would float, and that the small ones would sink, thus contradicting her own intuitive generalization.) Carl placed the big cakes of soap, big candle, big ball bearing, and big Montessori cylinder with the things that would float. The children's inability to separate weight from size is typical of children who have not yet dissociated weight from volume.

The Children's Explanations

Inhelder and Piaget state that children give different kinds of explanations at different stages as to why things sink or float. Preoperational children give multiple and often contradictory explanations without any awareness of the contradictions. Some of the examples they found in Geneva were the following: a boat floats because real boats float; a needle floats because it is little; an aluminum plate floats because it is light; a flat pebble floats because it is flat; a board floats because of its color; and a piece of wood floats because it floated before. In the next period, that of concrete operations, the children begin to assume the possibility of a coherent solution, and this expectation motivates them to try to resolve contradictions. Thus, they revise the concept of weight by integrating it with the concept of volume and say, for example, that a nail sinks "because it is light, but it is made of iron." In the period of formal operations, the last sources of contradiction are eliminated, i.e., the notion of absolute weight and reference to air as an explanation.

All the children we saw in Illinois used the rules they had learned to explain why objects sank or floated. However, all of them also gave the above multiple explanations that Inhelder and Piaget found in Geneva. Below is a list of the additional explanations each child gave either before or after verifying his prediction. They reveal the preoperational processes at work underneath the application of learned rules.

Ann: The small candle will float "because it's light."
The big candle will sink "because it's heavy."
The small piece of soap will float "because it's lighter."
An identical piece of soap will sink "because it's heavier."

Bill: All the objects in the float pile will float "because they are lighter."
All the objects in the sink pile will sink "because they are heavy."
The paper clip will sink "because it has cracks in it."
The little needle will float "because it's small."
The big ball will sink "because it's big."
The spice bottle will sink "because it's heavy."
The spice bottle sank "because it has water in it." (The spice bottle first floated with the cover screwed on, and then sank when the cover was removed.)

The metal plate will float "because it's skinny."
The metal plate sank "because I pushed it."

Carl: The block will float "because it's wood."
The little candle will float "because it's littler."
The big ball bearing will sink "because it is heavy."
The boat "floats like this (usual position), but it sinks like that (lying on its side)."
The spice bottle sank, when the cover was removed, "because the air went out."

Dan: The boat (and the closed spice bottle) will float "because it has air inside."
"I really don't know why (the tiny black ball will sink)."
The plate sank when it was filled with water "because it gets too heavy."

Interpretations of the Findings in the Light of Piaget's Theory of Sequential Development

To summarize the findings, although the children were taught a final hypothesis in the form of verbal rules, they persisted in making statements that characterize the preoperational child. Two interpretations can be made of this conclusion. One is that the rules were incomplete, and that better programming and a longer period of instruction were necessary. The other interpretation is that since the children did not have the prerequisite abilities for the construction of a single hypothesis, they could not possibly have attained the precise concept of specific gravity, no matter how long they had been taught many rules. The first interpretation is Engelmann's, the second is ours.

Since our interpretation of the findings is based on Piaget's theory of sequential development, the findings will be reviewed below in the light of the theory. Inhelder and Piaget state that formal operations are operations on concrete operations, which are achieved earlier. Each earlier achievement is a necessary-but-not-sufficient condition for the attainment of later abilities. The prerequisite abilities which are necessary but not sufficient for the construction of the notion of specific gravity include (1) the conservation of volume, (2) the conservation of weight, (3) the conservation of substance, (4) class inclusion, and (5) seriation. Chronologically speaking, the abilities that appear first are the conservation of substance, class inclusion, and seriation. The conservation of weight appears a little later (at about 8 years of age), and the conservation of volume is usually attained around 11 years of age by 50 percent of the children. Since the findings concerning conservation will be described later in this paper, a few comments will be made now only with regard to class inclusion and seriation.

It was stated above that the child in the period of concrete operations begins to assume the possibility of a noncontradictory explanation of why things sink or float. This expectation is made possible by the child's attainment of class inclusion. When he can distinguish between "some" and "all" because of the reversible operation of class inclusion, the child comes to see that small objects do not always weigh less than larger ones, i.e., that it is incorrect to consider all small objects as light and all large ones as heavy. The child comes to this conclusion by making a 2 x 2 table with the following four cells: (1) small-and-light objects, (2) small-and-nonlight objects, (3) large-and-light objects, and (4) large-and-nonlight objects. The cells of small-and-nonlight objects and of large-and-light objects lead the child to revise the hypotheses of absolute weight and absolute size.

Of the four children we tested, only one (Carl) had the reversible operation of class inclusion. We feel that this finding is one of the explanations as to why the children could not possibly have arrived at the concept of specific gravity.

To construct the hypothesis of specific gravity, the child must not only have at his disposal the above 2 x 2 table but also refine it into the multiple seriation of both variables (Inhelder & Piaget, 1958, pp. 31, 34). In other words, the above small-large and light-nonlight scheme has to be differentiated into a system of many different volumes for the same weight. The serial ordering of weights among objects of the same volume is not possible until late in the period of concrete operations (Piaget & Inhelder, 1962, p. 233).

We did not test any of the four children in seriation. However, the importance of seriation was seen when mercury was used as the medium instead of water. All four of the children (as well as the adults who were watching and the authors) were surprised to find out that a big, heavy ball bearing floated on mercury. All the children explained this phenomenon by saying, "Because it's lighter than a piece of mercury the same size." After hearing this explanation, we asked a child (Bill) whether or not he thought a small cake of soap would float on mercury. He said it would sink, and was surprised to find out that it floated. If he had had the structure of multiple seriation of weight and volume, he could have predicted that soap would float.

The findings concerning the four children's conservation will be presented in the next section. On the basis of what we saw in the four children in Illinois, we agree with Piaget that the construction of the ultimate single hypothesis of specific gravity is the result of the gradual elimination of earlier multiple hypotheses, which are in contradiction with each other. The very awareness of the contradiction grows out of the gradual integration of many prerequisite abilities. Our conclusion is a hypothesis which must be tested in contrast with that of Engelmann. His hypothesis states that rules can be programmed without following the developmental sequence that Piaget found. We hope to have an opportunity to test the two hypotheses.

Conservation

Findings

As can be seen in Chart 7-2, the four children generally did much better in conservation than could be expected of normal kindergarten children. Since no pretest was administered prior to instruction, it is not possible to determine how much of these achievements could be attributed to teaching.

Chart 7-2   The Various Conservation Tasks[a]

	Ann	Bill	Carl	Dan
Volume				
Explanation[b]	–	+	–	+
Transformations	almost	not quite	+	+
Countersuggestions		–		not quite
Weight				
Transformations	+	not quite	+	+
Countersuggestions	+		+	+
Liquid				
Transformations	not quite	+	+	+
Countersuggestions		–		+
Number				
Equivalence	+	– → +	+	+
Transformations	+	+	+	+

[a] "+" indicates "passed."
"almost" indicates a high-level intermediary stage.
"not quite" indicates a low-level intermediary stage.
"–" indicates "clearly failed."

[b] "Explanation" of volume refers to child's ability to explain why the water level rises when the clay ball is dropped into the water.

However, the above conclusion must be qualified in view of the fact that although the children were technically conserving, there was evidence that they did not necessarily understand what they were saying. The rules they had been taught apparently concerned identity ("It is (or was) the same size") and compensation ("It is longer this way but shorter this way"). In attempting to justify the conservation of volume, weight, or substance, the children's first statement was "Because it is (or was) the same size." This justification seemed reasonable in the past tense, but rather unrelated to reality in the present tense. Therefore, we told them that we could not see in what way the sausage (or pancake or pieces) was "the same size" as the ball, and asked them to show us what they meant. Their usual response was "It's longer this way but shorter this way" (indicating the two dimensions of the sausage with their hands). This argument fit the facts of the sausage and the ring. However, when the clay ball was transformed into a round "pancake," and the child (Carl) made the same gestures as for the sausage while saying, "It's longer this way but shorter this way," the justification could no longer be accepted. This reservation was confirmed when we further asked him to explain what he meant. This time, he made his finger go around the circumference of the "pancake" while saying, "It's longer this way." Rightly or wrongly, we gave a + to this kind of answer because, technically speaking, it was more correct than incorrect.

Although three children could more or less conserve volume, only one of the three, Dan, could explain why the water level goes up when the clay ball is immersed. He said the ball pushes the water, and the water goes up because it can't go sideways. When they were asked the same question, the other two children looked bothered, hesitated, and quickly answered, "It is heavier than a piece of water the same size" (an explanation that applied to the other experiment).

One of the questions concerning the conservation of volume involves putting into the child's hands a heavy ball bearing and a clay ball of the same size. The question that is then asked is, "Would the water come up as high here as here, or would the water go up higher in one glass?" Three of the children (Ann, Carl, and Dan) answered this question correctly. Bill said, "The heavier the ball is, the higher up the water will go" (a rule which is normally found among young children). This child was one of the two who could explain why dropping an object makes the water level rise. Two of the three children who could answer the question correctly were those who could not explain the displacement of water.

Implications

To summarize the findings, although the children were taught conservation in the form of verbal rules, their understanding was found to be limited. For example, they sometimes made statements which fit the rules but did not correspond to reality. Volume was sometimes "conserved" without an understanding of what volume is. As in the case of the Geneva children, an understanding of volume first seems to result in nonconservation and the construction of the wrong rule. The importance of going through this stage of constructing the wrong rule will be discussed in the next section.

Implications for Early Childhood Education

The Importance of the Sensorimotor Roots of Logical and Physical Knowledge

One of the most valuable things we observed in testing the children was the fact that hypothetico-deductive thinking is slowly built up from a sensorimotor base. It was instructive to see that the children's sensorimotor and intuitive concepts were more powerful than the overlay of verbal rules. The emerging notions of specific gravity will be selected below to illustrate this point.

Ann's responses exemplified a child trying to integrate her sensorimotor information with intuitive notions of absolute weight and volume and with the rules that had been taught.

The examiner picked up a small ball bearing ($\frac{1}{2}$ inch in diameter) from the group of objects Ann had predicted would float (presumably because she had equated "small" with "light"). She was asked why she thought the ball bearing would float.

Child:	It will sink. (She probably recalled the sensorimotor feeling of its weight.)
Examiner:	Let's change our minds, then (meaning let's put the ball bearing in the group of objects that will sink).
Child:	(Receiving the ball bearing from the examiner and feeling its weight,) This one will sink. (The sensorimotor concept of weight thus appears to be the deciding factor.)
Examiner:	Why?
Child:	It *feels* heavier. (She puts the ball bearing in the group of objects that will sink. Then picks up a small needle from the group of things that will float, and says,) This one will float. (She is back to equating "small" with "light.")

The overlay of rules was not integrated with this child's intuitive concept of specific gravity, and led her to the absurdity of saying on the next day that (1) two candles of different sizes have the same weight and (2) the big cake of soap must be lighter than the little cake of soap. Below is an abridged version of how the conversation took place.

Examiner:	(With big and tiny candles in hands) Are these made of the same thing?
Child:	Yes.
Examiner:	How do you know that?
Child:	Because I remember yesterday. They both floated because they are lighter than a piece of water the same size.
Examiner:	But isn't this one bigger than this one?

Child: Yes, one's bigger than the other.
Examiner: Then, isn't one heavier than the other?
Child: No, they weigh the same.
Examiner: Sure?
Child: Yes.
Examiner: Feel them in your hands.
Child: (Feeling them in both hands,) They both weigh the same.

The big cake of Ivory soap (which floated the day before) and the little cake of soap (that sank) were then reintroduced.

Examiner: Did both of these sink yesterday?
Child: Yes.
Examiner: Feel this big one and this little one in your hands.
Child: (Feeling the weight of the two pieces) The big one feels heavier.
Examiner: Will both of them sink?
Child: I think the little one will sink, too. (Her wording implies that although the little one is light because it is small, it will nevertheless sink.)
Examiner: Why?
Child: Because they are both soap.
Examiner: You put them in the water and see what happens.
Child: (Finding out that the big one floated and the little one sank,) I forgot yesterday!
Examiner: Remember you said the big one was heavier?
Child: The big one must be lighter, and the little one must be heavier (because the big one is lighter than a piece of water the same size, and the little one is heavier than a piece of water the same size).
Examiner: Do you think both are made from the same thing?
Child: I think they are made of the same thing.

Ann thus showed to us how deeply the notion of specific gravity is rooted in sensorimotor knowledge. With the ball bearing, she was demonstrating that she was intuitively coming to eliminate contradictions by coordinating concepts of size and weight. However, the candles and pieces of soap told a different story. When the child ends up saying that the big and little candles weigh the same, and that the big cake of soap must be lighter than the little cake of soap, the rules must be said to be interfering with the child's gradual modification of her sensorimotor concept of weight. We believe that early childhood education must build the child's sensorimotor knowledge, which is slowly modified and structured and makes the concept of specific gravity eventually possible.

The Progressive Structuring and Integration of Concepts

One of the fundamental principles to be discerned from Piaget's developmental theory is the fact that the concepts achieved earlier are necessary, albeit not sufficient, for the attainment of later concepts. Ann, whom we have just described above, showed that she had neither the earlier concepts nor the later concept of specific gravity in spite of the fact that she had been taught certain rules about specific gravity. As stated earlier in this paper, the necessary-but-not-sufficient conditions for the concept of specific gravity are (1) the conservation of volume, (2) the conservation of weight, (3) the conservation of substance, (4) class inclusion, and (5) seriation. None of the four children we saw in Illinois came anywhere near mastering half of the above five prerequisites. Contrary to what Engelmann maintains, the lesson we learned from these children was that teaching the rules does not necessarily result in the child's learning. The children did learn the rules, but the natural sequence of their development was not affected very much by them.

It has been stated in connection with the conservation-of-volume experiment that only Bill and Dan could explain why the water level goes up when an object is immersed. The explanation they gave was that the object *pushes* the water, and the water has to *go* somewhere. From the accompanying gestures of pushing the object down and pushing the water up, the sensorimotor roots of the concept of volume could clearly be seen. It can be seen from Chart 7-1 that Bill and Dan were also the only two who tended not to predict that the same object would sink if it is big and float if it is small. In contrast, the other two children (Ann and Carl) who superficially "conserved" volume without understanding the displacement of water were those who predicted that the big objects would sink and that the same objects would float if they were small. The importance of the notion of volume in the construction of specific gravity can thus be traced by comparing Ann and Carl on the one hand and Bill and Dan on the other.

The only statement that can be made here about the children's conservation of weight and substance is that although the surface verbalization resembled conservation, many *lacunae* were found by probing slightly below the surface.

Engelmann states that none of the children were taught class inclusion. As seen earlier, only Carl had attained this cognitive structure. It can be seen from Chart 7-1 that having the structure of class inclusion was not sufficient to attain the concept of specific gravity.

In conclusion, we would like to take issue with Engelmann's view that logic can be taught to young children without taking into account the natural developmental sequence that Piaget described. We feel that both logical and physical knowledge must be structured slowly beginning at the sensorimotor level and integrating all the intuitive concepts that are necessary for the attainment of later cognitive abilities.

"Thinking" as the Application of the Appropriate Rule(s)

Engelmann's conception of "thinking" is that its essence is the application of the appropriate rule(s). Early in his paper, he states, "The primary question, again, seems to be, 'What is the mechanism that induces change?' If we can specify this mechanism, we can control it." (By "inducing change," he meant inducing learning or development.) Below is a quotation from the same paper in which he discusses the mechanism of learning, the role of physical experience, and teaching according to the way suggested by the Piagetian model.

> The mechanism is actually quite simple. Children are taught. They may be taught through physical experiences. They may be taught through other types of experiences.
>
> It is possible to teach children a wide variety of discriminations, including those that involve logical structure. All red objects share a certain characteristic. This characteristic can be taught. It can be demonstrated in such a way that a child can generalize it. So it is with other rules, and to learn *red* is to learn a rule. All instances of compensating changes share a set of characteristics. These characteristics can be taught in quite the same way *red* is taught. The child is presented with instances of the concept and is taught the relationship between the characteristics and the language used to describe these. Unfortunately, I cannot go into great detail on the nature of concept analysis and the procedures by which generalization is induced, but I would like to stress that the most efficient way to teach is rarely the way suggested by the Piagetian model. Although a child must be exposed to instances of a particular concept before he can learn the concept, the physical experience often represents a noisy instance, one that is not well designed to teach what the salient characteristics of the concept are, or which aspect of the objects or events should be attended to. Many more instances of the noisy physical experience may have to be presented before the child learns the rule.

Our conception of the thinking of 6-year-old children is that it consists of the process of structuring knowledge by acting on objects.[4] Objects are far from being confusing "noise" in the child's processing of information. On the contrary, as demonstrated by Ann in the section on the sensorimotor roots of logical and physical knowledge, it was the rules that were interfering with the thinking process. If the child had not learned the rules, she would not have distorted her sensorimotor and intuitive concepts by thinking that the big and tiny candles must have the same weight, and that the big cake of soap must be lighter than the little cake of soap.

---

[4] The structuring of knowledge takes different forms depending on whether it concerns physical knowledge, social knowledge, or logical knowledge (see Kamii & Radin, in press; Sonquist, Kamii, & Derman, in press). However, the importance of acting on objects is common to all types of knowledge.

The four children we tested also seemed to be prevented from coming to grips with objects because the verbal rules blocked their intellectual contact with them. Instead of struggling with objects, the children tended to search their repertoire of rules. One example is the two children who "explained" why immersing an object makes the water level go up by first hesitating, and then saying, "It is heavier than a piece of water the same size." Another example is the child who ended up saying that a tiny piece of aluminum foil ($\frac{1}{2}$ inch x $\frac{1}{4}$ inch) was heavier than a larger piece of the same thing (approximately 3 inches x 2 inches). This conclusion was reached in the following way. The child saw a piece of aluminum foil floating on the water and explained this phenomenon by saying, "It's lighter than a piece of water the same size." We then tore off a tiny piece and made it sink to the bottom of the container by pushing it. The child's explanation of this phenomenon was "It's heavier than a piece of water the same size." When we looked puzzled and asked which piece was heavier, the child insisted to both Engelmann and us that the tiny piece was heavier because it sank.

When an object reacted in contradiction to the children's expectations, the children were surprised but quickly gave the rule ("It is lighter (or heavier) than a piece of water the same size"), no matter how much it differed from their own intuitive knowledge. One example is the following discussion (slightly abridged) with Carl while verifying his predictions:

Examiner:	(Picking up a large paper clip,) Why do you think this will float?
Child:	Because it is lighter than a piece of water the same size.
Examiner:	Okay. Shall we try it? You put it in and see if it will float. . . .Oops! So we've got to put it in with the things that sink. (Then, picking up a small piece of soap,) Why do you think this will float?
Child:	Because it is lighter than a piece of water the same size.
Examiner:	Okay, you try it. . . .What happened?
Child:	It sank.
Examiner:	But you told me it was lighter than a piece of water the same size.
Child:	But it sank.
Examiner:	Okay, then, how come?
Child:	It is heavier than a piece of water the same size.
Examiner:	Now, let's try the things that you think are going to sink.
Child:	(Tries the block.) It floated!
Examiner:	It's heavy, and it still floated?
Child:	Yes. (Tries the big candle. It floats.) How come everything in the sinking pile floats? (Picks up a big ball bearing, and says) This one will sink. . . .It did.
Examiner:	How come you were so sure that one would sink?

Child:	Because it is heavy. . . .(Puts large green bar of soap in the water.)
Examiner:	How come it sank?
Child:	Because it is heavier than a piece of water the same size.
Examiner:	(Picking up the bar of Ivory soap) Will this one sink?
Child:	Yes. (Tries it.)
Examiner:	How come this one didn't sink?
Child:	Because it is lighter than a piece of water the same size.

The contrast between Carl and Bill's handling of the metal plate vividly showed us how the imposition of rules can prevent children from thinking and discovering. While Engelmann had ranked Bill as the least able and most lackadaisical of the four children, we felt that he was the most active and creative thinker. Instead of reciting rules, he was constantly trying to come to grips with reality. (Engelmann had just joined the questioning.)

Engelmann:	Watch. (Makes the plate float.) What is the plate doing?
Child:	Floating.
Engelmann:	Now, watch. (Pushes it down.) What is it doing now?
Child:	Sinking.
Engelmann:	(Makes the plate float again.) All right, now, make it sink.
Child:	(Pushes the plate down.)
Engelmann:	Why did it float sometimes and sink at other times?
Child:	Because I made it sink.
Engelmann:	Why did it sink?
Child:	Because I pushed it.
Engelmann:	What did that do to the plate?
Child:	It made it sink.

While Bill's statements were thus preoperational, he was nevertheless always actively attempting to make sense of what he saw.

In contrast, Carl only referred to the rules as can be seen below.

Examiner:	Can you make it (the floating plate) sink?
Child:	Yes (Pushes it down.)
Examiner:	How come it floats when it is like this?
Child:	Because it is lighter than a piece of water the same size.
Examiner:	Does it get heavier when it sinks (pushing plate down)?
Child:	Yes.
Examiner:	How come it floats like this and sinks like this?
Child:	(No answer)
Examiner:	But can it sink when it goes like this (pushing plate down)?
Child:	Yes.
Examiner:	How come?
Child:	Because it is heavier than a piece of water the same size.

Some Piagetian Ideas about Teaching

The importance of the progressive structuring of knowledge from a sensorimotor base has already been discussed. The two additional points that we would like to make concern (1) the difference between short-term and long-term learning and (2) the importance of the child's going through stages of constructing wrong rules.

In the above quotation, Engelmann stated that "the most efficient way to teach is rarely the way suggested by the Piagetian model." There is perhaps a certain degree of truth in this statement in terms of the time it takes to teach concepts. As stated by Kohlberg (1968), the cognitive-developmental view of teaching aims at the building of broad, irreversible structures, rather than immediate gains which may be short-termed. The observations described in this paper confirmed our belief that learning is neither simple nor a quick process. In the long run, we feel that the imposition of rules is a less efficient way to teach than influencing the development of underlying cognitive processes that will eventually enable the child to construct his own rules. We consider teaching to be a method that helps the child to make his own discoveries by asking the right question at the right time. The "right" question is in precise harmony with what the child is thinking about at the moment. The "right" timing allows him enough time to integrate and consolidate a new discovery before the next question is introduced.

The importance of the child's construction of wrong hypotheses must be understood in the context of the progressive structuring and integration of knowledge. Wrong hypotheses are important to construct because they contain a certain degree of intuitive correctness, which must be incorporated into the ultimate hypothesis. For example, the four children tended to base their predictions (of floating and sinking) on the absolute weight of the objects. These predictions often turned out to be wrong, but they did take into account one of the attributes that is relevant to specific gravity. Compared to younger children, who gave the shape or color of the object as an explanation of floating and sinking, these 6-year-old children had progressed considerably. The hypothesis of absolute weight thus contains a great deal of correctness which must be brought out for the child to think about and eventually integrate into a higher-order hypothesis.

Bill, the most creative of the four children, explained that the metal plate sank "because I pushed it." This kind of wrong rule gives the teacher an opportunity to follow the child's line of thinking by saying, "Let's see if we can make everything else sink by pushing them." By verifying this hypothesis, the child can eventually come to a modified concept of weight that integrates the wrong intuition about the effects of pushing objects down to make them sink. The contradictory multiple hypotheses of the preoperational child can be eliminated only by their gradual integration. The imposition of rules may mask the multiple explanations, but the rules will not eliminate the child's intuition.

The lacunae that we observed underneath the rules need no further discussion. It is reasonable to assume that with such lacunae, the child cannot be expected to use the rules to create new higher-order hypotheses.

Our Piagetian idea of teaching is not to leave the child alone. Piaget's theory is not a maturationist theory. Neither is it an additive theory of learning. Rather, it is an interactionist theory (Kohlberg, 1968), which views learning as a continual process of assimilating new knowledge into old structures and accommodating the, old structures to new data. What we attempt to do in the Ypsilanti Early Education Program is to help the young child integrate the sensorimotor and intuitive knowledge he already has. By consolidating and articulating his preoperational knowledge, we feel that the child's chances of achieving the next stage are maximized.

IMPLICATIONS OF THE TEACHABILITY OF OPERATIONS FOR THE CONSTRUCTION OF ORDINAL SCALES OF COGNITIVE DEVELOPMENT

We would like to make only one point about this subject. Our experience convinced us of the importance of the exploratory (or clinical) method of testing. If we had questioned the children according to the instructions of a standardized test manual, we would have been forced to conclude that the children were, by and large, able to conserve substance, weight, and volume. We would also have concluded that the children had a single hypothesis explaining specific gravity. Because we used a flexible, exploratory method that followed the children's line of thinking, it was easy to find out that the children were preoperational in spite of an overlay of well-learned rules.

How young children learn is a complex question. Different researchers are attempting different approaches to answer this question. Just as in the specific-gravity experiment, we feel that only by verifying the various hypotheses can we hope to arrive at higher-order hypotheses. Out of such empirical verifications, we may someday come to discover the best possible way to teach young children.

Open Discussion

Attention was focused on different ways of looking at Engelmann's proposition that children can be taught to respond correctly to Piagetian tasks by teaching them a rule. Goldschmid felt that Engelmann was describing a procedure very much like teaching what Piaget calls a logical prerequisite and that perhaps one could consider reversibility a sort of a rule, just like addition or subtraction. Engelmann agreed in the sense that Piaget does carefully describe the structure of an operation, adding that one should make children aware of both the structure and the groups of objects to which those properties obtain.

Beilin noted that while he had found rule teaching a highly effective instructional procedure for teaching a particular kind of conservation, it unfortunately did not transfer to other kinds of conservation. A rule acts as a kind of algorithm which works only if the data are in a form consistent with the algorithm. However Beilin added that an operation is flexible and can be modified in relation to various inputs.

ENGELMANN

It is a function of the rule that you state. What you are saying—if I may restate it—is that if you give a rule that applies only to a certain set of objects or set of instances that have a particular set of characteristics, when you really want it to apply to a larger domain, then you have given the wrong rule. You have to use a more general rule such that you can plug in a variety of inputs initially to show how the rule is generalizable across this entire domain. Marion Blank, for instance, has a nice description of what may happen when children learn an inadequate rule. She asked a fourth grade class in which the children were studying about the characteristics of mammals:

"What do mammals do?"
"Well, they bear their young alive, and then they give milk. . ."
"Is this true of all mammals?"
"Yes."
"Well, does a mouse give milk?"
"Yes."
"When?"
"Well, after a mouse bears its young."
"And what about a rabbit?"
"Yes, same thing."
"And a horse?"
"Yes."
"Well, what about a cow?"
"No. Cows give milk."

This is a perfect example of the problem. The pupils learn a rule that does not cover the class initially, and then when they're presented with such an example, it is treated as an exception—this is faulty instruction. The appropriate rule had not been programmed in the first place. I'm not even postulating that you should always do it—some of these inconsistencies are inherent just in trying to deal with the immediate present.

BEILIN

I don't think there's any argument on that score. That's not really much of an issue. Of course, you have to get the appropriate kind of rule that will cover the instances. I know that in my own tests the rule that I chose for training of conservation was the reversibility rule tied to the addition-subtraction rule. I don't know what else you'd want to add if you're going to provide a rule. But I think the general question still remains. Certainly, it has to be an appropriate kind of rule. And if you don't get the results in your experiment, you'd have to look at that aspect of it first, as a simple procedural note.

Developmental Theory and Diagnostic Procedures[1]

CHAPTER EIGHT

BÄRBEL INHELDER
University of Geneva

Until recently, fundamental research in developmental psychology and attempts to evaluate cognitive functioning have followed separate paths. It is possible that today's encounter between specialists in these two different fields will lead to the convergence of theory and application; such a convergence promises to be fruitful. Fundamental research in developmental psychology has provided a considerable amount of experimental data which has led to the establishment of theory. There is a growing awareness of the need for sound theoretical bases which permit clinical diagnosis to do more than simply state achievements. A theory which is already firmly rooted in experimental fact will sooner or later receive wider application, and the wider its application, the more opportunities we shall have to test it in real-life situations.

Although my paper mainly concerns the links between theory and application, I shall begin with some introductory remarks on two fundamental principles of Piagetian theory: first, the genetic approach and the epistemological point of view; and second, the concept of structure and the biological aspect of this theory.

I shall then briefly discuss two points which have not yet been made explicit in the theory, that is to say, the relationships between partial structures and the influence of certain factors on cognitive development. The links between partial structures can be explored in different ways—for example, through new statistical methods or detailed learning studies. The individual factors influencing development can, up to a point, be distinguished and studied experimentally; for instance, we can explore the genesis of fundamental concepts in different cultural settings, or the role of language in the development of such concepts.

Finally, pathology constitutes another field where research based on the theoretical developmental approach can be fruitful. The study of the formation of the fundamental concepts and partial structures in psychotic children will be

[1] I take this opportunity to express my gratitude to Dr. H. Sinclair and Mrs. S. Wedgwood for their help in preparing this paper. Mrs. Wedgwood's collaboration was made possible by a grant from the Ford Foundation.

the subject of the last part of my paper. All these approaches which apply developmental psychological theory in very different fields are, we think, of twofold importance: the findings contribute to the theory, which itself provides a coherent framework within which it is possible to increase our understanding of cognitive mechanisms.

PIAGET'S CONCEPTION OF COGNITIVE DEVELOPMENT

Evidently, Piaget's (1967e) theory of development forms the basis of our research. Even if this theory is not yet complete to the last detail, it is, in my opinion, a fruitful explanatory psychological theory of cognitive development. It is, to my knowledge, the only theory which links the most basic biological mechanisms to the most superior achievements of human thought, and it does this through its concept of development as a continuous and progressive construction. Not only has this led Piaget to a detailed analysis of the construction of a number of fundamental concepts, but it has also enabled him to link cognitive structures to extremely early functions. For example, though the concept of conservation of quantity has always been considered a continuation of the permanency of the object, it was only quite recently that Piaget traced the slow evolution from this very first invariant to the conservation of quantity in the concrete operational stage. Early intuitions about qualititative identity have been uncovered and provide a deeper understanding of the development of this concept; a biological component has thus been added. It is only through a genuinely developmental approach that we can avoid mistaking the precocious appearance of an intuitive preparation for the operatory concept for the concept itself (Mehler & Bever, 1967). There are many such prenotions at an early age, but they are neither equivalent to the complete structure nor can they emerge without certain prior constructions.

This fundamentally developmental approach leads naturally to an interactionist epistemology, i.e., to interaction between the knower and the known. When one is aware of the fact that the knower changes continuously, then his interactions with known objects must also be seen as changing. In other words, the objects themselves lose their apparent invariance, since for the knower their implications do not remain the same. The classical alternative between empiricism and nativism presents itself only if behavior patterns are considered in isolation at a certain age; as soon as what preceded them and what will follow them is taken into account, only an interactionist or constructivist theory is possible. Verbal behavior patterns have recently been considered innate, because no associationist mechanism could possibly be sufficient to explain them. But here again we must consider what acquisitions preceded these verbal behavior patterns and to what more evolved structures they will lead. In the search for structures we should not ignore their formation; in fact, it seems rather as if the form of each structure is governed by the way it is constructed.

In this context, that is, with the emphasis on modes of construction and thus on the subject's activity, it is necessary to mention the two types of abstraction to which this activity leads.

On the one hand, there is the type of knowledge which is a result of a feedback from the subject's actions on objects when the objects are no more than a medium for this activity; that is, when their specific properties have no importance. The clearest example of this type of feedback is the development of the concept of number. The child who counts objects—first from object (a) to object (d), for instance, then from (d) to (a)—and finds that the result is always the same, gains knowledge from this activity; whether he acts on pebbles, marbles, or dolls is immaterial.

On the other hand, in the field of physical causality we have the example of the child who discovers something about elasticity. When he observes that a ball rebounds much higher from a hard floor than from soft sand, he also gets a feedback from his activity, but here the specific properties of the objects themselves are of prime importance.

Many of the controversies on what can be learned by feedback from the social or physical environment seem to stem from the fact that these two types of knowledge acquisition are not distinguished. In both cases, however, what is learned is acquired through the activity of the subject who, in the largest sense of the word, transforms reality.

In the sense that the acquisition of knowledge always involves the transformation of reality and is the result of continuously changing interactions with environment, Piaget's theory is profoundly biological. It was certainly fortunate that Piaget's first research concerned the adaptation of certain species in relation to their different environments (mollusks); it was also fortunate that, later on, he came into contact with Waddington's embryological research and the concept of epigenesis. But his psychological theory should in no way be regarded as simply contributing an intriguing analogy to biology; he has no reductionism of psychology to biology in mind, but rather a conviction that identical mechanisms are at work on the organic and on the mental level. On both planes, assimilation means that reality is incorporated into the organism's physiological or mental structure, and that this incorporation implies a transformation of reality as well as of the organism. A particularly striking example is that of the memory code, which has become of the greatest interest to both molecular biologists and psychologists. From both points of view, the transformational aspect is becoming clear; from our investigations it has become evident that during development important qualitative transformations take place in the subject's mnemonic code.

Thus, Piaget's (1968) structuralism is not mainly the result of a desire for logical formalization, as is maintained by many American psychologists, including our friend Bruner (1966); it has grown from his biological orientation which refuses to admit that a structure emerges *ex nihilo*. Every structure is based on an anterior structure, not only through logical derivation, but, far more profoundly, through biological growth.

NEW STATISTICAL PROCEDURES

After these preliminary remarks, I should like to describe one area of Genevan research which clearly shows how the convergence of theory and application can improve our understanding of the problem of partial structures.

One method of obtaining a more detailed insight into the way children who already possess a specific structure acquire a superior one and also into the links that exist between different fields of knowledge (concepts of space, conservation, logical and mathematical concepts, etc.) is to analyze our results by more sophisticated logistic or statistical techniques. My colleague, Professor Vinh Bang (1959), has been working on this problem for about 15 years from two different angles: (1) he is applying new methods of analysis to our former results; and, (2) he is using a set of already well-established tests in a different kind of experimentation in which each subject is presented with the complete set of tests. More than 40 standardized tests have been consistently applied to 25 subjects in each age group, and it is thus possible to plot the points of a developmental curve (or rather scale) by taking the age at which a specific behavior is observed as present in the group under study. Starting from these empirical results, it is possible to smooth the irregularities of the curve and to extrapolate it by means of a probit analysis (or as Finnley calls it, "small sample analysis").

The first task is to determine the developmental scale obtained for a particular test and to compare it with the behavior patterns obtained for the remainder of the tests. The patterns relating to a specific field of knowledge can be ordered by means of a Guttman scale. It is thus possible both to examine the order of appearance of the different behavior patterns within one specific field of knowledge and to compare the results of the whole set of tests, and therefore, to analyze the existing links between various fields. In this way, the chronological order of behavior patterns can be theoretically determined. However, many questions still remain. Does the contemporaneity of two behavior patterns or the exact coincidence of two curves mean that they are psychologically equivalent? Does the fact that one behavior pattern may be completed before another mean that the presence of the first is necessary for the development of the second? In addition, it still has to be determined to what degree the psychological development of a "real-life" child follows this theoretical pattern of development. This last problem is currently being investigated and we are already in a position to make a few important points.

The curves of our "theoretical" subjects serve as the normative pattern of the developmental hierarchy H_1. Thus H_1 represents the mean order of appearance of the behavior patterns and is calculated by taking the "50-percent success" point of each pattern. Thus for H_1, we could have the total order $a, b, c, d, \ldots$ meaning that behavior pattern a was acquired before b and b before c, etc.

It is obvious that this system is purely ordinal. Within the limits of our margins of error, i.e., the fiducial limits obtained by means of probit analysis, we can sometimes determine that certain behavior patterns are contemporaneous and must therefore be considered "equivalent." Here only a partial order may be established, i.e., *a* before *b* and *c* before *d*, the exact relationship between *b* and *c* remaining unknown.

In a second research program, each subject is presented with a whole set of tests. These tests are exactly the same as those used to establish the normative curve H_1, and it is therefore feasible to compare the new results with H_1. Some interesting factors have already emerged. It has been discovered that the order does not always strictly tally from group to group. Three categories of subjects may be distinguished: (1) subjects whose new results exactly tally with H_1 (approximately 25 percent); (2) subjects whose results show 10 percent inversions or errors (approximately 50 percent); and (3) subjects whose results differ almost completely from H_1 (approximately 25 percent). The frequency of occurrence of the results in each of these categories thus seems to validate the normative hierarchy H_1, and we are now trying to determine the coefficients of constancy.

The next problem was to see whether it was possible to establish a hierarchy for these new groups of subjects. In order to do this, the existence of H_1 was temporarily ignored and a hierarchy H_2, based on the new results, was established. The fact that it was possible to do this seems to demonstrate the existence of a certain consistency of the answers within each field.

We then compared the two hierarchies H_1 and H_2 in order to find·out whether there was a significant difference between the two sets of findings. Although all the results have not yet been analyzed, it does seem that the differences are not significant. However, as regards the results of individual subjects, we observed that both those of the young subjects situated in the upper part of the scale and those of the oldest children in the lower part are heterogeneous.

I hope that I have given you an idea of how we think the new method of analysis and experimentation used by Vinh Bang backs up to some extent Piaget's theory of cognitive development.

LEARNING AND DEVELOPMENT

The central biological question concerning learning is whether it constitutes the source or the result of development. It would certainly be the source were development to consist solely of an accumulation of acquisitions of external origin, as empiricists suppose. On the contrary, if development consists of a continuous construction of operatory structures through interaction between the subject's activities and external data, then the assimilation of these data will determine and direct the learning process which depends on the developmental stages. Consequently, in our view, it is development that directs learning rather than vice versa.

I should now like to describe an experiment through which we were able to determine the nature of the décalage between the acquisition of numerical and geometric structures (Inhelder et al., 1967). It concerns the acquisition of quantitative measurement in spatial configurations. One of the child's main difficulties in acquiring spatial structures resides in the fact that the elementary topological relationships (contiguity, order, and enclosure) have to be transformed to fit a graded system of geometric coordinates. Such transformation, by combining subdivision of length and displacement, leads to the concept of conservation of linear dimension, which is a prerequisite of the constitution of measurement units.

We ask ourselves the following two questions: first, can the acquisition of elementary spatial measurement be facilitated by exercises in which the child applies numerical operations to the evaluation of length? If so, what stages does the child go through? Second, can the children's behavior during learning sessions help us to understand what happens during the interval between the acquisition of number (generally at about 6 years of age) and length conservation (generally at about 9 years of age), and the nature of the specific difficulties a child finds in reasoning about discrete units on the one hand and about continuous quantities and dimensions on the other?

The procedure, designed by our research associate, Magali Bovet, was the following: both the experimenter and the subject have a number of matchsticks at their disposal, but the subject's matches are considerably shorter than those of the experimenter and are of a different color (seven of the subject's red matches add up to the same length as five of the experimenter's green ones). The experimenter constructs either a straight or a broken line, a "road", and asks the subject to construct a line of the same length ("just as long a road; just as far to walk, so that two people, one on each road, would be just as·tired"). Three situations are presented:

Situation (a)

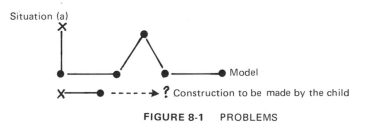

FIGURE 8-1   PROBLEMS

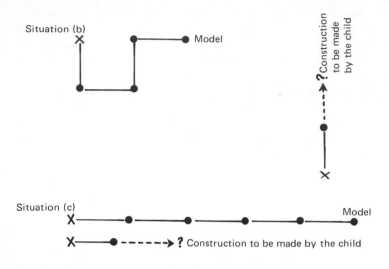

NB: The length of 5 of the model's matches = that of 7 of the child's matches

FIGURE 8-1 *(Continued)*

1.   The first situation is the most complex: the experimenter constructs a sort of zigzag line and the subject has to construct a straight line of the same length directly underneath. The figural pregnancy of the situation suggests a topological solution where beginning and end of both "roads" are congruent.

2.   In the second situation, the subject has again to construct a straight line of the same length as the experimenter's broken line but no longer directly underneath; this facilitates the problem slightly, since there is no longer a perceptual pregnancy that suggests a topological solution.

3.   The third is the easiest situation, since the experimenter's line is straight, and the subject is asked to construct a straight line directly underneath. Moreover, the experimenter uses the same number of matches (five) as in the first situation, so that this situation (seven of the subject's matches are needed to make a straight line of the same length) suggests a correct solution to both the first and second situations.

The three situations remain in front of the subject; after he has had his first attempt at each problem, he is encouraged to give explanations and eventually to reconsider his constructions, while the experimenter draws his attention to one situation after another.

The following reactions are typical of the subjects' behavior during the learning sessions:

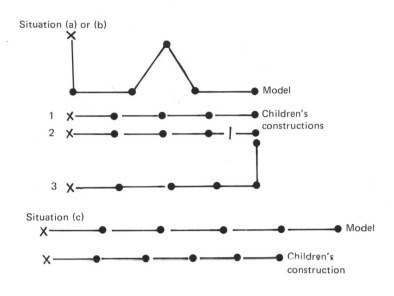

FIGURE 8-2   EXAMPLES OF SOLUTIONS

In the first situation, the most elementary solution is to construct a straight line with its extremities congruent with those of the experimenter's zigzag line. The child is convinced that the two lines are the same length, although his line is made up of four small matches and the experimenter's of five long matches.

In the second situation, the child has no ordinal or topological point of reference since he has to construct his line at some distance from that of the experimenter and he has no difficulty in using the numerical reference: he constructs his line using the same number of matches as the experimenter, regardless of the fact that his matches are shorter. When the experimenter now goes back to the first situation the child notices, with some embarrassment, that the line he previously considered of equal length does not contain the same number of matchsticks as that constructed by the experimenter.

At this point we often see amusing compromise solutions: for instance, in the first situation, the child may break one of his matches in two, thus creating a line with the same number of elements, without destroying the ordinal correspondence. Another solution, again clearly indicating the conflict between topological, ordinal, and numerical references, consists of adding one match, but putting it vertically instead of horizontally. When the child is then asked to construct his line in the third situation, he starts by using the same number of matches (five) as in the experimenter's line. Since this time both lines are straight and the second is directly under the model line, he sees immediately that this does not give the right solution; because his matches are shorter, his line does not reach as far as that of the model. Many children are perplexed at this point, and announce: "I can't do it; the red matches are smaller, it is impossible to get a road as long as the other." However, after a while, the child will usually realize that he can compensate for the difference in length by using more matchsticks, and will add two, thus giving the correct solution. He is now on the way to grasping the relationship between length and number of elements. Going back to the second situation he immediately says: "I will have to use more red matches to get the same road, because they are smaller." Those children who really acquire the concept will go even further: they will use the knowledge gained from the third situation (that seven red matches are equivalent in length to five green ones) in the first situation and will place their seven matches in a straight line without falling into the error of paying attention only to the ordinal aspect.

The main interest of this experiment is that, as in all our learning experiments, the children's reactions during the learning sessions show us, as through a magnifying glass, both the developmental processes and the specific difficulties they encounter. Cross-sectional experiments only rarely attain the fleeting, transitional stages, and though the general theory allows us to infer these gradual steps and the specific obstacles, the learning experiments show the development in a clearer and more detailed fashion.

As regards the specific problem of the links between numerical conservation and elementary measurement of continuous length, and the connected problem of the relationship between numerical and geometric fields of knowledge, we seem justified in concluding that it is indeed possible to make use of already acquired numerical operations to lead the child to spatial operations of measurement. However, even in the case of total acquisition, progress is slow, many obstacles are encountered in fitting the number concept to conservation of length problems. In some situations the ordinal and topological references are misleading, and before the two operational structures can strengthen each other, there is a period of conflict which can be overcome only through a constructive effort on the part of the child, who has to discover compensatory and coordinating actions. It is the feedback from these actions themselves which finally results in the acquisition of a structure of a higher order, and not the passive reading-off of a result.

Another problem which can be clarified through learning experiments concerns the influence the acquisition of one structure can have on that of another (Inhelder & Sinclair, 1969). Our class-inclusion learning experiment was undertaken with a twofold aim: first to study in more detail the substages in the acquisition of this concept, and second to study the eventual mutual influence between conservation and class inclusion. We therefore took two groups of subjects, both of which underwent identical pretests in number, liquid, and substance conservation and in class inclusion and class intersection. We selected subjects who possessed conservation of numerical equivalences, but none of the other conservations or class inclusion. One group received training on class inclusion problems and the other on conservation problems. As a posttest both groups were given the same items as the pretests, together with certain additional items. Two sessions a week were held and each subject took part in six. A second test was given 3 or 4 weeks after the posttest. Since then, we have studied a few control groups, i.e., groups which did not have the benefit of the learning sessions.

The learning procedure for conservation comprised a series of items of gradually increasing difficulty, progressing from discrete units to continuous quantities, composition of equalities and inequalities. The learning procedure for class inclusion was based on a preliminary experiment aimed at discovering substages by having the children execute verbal orders such as: "give the boy more apples than the girl, but he must have as many pieces of fruit as the girl" (in a situation where a girl doll has two apples and three pears, or two apples, one orange, one pear, and one peach).

Here I must point out that the plural of *fruit* in French, the language in which the experiment was conducted, is simply *fruits*. If conducted in English, flowers or candies, for example, would have to be used in order to avoid the "artificial" plural with *pieces*.

To succeed in these acting-out items, the subject has to compare subclass and total class, as in the test question: "Are there more daisies or more flowers?" in a bunch of twelve daisies and two tulips. The acting-out items are, however, easier because they do not demand comparison of a subclass to the total class in one collection only; the total class (the basket of fruit belonging to one of the dolls) remains visible as an object of comparison while the child constructs his subclasses (apples and other fruit) for the other doll. A series of items leads to questions on such comparisons in one collection: the doll has a basket containing four apples and two pears, and the child is asked: "What should he say to eat the most: *I want to eat my apples* or *I want to eat my fruit?*". Finally, the same question is asked as in the class-inclusion test: "Are there more apples or more pieces of fruit in the basket?". The posttests for both groups include some items not presented in the pretest and not exercised during the learning sessions: for conservation, there are problems of transitivity; for class inclusion, a three-stage inclusion (terriers, dogs, animals) and a question such as "Are there more dogs or more animals?" in a situation where *only* dogs are present. In that case, the usual answer "more animals than dogs" is no longer correct.

Although the main interest of this experiment lies in the careful analysis of each subject's reasoning and the gradual coordinations and integrations that are observed, the global results present a clear enough picture to make some general points.

1.   In both groups almost all the subjects made progress in the concept exercised during the learning sessions, no doubt because of the intensive and extended training (six sessions) and the rather advanced initial level of

the training group. Most of them were already at the intermediary stage as regards conservation of quantity.

2.   Progress in the exercised concept affected the subjects' reasoning about the nonexercised concept differently in the two groups. The conservation group subjects who progressed clearly in conservation showed progress in the inclusion tests in only a few cases, and even this progress was only partial. The other subjects showed no progress whatsoever in the class-inclusion problem, despite their success in the conservation tasks. By contrast, those children in the inclusion group who made clear progress in the inclusion problem also made remarkable progress in the conservation tasks, acquiring both conservation of quantity and conservation of weight. In several cases acquisition was complete, including transitivity of weight. Despite our very severe criteria as regards the interpretation of our results, some of our subjects acquired a completely operational structure.

3.   Progress was once again clearly related to the initial stage of development. Even subjects who in the pretest had given only answers of nonconservation often justified their answers in a way which indicated a difference in their level of reasoning. Compare, for instance, a subject who affirms for all the transformations of the ball of plasticine that there is no longer the same amount, but who says for the item where the one ball is divided into little pieces: "there is much more to eat with the little bits, they are much smaller, there are a lot more of them" with a subject who says "there is less to eat, those are only little bits." The first child mentions both that there are a lot of little bits and that these bits are small; even though he is incapable of using these data for a judgment of compensation, he is no longer, as is the second child, uniquely centered on one aspect of the situation. Other subjects, whom we considered more evolved, though still completely nonconservational in their answers, said in the same situation: "the boy has more to eat, with all the little bits; the girl should break her ball up, too." These subjects have already shifted from centering on the final state to taking into consideration the transformation itself, and even though this does not lead them to reversability, it does indicate an approach to the problem that is different from the simple consideration of two final states regarded as static.

Initial results in this experiment would point to the following conclusions. Progress in inclusion problems, obtained in learning sessions, has far more effect on conservation tasks than vice versa; in other words, appropriate training in a mainly logical field influences the child's reasoning in more physical problems despite the fact that these have not been touched upon in the learning sessions. Progress in conservation tasks, however, even clearly operational progress, only rarely (and then only partially) influences the child's approach to logical problems.

Second, we conclude that the lower the child's initial level (even if there are differences only within one stage) the more progress tends to be limited to one specific field or even to one specific type of problem. With some children we obtained excellent results during the training sessions, but the slightly different situations in the posttest (within the same field) were already less successfully solved, and the problems in the different fields were approached in exactly the same way as during the pretest. Only the subjects who mastered the operations of class inclusion and who had already shown some signs of decentration in the conservation pretests could use their newly acquired logical competence to succeed in conservation tasks. Finally, only the very exceptionally bright child could use newly acquired conservation concepts (even if they included transitivity of weight) as a basis for solving inclusion problems.

The results of this experiment show clearly the intricate nature of the relations betwen two different fields of knowledge. Moreover, once again it became clear that the influence of the progress made in one field on the other depends on the stage of development; as we have said, the lower the child's initial level, the more progress tends to be limited to one specific field.

LANGUAGE AND THOUGHT

Closely linked to the problem of learning is the question of the relationship between language and thought. Many authors affirm, and many educators behave as if it were true, that verbal learning can bring out progress in cognitive structure. It can be shown experimentally, however, that this is not the case. If a child has to learn to deal, for instance, with a logical multiplication of dimensions (length and width) we find (Sinclair, 1967) that to teach him to use the words "long" and "short" and "wide" and "narrow" in a consistent way is easy, even if at first he has no idea of doing so. But the result of such verbal training is limited to what Soviet psychologists call "orientation of attention"; in an experiment concerning conservation of quantity, the child now correctly describes a ball of clay which has been transformed into a sausage as "long and thin." However, this does not lead him *ipso facto* to the multiplication which is involved in compensation and conservation: "longer but thinner than the ball" and thus having the same quantity.

Thus it is not language which governs thought or forms operations. A group of research projects, involving children aged between 4.8 and 5.2, was directed towards finding out the eventual influence of language development on thought. It was found that a certain structuration takes place, often of elements which are already present, under the influence of operational development. Far from language structuring thought, we found that, at least in certain linguistic subsystems, the final structure is dependent on cognitive development, and that, moreover, the particular stage in verbal acquisition can be explained only by the operational development. If language developed autonomously, our results would be inexplicable.

A second group of research projects deals more directly with the learning of linguistic structures as such. As in all our other experiments, we found it necessary first to explore the appearance of such structures in a cross-sectional experiment. The technique used is as follows: the experimenter[2] gives the child a collection of toys, including dolls, cars, animals, sponges, marbles, and cups. After an introductory period during which the child names and tells the experimenter something about each object, he is asked to "act," using the objects, first a simple active and then a simple passive sentence. Various verbs are used and the sentences are sometimes "reversible" and sometimes "irreversible" (reversible: "Peter washes John" or "The red marble pushes the blue marble"; irreversible: "Peter washes his car").

Alternatively, the experimenter begins by performing an action with some of the toys and asking the child to tell him what happened. He tries to elicit passive sentences by asking the child to start his sentence with the noun indicating the object of the action performed (patient). For example, the experimenter acts the sentence "Peter washes his car" and then says to the child: "Now tell me what happened, but I would like you to start this way: the car . . ." Finally, the experimenter performs an action and at the same time himself describes it using the passive form; he then asks the child whether what he said was correct and asks him to repeat it.

This experiment is still continuing, but I should like to mention one particularly interesting type of behavior, which, however, we are still far from being able to interpret conclusively. At about $4\frac{1}{2}$ years old, several subjects decode a passive sentence into a reciprocal act. For example, the sentence "The boy knocks over the girl" is translated into an action during which the two dolls push each other and knock each other over; "Peter is washed by Mary" is acted so that Peter and Mary both take a sponge and wash each other. In the items where we try to elicit passive sentences, the children also produce sentences in this way: "Peter and Mary wash each other." Some children, however, say that what we ask them is impossible; when a 5-year-old was asked to start with the truck in his description of the action where the car is pushing the truck, she said: "I can't. The truck can't push the car when the car is pushing the truck." Another child said for the action where the boy washes the truck: "You can't; the truck hasn't got any hands."

After we had analyzed the results of our first experiment, we tried to simulate spontaneous development during two training sessions by giving our subjects a number of examples of passive sentences, and we observed how this information was used and integrated. The experiment is in the form of a game, where the child and the experimenter play different roles. Though we have only recently

[2]Sinclair, H. and Ferrero, E., research in progress.

started this approach, the results are intriguing. Certain children work through a series of hypotheses concerning the structure of the examples. For simple passive sentences, which are pronounced while an action is performed (for example, "The truck is pushed by the car"), we find subjects producing pairs of sentences like the following:

The first sentence is the child's own description, almost always a simple active sentence; the second is his attempt to imitate the style of the examples.

"The car pushes the truck."

"The car has pushed the truck."

In this case the child thought he should change from the present to the past. Or,

"The car pushes the truck."

"The car, it is pushing the truck." He has again made a change in the verb and also added a personal pronoun.

Both types of transformations are given several times for several different situations, until new examples induce a new hypothesis.

The main point of interest here is to see how the different hypotheses on a structure inferred from utterances spoken by the experimenter are integrated into already existing structures according to the level of the subject. Moreover, all the hypotheses found in the learning experiment are types of sentences already obtained in the preliminary experiment, where, without learning sessions, we investigated the understanding and production of passive sentences.

SOCIOCULTURAL RESEARCH

Another factor which has often been invoked is the influence of the various sociocultural environments on cognitive development, and recently many research projects have been initiated in this field. The results that have already been established vary and often conflict, but we feel that this diversity stems essentially from the great variety of theoretical approaches and the resulting methods of interpretation.

Research in this field is also being carried out by our research associate, Magali Bovet (1968), within the framework of the Genevan concept of intellectual development. We are trying to compare the results from different environments in order to bring to light any décalages (time lags) or synchronizations of the observable acquisitions. We are also tackling the more difficult problem of determining whether the underlying structures are always formed by the same processes in every cultural environment.

One example of this type of research is the study of the concepts of conservation of matter and length in unschooled Algerian children of illiterate parents. First, we presented these children with the standard conservation problems (the material was adapted so that the children were handling familiar objects). We then presented them with various complementary problems, one of which involved the anticipation of the height of the level when a quantity of liquid was transferred from one receptacle to another of different dimensions, and in another the child was asked to pour the same amount of liquid into glasses of varying shapes and sizes.

We obtained very different results in the two fields, conservation of matter and of length. As regards conservation of matter, 7- to 8-year-old Algerian children gave correct answers to the standard conservation problems, but (and this made us wonder about the reasoning structures underlying these answers) they were unable to answer the complementary questions correctly.

These results led us to question older children. In the 8- to 10-year-old group the answers to conservation problems were fluctuating, i.e., sometimes right and sometimes wrong. This corresponded to the behavior of Genevan children at an intermediary operatory level, as in fact did the Algerian children's answers to the complementary questions. It was only the 9- to 10-year-old Algerians who gave more or less consistently correct answers to both the conservation and complementary questions. The fact that the conservation of these 9- to 10-year-olds closely resembled that of our younger Genevan children, both as regards its elaboration and its final form, strengthened our belief that the initial conservation of the 7- to 8-year-olds had not been completely operatory.

Finally, the complementary problems constituted a form of "operatory" learning, and what we found particularly interesting was they had an apparently contradictory effect on the behavior of the 7- to 8-year-old group and on that of the two older groups. The children in the first group tended to give wrong answers in the final conservation tests, that is, *after* they had been presented with the complementary questions, whereas the children in the two older groups gave better answers after these complementary problems. The "regression" of the conservation answers seems to us in reality to constitute progress as regards the operatory development of the 7- to 8-year-olds. These children, who initially did not seem to take into account perceptual indexes, such as the level of the liquids and dimensions of the glasses (the apprehension of which is indispensable for operatory understanding of the conservation problem), seemed, in the final test, to pay attention to these factors. This led at first to nonconservation answers which were consistently based on one of the perceptual indexes. However, this nonconservation stage was followed by an intermediary and then a final stage of operatory conservation around 9 to 10 years, i.e., at a later age than in Geneva, thus constituting a deviation in comparison with development as we know it in our two countries.

By contrast, no such deviations in the course of development were observed in the reactions of Algerian children to problems of conservation of length. The only difference in this field between the two environments was one of developmental rate. All substages were reached at a slightly later age than in Geneva.

How can we account for the difference between the results in the field of conservation of matter and those in that of length? To answer this question complete-ly, we should need a whole team of psychologists, cultural anthropologists, and sociologists. However, we should like to suggest a possible reason for the "pseudo" conservation observed in the field of quantity.

In day-to-day life, children's activities as regards their handling of matter are quite different from their activities as regards measurement and comparison of length. Algerian children are present on occasions when adults evaluate quanti-ties of goods they wish to buy or sell. In the home, the mother distributes food which may be put in containers of various shapes and sizes and it is possible that the child pays far more attention to the initial act of distribution than to the perceptual indexes, i.e., the appearance of the food in the containers.

As far as measurement is concerned, however, Algerian children in their less sophisticated environment lack the kind of stimulation which results in more developed perceptual strategies, at least in this particular respect. They are not, as are our Genevan children, made aware at a very early age of differences in height, nor are they taught to compare length. This, we feel, probably explains the slower rate of development of this concept. The lack of stimulation is even more striking as regards the concept of time, which seems fragile even in unschooled Algerian adults.

Comparison between the study carried out by Bruner and Greenfield (1966) and that undertaken by Magali Bovet shows that this is one case where divergent methods of approach have led to an apparent convergence of results. The difference between the Genevan and the Harvard interpretation lies in the fact that we stress the underlying structures and the transformational processes from one stage to the next, rather than limiting ourselves to the study of the observable features of each individual stage.

OPERATORY THOUGHT PROCESSES IN PSYCHOTIC CHILDREN

Finally, I should like to discuss briefly the formation of the fundamental concepts and partial structures in psychotic children.

Many psychopathologists are interested in Piagetian theory, mostly from a psychoanalytical point of view. We think that this theory of cognitive develop-ment also plays an important part in highlighting abnormal aspects of cognition. Mental retardation has long been studied from this angle. Until recently, how-ever, child psychosis did not seem to lend itself to this approach. It might well seem that abnormal phenomena of the thought processes in child psychosis cannot be systematized as they may be in retardates. Recently, however, this approach has proved fruitful in the study of senile dementia and sensory deficit (blind or deaf children). Since then, I have been using this approach in a study of psychotic children. At first sight, it seems as if the pervading character of the very individual meanings these children attach to their physical environment and to the human beings who surround them makes it impossible to diagnose the cognitive levels and operatory thought processes. However, we have been able to distinguish some general characteristics from among the welter of individual particularities.

We[3] selected three types of experiments to be carried out with our first group of boys, aged between 10.4 and 15 years. All these subjects were able to communicate verbally, though often in a very limited manner due to their illness. They had all been under psychiatric care for about 10 years and the majority had experienced hallucinations.

The first type of experiment required logical class operations and took the form of inclusion and class-intersection problems. We used pictures in these experiments. The second required the physical or spatiotemporal operations underlying the concepts of conservation of matter. These experiments involved the transformation of a ball of plasticine or the dissolution of a lump of sugar in water. The third required the combinatory operations underlying the concept of probability. The child's probabilistic knowledge was tested by means of one experiment using counters with a circle on one side and a cross on the other (a sort of "heads or tails" experiment); another involved drawing lots and a third used what was essentially a roulette wheel.

Our *method of investigation* is as follows: while we carry out the experiments we keep up a continual clinical dialogue with the child. Although we follow the wandering thought of the young patient, we nevertheless try to center the child's attention on cognitive problems. Since the child sometimes becomes disturbed through our insistence on his giving reasons for his answers, he does not always give as good an answer as he might otherwise have done, but by this method we can discover the child's particular difficulties. These bear on his relationship with other people and his deformation and subjective assimilation of reality.

For this brief discussion, I should like to limit myself to describing some striking phenomena in subjects ranging from children at the level of elementary concrete operations to those who have reached the transition to formal operations. Between these two categories, we know, there is a wide range of concrete thought operations. We already know which of these operations are developed synchronously and where décalages occur in normal children. On one hand, we have the logico-arithmetic operations which are acquired when a child, for whom material objects only exist to be acted upon (classifying, ordering, counting), becomes able to coordinate his own actions; on the other, we have the physical operations which are also known as spatiotemporal or infralogical operations. The latter are also developed from the subject's actions, but this time the actions transform reality and in return are themselves modified by reality.

Probabilistic reasoning, which aims at organizing "chance events," cannot be worked out deductively. It requires the development of concrete and formal

[3] This study forms part of a research project undertaken in collaboration with Professor Ajuriaguerra and his colleagues from the Geneva University Psychiatric Clinic.

operations, even though these cannot be applied directly to chance events. By analyzing the thought of young patients in this developmental framework, we think it is possible to determine some abnormal constants. I shall describe some of the most striking. The most salient characteristics are the great "ups and downs" observed even during the space of one relatively short interview.

We believe that we can distinguish two groups of children from among our sample population: those whose thought structure is perfectly integrated (and either corresponds to their age level or is even more advanced) and those whose integration is only partial and consequently extremely fragile. The first abnormal constant is that these children cannot understand and assimilate chance phenomena and refuse to reason in probabilistic terms.

Even the children in the first category who have acquired the first formal operations and who show by their reasoning that their concrete operations are completely integrated (in fact only one case out of ten) are particularly reticent when it comes to chance phenomena. They act as if they consider everything in the world to be deducible. Therefore, as soon as they can no longer assimilate reality to simple causal sequences or predictible frequency of occurrence, they refuse to guess or to give a probabilistic judgment. Clearly, they do not lack the ability to work out the logicomathematical operations underlying the chance concepts (combinatory and proportion operations). Their difficulty stems simply from the fact that they find themselves face to face with uncertainty. The children who are at a less advanced operatory stage often imagine that there is some magical force at work or that the experimenter is tricking them. The boundary between the physical and the human world seems at times to be extremely woolly, the psychotic child sometimes falling back into primitive adualism of thought.

The second abnormal characteristic is the relative inferiority of physical operations in relation to logico-arithmetical operations. With children whose concrete operations are only partially developed, we notice, to varying degrees, a discordance illustrating an abnormal décalage between the capability of carrying out logical inclusion operations and those of conservation of matter at the corresponding level. With the mentally deficient child, we have noticed that the décalage is rather the other way round, since this child does less well in experiments concerning logic than those concerning physical matter. Hatwell (1966) also found this greater difficulty in coordinating actions concerned with transformations and compositions in the physical world in children who were either born blind or became blind very early in life. Stambak (1964) also found this (but to a lesser degree) in the dyspraxic children she studied. In young psychotic children, as in those with sensorimotor or praxic deficiency, exchanges with the physical world are more or less deeply disturbed and their thought operations seem to be affected by this.

The third abnormal constant concerned the difficulty these children find in handling logical relations and more particularly the concept of conservation of continuous quantity. The physical concepts of conservation, or rather the structures underlying them, are extremely stable in normal thought. By contrast, in a psychotic child these concepts seem very fragile. It often happens that when the child has at long last acquired them, he suddenly reverts back to a much earlier stage of thought. And even in the rare cases where these concepts seem firmly established, we find that the operatory processes which underlie their formation are hardly ever the same as those of normal children. With the latter, the arguments which reveal these formative processes bear both on the compensations of the transformations (reciprocal operations) and on reversibility (canceling) and identity. In psychotic children whose reasoning is not completely integrated, we note almost exclusively arguments of identity, only exceptionally arguments of reversibility, and no valid arguments of compensation in the transformation of the dimensions of the type "longer but thinner," etc. It looks as if these children tend to mentally break up contents into fragments, or even countable units, but find themselves incapable when it comes to mastering the concept of conservation of continuous quantity.

Their difficulty is shown clearly, for instance, in the abnormally wide décalage between their solution of the conservation problem in the experiment concerning the changing shape of the ball of plasticine and that concerning the dissolution of sugar. The psychotic child, due in fact to his need to deal with fragments, easily brings a certain atomistic intuition to bear on the question and can picture the sugar in the form of little grains to count, but cannot represent the continuous process of transformation linking the initial to the final state and vice versa. This system of operations in the normal child precedes an attempt at an atomistic explanation. For the psychotic child, the sugar is first of all there and then suddenly it is "dead" as some of them say.

It is possible—but this remains to be proved through more adequate experiments—that beyond the particular difficulty of mentally compensating for the transformations carried out and grasped by the reciprocal mental operations, the psychotic child has more difficulty in handling logical relations than logical classes. His language is in fact poor in comparative terms and is more like that of the children at a preoperatory level studied by Sinclair (1967).

The last abnormal constant I shall mention concerns the fixed aspect of the symbolic function and the particular difficulties these children find in reasoning from assumptions.

To understand the operatory tests, the child must accept the make-believe put forward by the experimenter: we shall play with the plasticine as if it were a cake; we shall pretend that the Indians have chased all the birds. To abstract a common characteristic (for instance color) we show pictures of green (or some other color) leaves, cats, etc. It is strange to find that children between 10 and 15 years old, who seem to be living in an imaginary world full of phantoms, have such great difficulty in indulging in the make-believe so popular with normal young children. But it is one thing to be enclosed in one's own imaginary world and quite another to share other people's imaginary worlds, and especially that of one's questioner. First, the psychotic child has great difficulty in getting away from himself and his subjective world. In addition, for the child to have a full range of possible actions from which he can freely choose within his grasp, his semiotic function must be operating normally. He must also be able to substitute symbols and signs for reality, have an elementary knowledge about the difference between the signifier and the significate, and realise that symbols are not part of reality itself but indicate it. In fact, everything leads us to believe that it is the symbolic function which is disturbed or has become static in these young patients. Their thoughts often lack consistency and they cannot conform to the behavior standards of their group. In addition, they also lack creativity, despite the fact that their thought is often full of imagery.

The dominant characteristics concerning the functioning of thought which we have briefly described stem from three types of troubles: (1) disturbance of the relationship with others (revealed in an inability to decentrate), (2) disturbance in the mastering of the physical world (revealed by the instability of the adualism), and (3) by disturbances of symbolic activity (characterised by the various ways the child is unable to differentiate between symbols and signs on the one hand and reality on the other).

These studies are, however, only in the early stages, and it is far too early to draw clear conclusions. Nevertheless, I should like to emphasize two points: first, as is so often the case, results from psychopathological studies can contribute to the explanatory aspect of developmental psychology through the dissociation of factors which often takes place in pathology; second, our procedures and assessment methods make it possible, at least to a certain degree, to avoid the widespread tendency to explore cognitive and emotional phenomena by means of totally different tests and methods. It is true that nobody would deny the link between cognition and personality structure, but the relationship between the two and even their partial similarity can be demonstrated in a particularly clear fashion by using the developmental frame of reference. On the one hand, the disturbing and sometimes spectacular cases of child psychosis can, through this kind of analysis, throw light on the normal mechanisms, and on the other, our comprehension of normal development gives us a better understanding of the dissociations and abnormal functioning found in pathology.

SUMMARY

Although the various examples I have given may seem rather disparate, they are nevertheless linked both by the experimental approach and by the underlying theoretical concepts. In fact, the convergence of fundamental research and its application for diagnostic purposes is illustrated in each of the three fields I have briefly described.

In the last example, concept formation in psychotic children, I have tried to show that a better understanding of their reasoning processes can be obtained by taking into account those found in normal children. Inconsistencies both in temporal succession and between different fields of knowledge can be interpreted in a more meaningful way when they are compared with what we know of the temporal lags and the links between fields of knowledge in normal children. These links have become far clearer through our detailed investigations in the learning experiments, as I hope I have shown in the second part of my paper. Many of the new interpretations we were able to make from these learning experiments have been confirmed by a very different approach, that is, the new methods of statistical analysis which I described in the first part of my talk. It seems significant that the results from statistical studies, learning experiments, and psychopathological investigations, all point in the same direction. In this way, the structural approach to the study of development can be completed by a more dynamic approach that will clarify the relationship between the theoretical formalization of structures and dynamic real-life acts of thought.

In the study of these acts of thought, several factors of development have traditionally been distinguished. I think it is significant that all our research projects, the learning experiments as much as the linguistic and intercultural studies, show that it is impossible to separate these factors. In every field, it has become clear that to reach a certain measure of explanatory adequacy we must consider total development and not lose sight of the fundamental processes as they are elucidated by developmental psychology. From this point of view, a more urgent problem of the greatest importance is the need for tests which are adapted to different cultural and linguistic environments, but which remain directed towards the investigation of basic cognitive mechanisms rather than more superficial achievements. We hope we have made a valid contribution in this sphere.

Comments on Inhelder's Paper
by David Elkind
University of Rochester

I have been asked to respond to Professor Inhelder's excellent paper. Since my position vis-à-vis the Genevan school is not entirely neutral, this request places me in a delicate position. If I praise Inhelder's paper I might be accused of being partial, whereas if I am critical of it, I might be said to be disloyal. Hopefully if I say something both laudatory and critical, my partiality will cancel out my disloyalty and I will again be in equilibrium with all concerned.

It is easy to find good things to say about Inhelder's paper. Indeed, the paper contains so much that is new and rich in psychological implications that one hardly knows where to begin. Under the circumstances it might be just as well to say something general. One of the most impressive things about the work on memory, to me at any rate, is that it demonstrates how inadequate is a purely associationist model of recall and recognition. Let me be more explicit.

All associative learning presupposes a cognitive organization or system within which the associative elements are linked. To illustrate, even the learning of a list of words or nonsense syllables presupposes an organizational schema of the form $A > B > C$ or A before B, B before C, and so on. These organizing frameworks or systems tend to be ignored by those concerned with associative learning. To be sure, Gestalt psychology emphasized the importance of organizational factors in learning, but the impact of Gestalt psychology was muffled by its tacit acceptance of these structures as more or less fixed or permanent.

Now all of Piaget's work in cognitive development has emphasized that the mental organizations within which associative learning takes place develop and change with age. This work has been in a different area than most associative learning studies, but in the memory studies the Genevans have dealt with a problem central to the associative learning model. Accordingly, my guess is that the work on memory may have a greater impact upon the psychology of learning, so dominant in America, than any of the earlier work that has emanated from Geneva.

Let me now be critical for a moment, or perhaps quizzical would be a better word. One term that has bothered me in reading Piaget, and again in reading Inhelder, is the concept of abstraction. Somehow this term seems foreign to me in the context of Piaget's theory since, to my mind, it derives from English associationist psychology. What I am afraid of, I suppose, is that by using the term abstraction, association is let in through the back door. Perhaps it is my narrow conception of abstraction and insularity which makes me react this way to the term, and I would very much like to hear Professor Inhelder's interpretation of the term as it is used in Geneva.

Open Discussion

The discussion of Professor Inhelder's paper was devoted primarily to further clarification of the material she had presented. The discussion was opened by Inhelder who, in response to Elkind's question, wished to clarify further the nature of the two kinds of abstractions which she had described. Using the language of "blackboxes," she noted that there is input *from* the environment and output *to* the environment. There are two kinds of abstraction which act as input. One concerns the activities themselves which act on the transformation processes in the blackbox. But the environment is transformed by our activity and so there is also the other kind of abstraction, that from the environment itself, but as a new input which is transformed by our activity. Thus there are two kinds of feedback and two kinds of abstraction: physical abstraction, from the environment itself, and reflexive abstraction (or logical, mathematical abstraction) from the activity of the subject.

Heider then asked in what way children falling into the low group on the Genevan tests have individual sequences that differ from the theoretical sequences of development. Inhelder explained that the relationship between the different fields of knowledge is a less close one in the poor group than in the good and medium groups. This means that the poor group has to be given more tests in order to be sure about the significance of the results. However, even in general, the connection between the different fields of knowledge is not equally close in all cases. For instance, the link is looser between spatial problems and logic than between logic and conservation of physical quantities.

Flavell suggested that there might be two possible interpretations of the low group's performance. The first is that perhaps what we think the necessary conditions for the next step ought to be may not be so necessary and can be bypassed. This would pose a rather serious problem for the theory. The second possibility is that the test's ability to assess what the child knows is less in the case of the duller child.

Inhelder felt, based on her experience, that it is highly probable that the relationship between performance and competence is not exactly the same with the lower group as with the others. She commented that all kinds of disparate results are obtained with the lower group, but they are still normal children—they are normal in school settings. This necessitates a much more detailed diagnosis of these children to bring out the relationship between performance and competence. To grasp their real capabilities, it is necessary to use a very detailed clinical method.

Flavell suggested that when you pose a problem to a child, one of his rules has to be to treat this as a problem for which thinking is necessary; otherwise you don't gain any access to what he knows.

Inhelder commented that there are relatively few cases where they find complete inversions as compared with the theoretical order. Inversions are possible in the sense that a subject succeeds in a problem which, in general, is solved later, and fails in another problem which is generally solved earlier. However, this does *not* mean that such a child would show a lower level of reasoning for the same problem presented at a later period in his development. The Geneva group found no genuine regressions either in their longitudinal studies or in the learning procedures.

Stephens noted that most of the conference participants were interested in determining the relationships which exist among Piagetian measures of reasoning. She described her recent factor analysis, done in conjunction with Gene Glass, of scores from Piaget's reasoning tasks, subscores from the Wechsler Intelligence Scale for Children (WISC), and subscores from the Wide Range Achievement Test (WRAT). Five factors were derived. The first, which was defined by WISC and WRAT subscores, was a general intelligence and school achievement factor. The second was a Piagetian operational thought factor defined by loadings from measures of conservation, categorical manipulation, combinatory logic, and spatial organization. Loadings from a class-inclusion task defined the third factor. The fourth had loadings from mental age, chronological age, and Rotation of Squares, a measure of the ability to anticipate the positions of objects as they are rotated in space. The fifth was a separate Wechsler visual-perceptual synthesis factor. Intercorrelations of factors served to substantiate findings by Tuddenham and Almy. It was Stephens' feeling that as these relationships are further explored, some answers may be provided to questions concerning generalizations in learning.

Returning to the question of the two kinds of feedback, Smock wondered if any of the language experiments in Geneva had dealt with the functional role of language in the acquisition of structures relevant to these distinct kinds of feedback conditions.

Inhelder felt that this was an important question. However, the only experiments they did on the influence of language on the acquisition of concepts concerned conservation problems, where the distinction between the two kinds of feedback is difficult to make. She noted, however, that it seems that experiments which purport to show the influence of language on concept formation always involve the kind of feedback in which the properties of objects are important.

Goldschmid noted that Inhelder had found a lack of relationship between conservation of matter and of length (in unschooled Algerian children). He commented that Bentler and he had gotten a similar result, namely, that conservation of continuous matter was on one dimension and conservation of length on another. They were correlated .73 but were clearly separate dimensions.

The discussion concluded with Inhelder's comment that when considering conservation of length, it is necessary to distinguish between the conservation of geometric dimensions and the identity of the same object being displaced, and this is often difficult. The former comes much later. In conservation of length, there is a spatial relationship—you have to overcome the ordinal aspect of it, the topological aspect of it, the image of it.

Developmental Stages and Developmental Processes[1]

CHAPTER NINE

HARRY BEILIN
The City University of New York

After an era characterized by much disagreement over the stage concept in cognitive development, it is appropriate to consider whether the notion has lived up to its claims and is meaningful to further research. An assessment of these claims has to be made against the background of recurrent assertions that the stage construct and the related continuity-discontinuity issue (1) are false issues incapable of being empirically tested; (2) are only reflections of a methodological problem that results from the way developmental data are treated; (3) introduce distinctions which lead to no differences in the predictions that are made about developing thought or behavior, and (4) are issues, both trivial and intractable, that divert energies from problems which are solvable and meaningful.

The meaningfulness of the concept for psychological investigation is associated with the philosophic distinction between meaning and truth, and between explanation and verification. I propose that a judgment as to whether the stage construct has utility for psychology depends upon whether the term has legitimate conceptual status within a theoretical conception of development, whether the defined characteristics of the term are in accord with empirical evidence, and whether developmental data are adequately explained by the construct as well as the theory of development of which it is a part. If none of those conditions is met, then the construct has little value for psychology, but if even one is, then the stage construct has more than a little value.

The term "stage" has two kinds of status: first, as representing an empirical generalization of a type of developmental data and, second, as a construct within a formal developmental theory whose principal function is that of explaining

[1] The preparation of this paper was supported in part by the National Institute of Child Health and Human Development grant HD-00925-08. The author is indebted to Ruth S. Mechaneck, who aided in its preparation.

developmental phenomena. With respect to the latter, the stage notion is sometimes thought of as an "ideal construct" designed to facilitate analysis, whereas the former notion is considered a "schematic" representation of actual development (Hoselitz, 1960). Although most psychologists treat the term as a direct reflection of reality, others like Heinz Werner (1965) contend that the concept of development (and by implication the stage concept) is not a descriptive entity at all but represents a "certain manner of viewing behavior." He considered his orthogenetic principle of development, for example, as a "heuristic definition . . . not subject to empirical test [which would be] valuable to developmental psychologists in leading to a determination of the actual range of applicability of developmental concepts to the behavior of organisms." Kaplan, who shares Werner's position, defines developmental progressions as standards or idealizations (sequences of ideal-type constructs) against which to relate actual behavioral change (Kaplan, 1965). In a philosophic sense, "stage" is a construct within a theory of development whose relations with other constructs and propositions within the theory help to define its meaning. The construct may obtain its meaning solely within the context of a particular developmental theory, such as Piaget's, or from a more general theory that, within its explanatory scope, encompasses the developmental theory (e.g., a mechanistic or organismic theory that in turn would explain Piaget's theory). The principal function of both the stage construct and its more general developmental theory is explanatory. This category of explanation is offered "for the recurring events and invariable and statistical regularities in human behavior" (Nagel, 1957). In this sense the stage construct is not an empirical or inductive generalization from observed data, but part of a formulation of an abstract relational structure. Although few, if any, psychological constructions will fit the requirements of formal theory, such as having an "abstract calculus" as an essential component, some important psychological conceptions come closer to being in the realm of such theories than to being empirical generalizations. In any case, the stage notion could have a hypothetical status in psychological theory and serve a meaningful purpose if it led deductively to new explanatory statements, if it aided in the explanation of observed phenomena, or if it led to new ways of exploring or analyzing data. If the value of the stage construct were solely that it led to the formulation of other hypothetical constructs, it would be of limited interest, for its persisting importance lies in the implication that it pertains to real entities. Whether "stages" do in fact represent real entities, i.e., whether the term is inductively congruent with empirical evidence, has to be examined in relation to claims for that status.

One may conclude, then, that the stage notion, by virtue of its status in certain developmental theories may be meaningful for the role it plays in making other constructs and propositions within these theories meaningful. The stage idea in Piaget's theory is crucial to the theory, and other significant features of the theory are crucial to the conception of stages. In addition, the stage construct has even greater value in the explanation of developmental data. In this respect the stage notion provides a point of view that leads not only to a different type of interpretation of data but to different ways of treating data.

THE STAGE CONCEPT AND
THE MEANING OF THE TERM "DEVELOPMENT"

Since the stage construct obtains its meaning largely in relation to theories of development, it is normally tied to both continuity and discontinuity conceptions of development. It would be quite difficult, in fact, to define "development" so as to avoid the continuity-discontinuity distinction, i.e., so that its properties would be common to any developmental theory. This is clear from the manner in which Nagel (1957) defines the essential components in the connotative meaning of the term "development."

First, he says, it refers to a system possessing a definite structure and a definite set of preexisting capacities. Second, it refers to "the notion of a sequential set of changes in the system, yielding relatively permanent but novel increments not only in structure but in its modes of operation as well" (Nagel, 1957, p. 17).

This latter point implies "emergence" and the idea of preformationism usually associated with the maturationist and nativist traditions. Although Nagel's analysis attempts to neutralize the meaning of the term "development" relative to the continuity-discontinuity question, it nevertheless retains a discontinuity flavor, as is evident in the references to "structure," "preexisting capacities," and "novel increments." This impression is reinforced by his more specific explication of the meanings psychologists, developmental biologists, and others associate with the term:

1. Developmental processes make progressively manifest something which is latent or "hidden"—a sequence of continuous changes eventuating in some outcome which is somehow potentially present in the earlier stages of the process (the "epigenetic" implication).
2. A sequence of change is developmental only if it contributes to the generation of some more or less specifically characterized system of things or properties of things (the "teleological" implication).
3. Changes must be cumulative and irreversible to be considered developmental.
4. Changes must yield not just greater numerical complexity but eventuate in modes of organization not previously manifest in its history such that the system acquires increased capacity for self-regulation, etc.

Nagel, in the dominant tradition of contemporary philosophy of science, enunciates the thesis that to be understood as developmental phenomena, particular concepts such as "novelty," "self-regulation," and "additivity" need to be interpreted relative to a specific developmental theory or some specific set of theoretical assumptions concerning development. In his attempt to be all-inclusive, and in particular to account for the usage of the developmental biologist, his characterization will fail to satisfy some psychologists. A behaviorist such as Bijou (1965, 1968) offers a definition with fewer theoretical assumptions and devoid of properties indicated in the "emergent implication." In differentiating behavioral from biological development, Bijou defines behavioral development as "progressive changes in interactions between a child's responses and the stimulus events and setting conditions which make up his environment." Behavioral development resulting from the interaction between the organism, its biological characteristics, and the environment yields a series of stages which are identified, following Kantor (1959), as a sequence of three general periods (Universal, Basic, and Societal). Biological influences are viewed as producing internal stimuli, setting limits on behavior by limiting the classes of responses possible, limiting the range of responses at developmental stages, and providing the source of stimulation to others whose behavior in turn influences the actor. At the same time, Bijou emphatically denies that the mechanisms of psychological development are congruent with those of biological development. Instead, the mechanisms of psychological development are connected only to the *acts* and interactions of the organism. The principal impetus for developmental change comes not from maturational processes but from learning processes that are also available from birth, namely, operant and respondent conditioning. The kind of control that results from biological change is not clear in this kind of formulation. It is the dilemma of the empiricist that he is forced to accept the facts of maturation but is unwilling to concede to it a central control function.

Bijou, as a developmental behaviorist, then, is not likely to accept the notion of emergence as a basis for stage progression nor some of the "organization" criteria implicit in Nagel's definition of development. What he does accept is the idea of cumulative change leading to greater complexity.

In an attempt to bridge the seemingly wide gap between general behavior theory (of the Hullian type) and developmental theory, Kessen (1962) proposes a common interpretive rubric which, although inclined toward behaviorism, is less positivist than Bijou's (i.e., more Hullian than Skinnerian). Kessen also reflects the view that stage and development constructs are meaningful only in relation to a set of theoretical assumptions. For each stage (or "state"—a term which more adequately reflects for him the momentary character of organization within continuous development) there is a theoretical characterization, in effect a miniature theory, which explains the behavior of that stage or state. Specifically, Kessen hypothesizes that stages represent parametric variations in the basic formulas of development: "If a theorist aims at a fully generalizable theory of behavior, it will be necessary to make changes in the generalized constants of the fundamental equations in order to predict variation with age."

The basic formulas derive from assumptions of such theories as psychoanalytic theory, learning theory, or Piagetian cognitive theory. The principal parameters of each theory differ, of course, but the proposition that Kessen offers is that these basic formulas represent the basic processes that operate in all development. These processes are not those that "create" the stages, however, that is, that impose the variation on the parameters of development. Another set of rules applies to the stage-to-stage transitions. These transition rules identify processes related to learning which ostensibly impel stage-to-stage change. It is not clear from Kessen's account whether "transition rules" share the burden of accounting for parametric variation as part of the basic mechanisms of development or are independent mechanisms of transport. Since he apparently accepts the idea that Piaget's basic developmental mechanisms (assimilation, accommodation, and equilibration) operate continuously in development, it is not clear why an added set of mechanisms is necessary to account for the transitions, particularly when stages represent for him only parametric variation and not discontinuities or the emergents of new processes. There is no reason why the developmental processes that act continuously cannot at the same time incorporate rules that determine "parametric variation."

The Nagel and Kessen formulations are explicit in the philosophic position that stages are constructions interpretable only in relation to a set of theoretical assumptions. Bijou's formulation, which is in the tradition of Skinnerian antitheoretical behaviorism, is nevertheless a stage conception with an implicit set of theoretical assumptions. The assertion that stages result from the interaction between organism, biological characteristics, and environment is almost out of Piaget or Freud, and, while the emphasis upon conditioning shows how it is different, the underlying assumptions are still of a theoretical nature. It is questionable, then, whether any meaningful statements can be made about development which are not based upon some set of theoretical assumptions.

THEORETICAL PROPERTIES OF DEVELOPMENTAL STAGES— THE EMERGENT IMPLICATION

The property of emergence, or the epigenetic thesis, while intimately associated in the minds of many with the conception of development, is the principal target of those who usually support continuity theories of development. Emergence or epigenesis is a property of theories of maturation and is usually considered a byproduct of preformationist theories. Such theories are often rejected by psychologists. Even Piaget who accepts a role for maturation in development rejects the preformationist thesis in favor of a kind of interactionism or transactionism. Few psychologists, however, are either nativists or radical empiricists. Each recognizes the influence of both biological and experiential phenomena. As Kohlberg (1968) points out, the real issue is not over an either/or choice, but over which mechanisms or processes are the causal agents in development (i.e., are the "source of basic patterning"). To the environmentalist, the rules represented in the organism's external or internal environment determine such patterning; to the nativist, the programming and coding functions of genetic structure determine the course and nature of development as well as the outcome of the organism's encounter with the environment. Although nativist and maturationist theories share the idea of genetic preprogramming, they differ in their views of the timing and availability of fully formed capacities. Maturation refers to the progressive emergence or "unfolding" of a set of processes or products over time, while the nativist assumes that "prewired" structures and processes become operational at birth with only minor physiological change or external stimulation. While many processes are functional at birth, others such as language may have to wait for the development of a supporting physical architecture. The nativist view is generally shared by Gestaltists, some ethologists, and is presently being championed by Chomsky and other generative-transformational linguists. Chomsky has also declared his faith in the doctrine of "innate ideas," although not as broadly as Descartes. "There is nothing incomprehensible" (Chomsky says, in reply to Goodman who thinks there is) "in the view that stimulation provides the occasion for the mind to apply certain innate interpretive principles, certain concepts that proceed from the 'power of understanding' itself, from the faculty of thinking rather than from external objects directly" (Chomsky, 1968b, p. 72). Although nativist in regard to both language and cognition, Chomsky accepts the possibility that by maturation, language and cognition may evolve in stages (Chomsky, 1968b, p. 76; 1965, p. 202), but not by virtue of the controlling influence of experience and stimulation.

Piaget takes exception to Chomsky's conception of the origins of language and cognition and to nativism in general (Piaget, 1968a). He argues that nativism cannot explain the details of the mechanisms at work in cognitive development. If Piaget means it is not in theory possible, then he makes a questionable assertion, since the recent developments in molecular biology demonstrate that the mechanisms of genetic coding and transmission account in large measure for the control of the processes and structures of biological development. While environmental (i.e., cytoplasmic) control processes are not excluded from these genetic explanations, they are nevertheless subsidiary to them. At the least, it is clear that the mechanisms of innate control are specifiable and no reason exists to suppose that analogous mechanisms cannot account for cognitive development.

While denying the nativist thesis and accepting a role for maturation, Piaget proposes that the essential control of development resides in a self-regulating mechanism that derives information from both genetic and experiential sources. At the same time, Piaget accepts the idea of "permanent functional mechanisms of ordering, embedding, establishing correspondences and equivalences" (1968a,

p. 979), all of which presume an innate neurological and organic substructure. Yet Piaget rejects "structural hereditary programmation" as part of this scheme. What he seems to be saying is that specific cognitive structures are not preprogrammed as such. The structures associated with the conservation of number, for example, are not genetically given but are constructed out of an active encounter with the environment. The idea of "permanent functional mechanics" implies, however, that a preprogrammed rule system controls the transaction with reality that leads to the construction of only very limited types of structure. If Piaget were to assert that external conditions, and action carried out in response to such conditions, were the source of the rules that determine thought and action, then the organism would be under the control of and "copying" reality, a thesis which Piaget would reject. The issue reduces itself to whether the rule system by which cognitive structures are constructed is determined by external reality or internally by genetic structure. Since Piaget would accept internal programming as a source of functional mechanics and would probably reject an external rule system as the basis for structure determination, it is difficult to avoid the conclusion that Piaget's position is fundamentally a maturationist position—and that in the transaction with the environment, experience and action are principally facilitating agencies. Piaget's recourse to a self-regulatory mechanism and equilibrium as explanatory theoretical assumptions for the construction of cognitive structure only begs the question of innate programming or environmental rule determination. It is apparent from Piaget's specification of these self-regulating mechanisms (equilibration, accommodation, and assimilation) that they themselves are innately determined. Piaget's primary criterion for the theory of stages, the invariant order of structural achievements, to which Piaget accepts no qualification, suggests, in fact almost requires, an explanation defined in terms of genetic control. When the effects of experience are accepted only in the rate of structure acquisition, it is difficult to see why Piaget would explain structural achievement other than by genetically controlled mechanisms. As Mehler and Bever (1968) put it, Piaget's postulation of a "reflective abstraction process" that extracts the regularities, rules, operations, and coordinations of the child's actions and transfers these to the cognitive domain "entails powerful nativist assumptions because it must have internal structure, already defined domains of application, and built-in capacity to segment actions and their coordinations." Mehler and Bever in turn approve of what they consider to be Piaget's emphasis on functional innateness (i.e., on given processes which abstract structure from experience), rather than on innate structure of the Chomsky type which they associate with preformationism. The fact is, however, that Piaget's position is essentially preformationist too. One may look to the nature of DNA genetic coding for an analogue. Genetic coding (within given molecular structures) controls enzyme actions that in turn lead to the selective use of environmental material for the construction of predetermined cell, tissue, and organ structures (Gottlieb, 1966). Inherent in this is a system of "functional innateness" which programs according to hereditarily determined gene structure. The preformed structure of the gene thus codes both the functional mechanism that deals with the environment and the final structural output. At the same time, although Chomsky proposes the existence of innate linguistic structure (i.e., innate ideas, a base-structure grammar, etc.) he too proposes that this rule system becomes functional through the construction of a surface structure grammar out of the selective use of environmental input. This conception is not much different from Piaget's delineation of functional mechanisms which extract regularities from the organism's actions. Since these processes require innate programming for their very existence, it is evident that Piaget and Chomsky are not as far apart from each other as both Piaget and Chomsky claim.

In Piaget's cognitive stage theory, new properties of thought and action are the emergents. These properties result from the coordination of already existing schemes of a prior level with new properties acquired in acting upon the environment. An unspecified set of emergents exists as well within presumed maturational change. If one were able to specify, in Piagetian terms, the actions out of which cognitive constructions arise, it should be equally possible to specify the emergent properties that arise out of the maturational process. The large body of research in the training of conservation is, I think, instructive in this regard. It is increasingly evident that efforts to induce conservation by deliberate training lead to artifactual or algorithmic learning, or none at all (Beilin, 1969). Where legitimately inferred change is observed, it is invariably in subjects who are already partially conserving. The only reasonable inference to draw from this is that achievement of conservation is not under the control of the actions or experience of the child. Induced action, verbalization, and perceptual training lead to little effective conservation. Since no one seems able to identify the parameters of natural experience that result in the construction of conservation operations, one can only conclude that much more of the burden of explanation must be borne by the maturation of relevant data-processing mechanisms and the nonspecific effects of experience.

Piaget's identification of two categories of developmental change—(1) functional mechanisms that operate through the life span (the self-regulatory equilibration mechanism; the "reflective abstractive process," etc.), and (2) structures and operations which stabilize temporarily—is paralleled in other developmental theories, of which Heinz Werner's (1957) is an example. Werner distinguishes between continuous aspects of change, usually seen as changes in quantitative aspects of behavior (i.e., magnitude, frequency, and efficiency of response), and qualitative change which, by definition, is associated with discontinuity. Discontinuity which is reserved only for qualitative change is defined by two characteristics: "emergence," which Werner characterizes as the irreducibility of later stages to earlier ones, and "gappiness," or abruptness—the lack of intermediate stages between later and earlier ones. Two types of emergence are distinguished:

(1) the emergence of a new operation or function, and (2) the emergence of a novel pattern or operation through reorganization of existing elements within a pattern or through the integration of a new operation with an existing pattern.

Werner's distinction between continuous and discontinuous development clarifies one issue traditionally raised against discontinuity theories: that developmental change is usually continuous and not abrupt.[2] A corollary of this view is that continuity and discontinuity are a function of how developmental data are treated. This assertion is in part true, for by segmenting time periods appropriately one can obtain different characterizations of developmental change.[3] The manipulation of time segments, however, may mask differences in the processes, operations, or structures which give rise to the behaviors represented in these descriptions of developmental change. Werner and others (Gollin & Saravo, in press; Kendler & Kendler, 1962) have shown that some developmental processes may decline while others advance within the context of the same type of cognitive behavior [as with the developmental emergence of verbal mediation against a base of associational learning in a single type of discrimination learning (Kendler & Kendler, 1962)].

Four kinds of discontinuity describe developmental phenomena: (1) The processes of development remain the same but give rise to structures and properties which differ at different ages (the Piagetian view). (2) All processes and functional properties are available at birth but selected variables become dominant at different stages as the organism matures (typical of Freudian types of developmental theory).[4] (3) New processes emerge against a base of more

---

[2] Although it is usually argued that discontinuity is imposed upon continuous data, LeComte de Nouy (Werner, 1956) argued to the contrary that continuity is manufactured by the data of experience. This was one of the "roles of consciousness." In more contemporary fashion, Schrödinger (1956) cites the data and principles of quantum mechanics in asserting reality to be basically discontinuous.

[3] Werner cites several errors that are made in attributing continuity to discontinuous development: (1) A change may be metrically continuous but qualitatively discontinuous (e.g., walking cannot be reduced to crawling). (2) A qualitative or quantitative change may be small but that in itself does not make it continuous (a mutation is a slight change usually and is discontinuous in that there are no intermediate forms). (3) Continuity shows up in averaged or composite developmental curves where discontinuity exists in individual curves. (4) The interpretative framework can determine whether a change is continuous or discontinuous (color hues interpreted as wave lengths are continuous; as colors they are discontinuous). (5) There is no logical necessity for concordance in terms of continuity between qualitative and quantitative aspects of change: (a) discontinuous qualitative change may become distinct gradually; (b) sudden change upward or downward in a developmental curve need not imply novel process formation. Actually, Piaget and Werner differ in their interpretation of the continuity-discontinuity issue. Piaget says: ". . . continuity would depend fundamentally on a question of scale; for a certain scale of measurement we obtain discontinuity when with a finer scale we should get continuity" (1960, p. 121). For Werner, one gets continuity with a certain scale and discontinuity with another type of scale.

[4] Erikson postulates that the dominant mode of behaving comes about "by way of a newly matured executive part of the organism" (1960, p. 137).

primitive process (the view of the verbal mediationists,[5] and Werner). (4) Curves that represent change in particular parameters of development show periods in which the rate of development changes. These periods of relative stability are seen as pacing variations in the operation of basic processes available from birth. Physical growth is taken as an example of this (Tanner, 1960).

The empirical criterion of emergence is defined by qualitative differences in behavior between two time periods. The conceptual criterion of emergence, on the other hand, is defined by the theoretical assumptions concerning the developmental processes which create the emergents. The empirical identification of qualitative differences alone will not provide an adequate basis for establishing that the qualitative differences are in fact emergents. Some recourse to a set of theoretical propositions which make such data interpretable is required to establish their validity.

THE TELEOLOGICAL IMPLICATION OF DEVELOPMENT

The teleological emphasis in a well-delineated developmental scheme such as Piaget's is considerable. The theoretical formulation is based upon the thesis that with appropriate experience a well-defined set of cognitive outcomes will be achieved. Although the limits of human cognition are not defined and the content of cognition is not fully specified, it is implied that in the larger categories of thought the theoretical system accounts for its totality. The period of concrete operations, for example, is not likely to have logical categories in addition to the logic of classes, the logic of relations, and the infralogical operations carried over from the period of prelogical thought. In this sense, development may be said to be aimed at the achievement of particular thought forms. Variation from these forms is strictly limited. Even though there is great variability in environmental conditions which human beings experience, there is relatively little variability, if any, in the logical categories represented in their thought.

If the explanation for these end-products of development is not to fall into vitalistic or metaphysical explanation, the phenomena are best accounted for in terms of genetic preprogramming mechanisms. The well-articulated, logically ordered, and invariant sequences argue more for a genetic, i.e., maturational, model than for either environmental determinism or interactionism. If the environmental side of the transaction were really to play a significant causal role, one might expect, as has already been pointed out, greater environmental influence on structure determination, and not just in variation of time of onset or in rate of acquisition.

[5] To some mediationists, language mediation requires the operation of no new learning or thought process. Association is sufficient to describe the basic operation in verbal mediation. Piaget, for whom language is a representation of the symbolic function, probably would consider language an emergent, but only in reference to a system of representation and not as a separate process of thought.

Since a role for experience in development is not denied by anyone, not even nativists, it is appropriate to enquire as to the role that experience does play in cognitive development. One unquestioned function is to provide the content of thought (e.g., the data for developing the concepts of mass, volume, etc.), as well as information of extent, i.e., magnitude and variability. These parametric and content variables also act in relation to another function, namely that of switching or triggering, which is related to what Baldwin (1955) calls "stimulus-induced maturation." Stimulus-induced maturation refers to the observation that maturational change is not likely to occur without appropriate environmental stimulation. The mechanism for this is suggested by recent evidence from the study of the gene function, which indicates the existence of "timing genes" that act to synchronize the activity of other genes in developmental programming, as well as the existence of genetic switch mechanisms, which are activated by external or internal agents (Gottlieb, 1966). The activity of some genetic switch mechanisms is stimulated by relatively unspecific agents and it seems likely that in behavioral development relatively nonspecific stimulation within stimulus categories can activate processes already programmed to respond to such stimulation. The processes that lead to the acquisition of concrete operations may thus be initiated by encounters with a wide variety of stimulation. Such switch mechanisms, although responsive to external stimulation, are nevertheless under genetic control since, as the conservation learning studies suggest, specific training alone will not ensure the triggering of these functions. At the same time, switch mechanisms are well differentiated in their response to categories of environmental inputs since in some related functions operational achievement is highly differential. In area and length qualitative measurement, for example, training children in the first and third grades shows that first grade children are completely unable to profit from area training but do very well in learning qualitative length measurement, whereas older third graders easily reach criterion level in both tasks (Beilin & Franklin, 1962). The differential effect of training is attributable to a difference in internal programming, and training will not switch on a mechanism that is not primed for it.

CUMULATIVE AND IRREVERSIBLE DEVELOPMENTAL PROPERTIES

Most continuity and discontinuity theories accept the fact that developmental change is cumulative even though beyond particular ages some changes superficially appear to be subtractive. These behavioral decrements result from loss or deterioration of sensorimotor function. Such developments are cumulative, nevertheless, in that deterioration is usually the result of damage or the accumulation of function-retarding products. The cumulation issue is not so much one of addition and retention but of the organization of the processes and products of cumulation. There seems to be some agreement among theorists that cumulative change occurs in an organized fashion, although there are some dissenters (Russell, 1957). Nevertheless there is not much consensus as to the nature and form of organization. Gagné (1968), who offers a learning theory explanation of cognitive development as an alternative to Piagetian theory, posits a hierarchic organization of development in terms of a series of stages derived from the additive combination of simpler processes. Stages of development in this theory are not age-related but specific experience-related, and evolve from the operation of basic behavioral processes (discrimination, memory, and generalization). While he differs from some other behaviorists in his interest in hierarchic systems of organization, his theory also differs in an important way from the organization theories of Piaget and Werner. Gagné assumes that two or more learned sequences add together to form a more complex thought unit and, conversely, more complex levels reduce to the simpler components. The cumulation of elements involves no assumptions other than those of learning and addition. In regard to the acquisition of conservation, Gagné argues that it is achieved by the successive addition of constituent abilities. Piaget argues contrariwise that even in the condition in which a child may demonstrate independent knowledge of the components of conservation (i.e., knowledge of the effects of variation in length, height, and width), if he is a "nonconserver" he will be unable to integrate these independent capacities into the appropriate reversible-compensatory operations that make conservation possible. It is assumed that the child is operationally incapable of doing so, even with training. Other investigators who have attempted to test this assertion confirm it (Sigel & Hooper, 1968), although a limited number of studies stand in contradiction. Although Piaget grants that training will have positive effects in some circumstances, he argues against anticipating fundamental cognitive change through training.

The common assertion of the irreversibility of development is important only in its reference to basic developmental process. For one, reversibility is a question of how one defines the processes and states of development. If it is assumed that any cumulation of experience or growth makes a later state different from a prior one, then by definition development is irreversible, but not much is added by saying so. If one means, however, that the organization of behavior or thought will manifest itself in identical qualities in early and later states, while different qualities of thought exist in intermediate stages, then it represents a testable theoretical possibility. In biological development (particularly in differentiation) it is recognized that reversibility is possible, at least in some rather limited circumstances (Waddington, 1966), although it is not at all easy to achieve. At the same time, Waddington holds that differentiation in some kinds of cells, e.g., nerve cells, is practically irreversible. The biological substrate of psychological development should follow the same rules. Where psychological development is tied closely to neurological development, reversibility may be practically impossible. In deviant psychological development and in unusual environmental conditions, reorganization of behavior and thought may occur, but since growth and experience would have intervened between the earlier and later stages, it is unlikely that the later stage will be simply a duplicate of the first, even though they may be equivalent in some functional attributes.

The reason for interest in reversibility, aside from the practical one of explaining the nature of deviant behavior, is that it is theoretically associated with emergence and maturation. It is an assumption of maturationist theories that development under the control of genetic mechanisms and capable of yielding only particular species-specific structures proceeds only in the direction of the development of such structures. This neutral teleology is unacceptable to copy theorists and empiricists who expect the organism's development to reflect environmental control, which should make reversibility possible.

Irreversibility of development is viewed with suspicion also by those who apply a moral interpretation to development, an attitude which has its origin in the Enlightenment when development became associated with the idea of progress, and progress was taken to be good. In this cynical age, when progress is as evil as good, there is a disposition to interpret the notion of irreversibility as evil, too. The issue of reversibility and irreversibility should be approached, however, as morally neutral.

DEVELOPMENTAL PROCESSES AND MECHANISMS

Present explanations of psychological development do nothing to specify the nature of developmental mechanisms. They allude to such mechanisms and detail certain properties and general rules that must govern them, but their specification is left open. The characterization of system output in the form of behavior or (implied) thought is much more adequate. Werner's principle of differentiation and hierarchic integration, for example, defines the outcome of development but only implies the existence of processes or mechanisms that lead to such outcomes. Hierarchic integration is not so much a mechanism of development as a characterization of the product. Piaget's specification of accommodation, assimilation, and equilibration as the key processes in cognitive development is in the same category, as is the empiricist's identification of discrimination and generalization as basic processes. These process identifications really represent place-holding constructs that stand as explanations till it is possible by specific rule writing to fill in the details that can account for the generation of specific forms of thought. Some of the present excitement over the work of Chomsky and the generative-transformational grammar group is in their proposed set of linguistic rules (the base-structure grammar and transformation rules) which stand in a logical relationship to the acceptable and unacceptable sentences generated by a speaker. These rules are of great precision and economy. Most important, they have powerful explanatory value. At the same time, in spite of the achievements of the generative-transformational linguists and psychologists, the mechanisms by which sentences are generated or understood remain unknown (Sutherland, 1966).

In cognitive development, the most sophisticated rule system for defining the cognitive behavior of the developing child is undoubtedly the one provided by Piaget. In spite of its explanatory limitations, it is a long stride in the effort to specify the rule system for logical thought. Its explanatory structure is at two levels. First, there is the level of specifying the logical forms, such as the logic of classes, logic of relations and the four-group, that lead to such specific thinking and reasoning as is found in ordering, classifying, concept formation, and problem solving. In this sense Piagetian theory asserts that any cognitive behavior seen in the child at a particular developmental period conforms to the regularities of these logical rules. A corollary to this is that the rules for the determination of the forms of thought will differ for each developmental stage. Second, there is a more fundamental level of explanation that attempts to specify how the rules of logical form come into being. This level of specification refers to the existence of the self-regulatory mechanism that derives rules from maturational programming and from action in relation to objects.

There are potentially analogous levels of explanation for language development. The (universal) base structure rules which specify the constraints placed upon sentence generation also define the logical properties of sentences in a manner analogous to the way the logical rules of thought specify the products of thought and their regularities. There are no specified mechanisms of language generation, however, analogous to Piaget's self-regulating mechanisms, although it is asserted that base structure rules are innately specified. It may be discovered someday that the mechanisms by which language is generated are intimately related to the mechanisms by which thought is generated.

In any case, it is strongly suggested by the evidence and the theory that Piaget's (universal) logical rule system derives from innate mechanisms—as emergent processes programmed by an innate genetic structure. The impetus to cognitive growth comes from both the biological mechanisms and environmental input. Cognitive development under the control of the self-regulatory mechanisms yields particular products whose properties are defined by the rules of logical thought (not necessarily of all thought). Such development does not end as a result of achieving structural integration, since as part of an open system integration and reintegration continue as long as the system exists. In this context, the presently popular game of asserting that Piaget has no theory to account for the transition between stages is difficult to understand, unless it is because Piaget is not emphatic enough in emphasizing that development proceeds according to genetic requirements. It is clearly implied that continuous additions to the cognitive system by virtue of both maturation and experience soon unbalance whatever stability is achieved through integrated structures. Those who claim that Piaget has no explanation for transitions do not recognize or are unwilling to accept the maturationist and self-regulatory-system claims of the theory. Some desire to substitute counterclaims more in accord with environ-mentalist theory (Gagné, 1968) or wish to press an accommodation between Piagetian and behaviorist theory (Kessen, 1962). Assertions that the nature of these transitions is not specified by fully described self-regulatory and equilibrium mechanisms is correct, but that is different from the claim that transitions are not fully accounted for by the self-regulatory and equilibrium mechanisms.

THEORETICAL MEANINGFULNESS OF THE STAGE CONCEPT

The import of these observations to whether the stage notion is meaningful lies in the ability of the stage construct to explain developmental change as part of a theory of development. In the Piaget system, stages represent, on one level, a description of cognitive behaviors qualitatively different from one another. This description is related to a set of theoretical assumptions represented by a logical rule system that explains the form of the described behaviors, and these in turn are related to another set of assumptions that account for the generation of the logical rule system. The explanatory power of these logical rules is quite considerable. At the same time, there are important areas of cognitive develop-ment that are not fully explained. The theory, as it presently stands, does not appear sufficient to account for the ability of the 4-year-old child to generate an infinite number of meaningful sentences in accord with an apparently sophisti-cated set of linguistic rules, when the cognitive prelogical apparatus available to him, detailed in Piaget's theory, appears too limited for that task. This seeming paradox suggests the need for further development of the Piagetian theory.

EMPIRICAL VALIDITY

The question of whether stages "exist" has to be answered in the same way as the question as to whether development "exists." It requires two kinds of definition—a conceptual definition, albeit at the level of inductive generalization, and an operational definition (i.e., a specification of an appropriate measure-ment). The measurement of the phenomena of development should provide data that can be related appropriately to the defined constructs.

By common agreement, stages, at the minimum, require the specification and identification of qualitative differences in behavior. The change need not be saltatory, but a differentiable difference in behavior is required nevertheless. It is often observed, as already pointed out, that the appropriate segmentation of developmental data will give such differentiation, and in saying so it is implied that the result is necessarily artifactual. This is not so. For one, it could be just as legitimately argued that a developmental sequence which is "naturally" segmented may have its stagelike appearance made continuous by resegmentation. The question as to which segmentation would be "true" in the identification of "reality," the stagelike or continuity characterization, can be answered only by reference to some explanatory system which at the same time explains more, and more adequately, additional facts of development than just the stage- or nonstagelike features of the data. The validity of either continuity or discontinuity theory will be determined by the ability of these theories to explain the totality of developmental data and not stage data alone.

Piaget's stage theory demands more than the requirement of qualitative difference between stage behaviors. It requires invariance in the serial order of stages as well as other criteria related to his theory of cognitive development (Piaget, 1956).[6]

Piaget's empirical characterization of developmental stages includes a description of the child's response to the experimenter's questions and the experimenter's manipulation of objects. One has to infer from these data, which are usually presented as individual illustrative protocols, how the stage characterizations were arrived at. One assumes that the differentiation of qualitative differences was developed inductively by delineating the salient and common properties in the variety of protocols. The extent to which these generalizations apply to the total data of an age period is not clear. Two kinds of generalization are made from the stage data. First, a stage is characterized by a certain set of common properties. These common properties reflect the development of a hypothesized total structure. The common properties of the period of concrete operations, for example, for which there is a wide variety of cognitive behavior, suggests that at least a part of each cognitive behavior has within it the operation of these common concrete operational structures. A second type of generalization is made. Since each structure operates in relation to a different context (in conservation it is in relation to length, mass, volume, etc.), context differences lead to acquisition differences and a lack of performance generalization across these contexts.[7]

The same data, then, lead to a generalization concerning common structure from properties which are ostensibly differentiated from those of earlier and later periods, and also to a generalization that performance within a defined stage is not generalizable because of context differences within the stage. A difficult measurement problem exists when one tries to substantiate a thesis

---

[6] There are five criteria specified for stages: (1) invariant order of succession; (2) integration of the structures of a higher level such that the equivalent of the earlier structure can be found in the later; (3) distinguishing an aspect of achievement with respect to stages going before and an aspect of preparation with respect to stages coming after; (4) characterization by the existence of a general or total structure which relates the preparation and achievement of a stage; and (5) a series of equilibrium levels where the range of operation becomes greater and more mobile with successive levels, and stability of the equilibrium depends upon degree of integration and emergent structure.

[7] The well-known distinction between vertical and horizontal décalage.

based upon this type of differentiation. The way this problem has been handled, to date, has been to treat successive order based upon qualitatively differentiable properties by scalogram analysis, on the assumption that such data most aptly meet the criteria of ordinal scaling (i.e., connectedness, asymmetry, and transitivity). This is now a fairly common procedure with the use of the Guttman scale (1954b), the Green index of consistency (1956), and Loevinger's index of homogeneity (1947). In addition to the measurement of succession, scalogram analysis has been used as a measure of homogeneity within levels as an indication of "unitary dimensionality" (Nassefat, 1963).

Parametric and nonparametric correlational analysis of within-stage data has been used to test for generality across tasks, as has the analysis of variance (Uzgiris, 1964). It is not frequently considered whether the scaling assumptions inherent in these analyses are in accord with the theory assumptions that are tested by these analyses (as distinct from the specific assumptions of the statistical tests). It is questionable whether Piagetian theory based upon discontinuity assumptions is testable by parametric tests based upon continuity and additivity assumptions (unless, of course, Piaget is correct in assuming that continuity-discontinuity is simply a matter of scale refinement—in which case, an ordinal scale application would be considered an approximation to an interval scale statistic). What basically has to be answered is whether magnitude differences are related to qualitative changes identified with stage structures. To the extent that magnitude differences and quality differences relate to aspects of development which suggest two different types of process, it may be that parametric and nonparametric methods should be used only in relation to the discontinuity-continuity assumptions of the theory they are testing.

The invariance of cognitive developmental stages has been tested by a number of investigators (see Sigel & Hooper, 1968). Aside from the internal difficulties of specific scaling methods, there is a problem of treating the entire developmental scheme as a multiordinal scaling problem with the additional assumptions of response variability due to context, and response variability due to subject differences. In spite of this, by selecting the dimensions for test without overcomplicating them, it has been possible to confirm, in the main, the invariant sequence assertions of the Piagetian theory. Were the data reorganized to conform to the assumptions of Freudian-type developmental theory or treated according to an additive learning theory model, it is not clear whether confirmation would be equally forthcoming. A number of recent studies have been employing parametric methods in application to Piagetian concepts and procedures, but it would be theoretically and empirically instructive if psychometric comparison of all major models could be made. From what I have suggested, each of these empirical tests could turn out to be confirming of its assumptions, at least for some limited sample of the data, and yet differ in their explanatory power or value. Again, whether continuity or discontinuity assumptions about developmental change are correct will be determined more by the explanatory power of the entire theory than by the stage construct alone.

On the whole, the extent to which Piaget's stage description accounts for all the logical thought data of a stage is not clear even with the fairly large number of validation studies already carried out, if only because the scope of the Piaget system is so vast as to make the task too time-consuming. It is doubtful whether much of the system will be validated or for that matter should be. In all likelihood the pace of validation studies should reduce as the results become more redundant, and this is already evident. Investigation into the nature and explanatory adequacy of the rule systems governing the developmental stages, however, offers a more fruitful area of research interest.

EMPIRICAL MEANINGFULNESS OF THE STAGE CONCEPT

As implied, empirical meaningfulness of the stage concept is limited without reference to the assumptions of some theory. At the same time the scientific meaningfulness of stages within a conceptual system of development will have little significance without reference to the data of development. To date, the impression which emerges is that the stage notion has been of greater interest and significance as a theoretical construct than as an empirical generalization. This may be from lack of sufficient attention to the empirical problem or because the empirical problem is difficult to handle. For the moment at least it would seem that a limited body of empirical data have to carry a heavy theoretical burden.

Comments on Beilin's Paper
by John H. Flavell
University of Minnesota

Beilin's paper reflects a kind of symptom of the Zeitgeist. I think that in the next few years we will see more papers and books like this. That is, there will be more efforts of the sort that tries to stand back about three paces from the data to get some feeling for what the whole shape of development is like—what the morphology of development is like—rather than simply burrowing into the data, looking at this or that Piagetian acquisition, trying to replicate it or extend it, and so forth. I think we're beginning to get the dim outlines of perhaps a new conception, or at least of a modified conception, of how development in general goes. Piaget has been working on such a conception for years, but I think it's time for the rest of us also to take a hand at it.

Beilin's paper really is excellent, which is to say that it agrees with my biases in most respects! Hence I will limit myself to comments on only a few specific points of his paper. For example, on page 175 he makes the following statement: "The kind of control that results from biological change is not clear [within an empiricist, S-R kind of a model]. It is the dilemma of the empiricist that he is forced to accept the facts of maturation but is unwilling to concede to it a central control function." It seems to me that this is a very important point and very well taken. While S-R people always admit the importance of maturational forces, they never really want to accord them any kind of systematic role in the theory itself.

Now, he made some comments later on which I also found interesting. These concern his reinterpretation of Piaget's theory as essentially maturationist, a reinterpretation with which I am largely in accord although I didn't realize it until last year or so. First, he speaks of "... a preprogrammed rule system [that] controls the transaction with reality that leads to the construction of only very limited types of structure" (p. 178). The idea is that development is just not going to lead into basic thought forms other than the ones that you specify in your theory, no matter what the interaction with the environment. That is an important point. He also asserts that "... it is difficult to avoid the conclusion that Piaget's position is fundamentally a maturationist position—and that in the transaction with the environment, experience and action are principally facilitating agencies" (p. 178).

I wonder if it may be that, in the course of development, the constraining role of maturation or endogenous factors actually decreases rather than increases. Now, we usually think that what's really important is the kind of stimulation a child gets in infancy, and that once that's taken care of, you don't have to worry so much about the rest of development. We think of infancy, in other words, as *the* critical period for cognitive development. But if you actually look at the facts in the Piagetian domain, it turns out that it is far more certain, and I think more biologically guaranteed, that a child is going to achieve sensorimotor acquisitions than it is that he will acquire formal operations. The evidence suggests that whether or to what extent you get formal operations will depend much more upon the specific encounters the child has with his milieu than would be the case for sensorimotor actions or even concrete operations.

My image of development is thus a sort of cone or megaphone, with its small end towards birth and its large end towards maturity. The circumference of the walls represents the constraints on what the child can develop into at each age period—thus, there are tighter constraints in infancy and looser ones towards adulthood. I am simply impressed with the fact, as Beilin is, that there have to be some deeply rooted biological constraints or governors on the form of childhood cognitive growth. Cognitive changes during childhood have formal "morphogenetic" properties which I think must have a biological growth process as their substrate. The major cognitive changes are, in neurologically intact children, largely *inevitable, momentous, directional, uniform,* and *irreversible.* Adult cognitive changes appear to lack these properties, despite the fact that adults, like children, are continually subject to a wide variety of environmental inputs. I think that such considerations pose real problems for psychologists who are prone to stress nurture at the expense of nature.

Beilin also discusses Gagné's model and talks about a difference between Gagné's point of view—which looks superficially something like the Piagetian one—and the actual Piagetian one. I would like to point to one other difference between the two. Gagné thinks that the tempo of development is constrained only by the fact that learning takes time and there is so much to learn. I rather suspect, as I believe Piaget and other people of a maturationist bent do, that there are in fact some basic temporal governors on the rate of development. In other words, it is not just a matter of the number of things a child has to acquire, but also of some kind of governing, rate-constraining process having to do with the passage of biological time.

Finally, Beilin speaks of Piaget's concept of equilibration as the fundamental process or mechanism of cognitive change from one stage to the next. I think most people who have looked at Piaget's theory long and hard have the feeling that he must be partly right—that there is something intuitively correct about that kind of model. But I also agree with Beilin when he says that presently we can't be very specific about it. If you've ever had the experience of trying to explain exactly what Piaget means by "equilibration" to a class of students, you know that that concept is far from clear. What we need to do, obviously, is to specify the meaning of this concept clearly and concretely enough to be able to research it—to actually find out if it has any real promise as an explanatory construct. And on this same point, a concept that has always eluded me (in its entirety at least) is Piaget's notion of *structures d'ensemble*—of structural integration. It seems to me exactly what that implies is also not yet clear, and that we should work towards its clarification.

Open Discussion

There was a long and lively discussion of Beilin's stimulating paper. The discussion centered around the problem of how to account for novelty, or emergent processes in development, and the related questions of genetic, environmental, and transactional influences. Several other matters were discussed briefly.

Piaget opened the discussion with a detailed explanation of his position on the issue of novelty raised by Beilin's paper.

PIAGET

I should like to say how delighted I was to hear you speak. My friend, Daniel Berlyne, wrote an article maintaining that I was a neobehaviorist, and today Beilin has read a paper showing that I am a maturationist. In fact, I am neither one nor the other. I refuse to admit the necessity of a choice between these alternatives, and Beilin's paper has proved very instructive in that it has shown how difficult it is for me to make myself understood.

I refuse to make this choice for the following reasons. Let us take a characteristic which appears at a specific moment in a child's development, for instance, conservation. You could then reason along the following lines: this characteristic must either stem from already existing properties of the world of reality, with the organism simply registering them, or it has been genetically preformed and is therefore already present in the subject's hereditary genetic structure. In both cases, the characteristic is not new. It either comes from the external world and information is obtained by simple abstraction bearing on external objects, or it is genetically preformed and information is abstracted "internally"; according to this way of thinking, it must be one or the other.

I consider the problem quite differently. For me, the real problem is how to explain novelties. I think that novelties, i.e., creations, constantly intervene in development. New structures, not preformed either in the external world or in genetic structure, are constantly appearing. My problem is how to explain the novelties. I think there are two or three points which may be made in this connection, first from the biological and then from the psychological point of view.

Biologically, it is indisputable that novelties are created. I believe that, from the phylogenetic point of view, it is impossible to think that man is preformed in the protozoa or that the elephant is already contained in the bacteria. There are novelties which are constantly being created during evolution, and it is on this, as yet unsolved, problem that modern biologists are concentrating.

Second, from the biological point of view, there is the development of the individual, i.e., the formation of a phenotype, which is not simply the actualization of hereditary characteristics. A phenotype, as maintained by both Dobzhansky and Waddington, is the genotype's response to environmental pressures. This response is new. In contemporary genetics, there is the important concept of the "reaction norms" of a given genotype which gives us the range and distribution of all its possible variations; these variations represent all the possible reactions which may be constructed through interaction with the environment.

The third biologically oriented remark I should like to make concerns permanent functions; these exist in biology just as, I believe, there are in psychology such permanent functions as assimilation and accommodation, and so forth. A permanent function does not contain an already formed structure; this structure must be constructed. For example, all animals possess the function of nutrition—they all feed themselves. They all assimilate food, but that does not mean that the function of nutrition presupposes the existence of a digestive tube or stomach. The construction of a structure is thus not the same thing as the permanence of the function. Those are the three "biological" comments I wanted to make; I shall now go on to the "psychological" ones.

Here again, I think three points may be raised. The first is that maturation as regards cognitive functions—knowledge—simply determines the range of possibilities at a specific stage. It does not cause the actualization of the structures. Maturation simply indicates whether or not the construction of a specific structure is possible at a specific stage. It does not itself contain a preformed structure, but simply opens up possibilities—the new reality still has to be constructed.

Secondly, when we speak of reflexive abstraction (as opposed to "simple" abstraction, which consists of retaining the interesting properties of objects by separating them from others which are ignored), we use the word "reflexive" in both senses of the term. First, in the physical sense, the results of abstractions carried out on an inferior level are reflected (like a ray reflected by a mirror) onto a superior one. Consequently, it is necessary to reconstruct on this superior plane that which existed on the inferior one. And here lies the importance of the second sense (mental) of "reflexion": in order to reconstruct this structure on the superior level, richer and new constructions have to be made, since it is not just a question of translating the inferior into the superior, but of simultaneously adding the operations which make possible the passage from the inferior to the superior level. This is why the reflexive abstraction does not (as does "simple" abstraction) involve only the use of elementary data already present at the inferior level. A reflexive abstraction is always a construction of new realities.

My third comment concerns an example of these abstractions. Take, for example, the function of establishing correspondences, which is found at the sensorimotor level. When a baby learns to imitate using facial movements, he is already, for example, putting the model's nose into correspondence with his own nose, or the model's hair with his own hair. Does this elementary correspondence contain all the higher forms of correspondence? The answer is obviously "no." Take, for example, Cantor's theory of sets and in particular his creation of "transfinite" numbers. One, two, three, four, can be matched with two, four, six, eight, etc. In common in the two series is the first transfinite cardinal number, i.e., aleph null. Can we say that aleph null was contained in advance in the reactions of the baby who is starting to establish correspondences? Of course not; the correspondence simply gives us a functioning—a functioning which, although it has deep roots in the organism, does not, because of this, already contain all that may in the future be drawn from it.

To conclude, it is possible to maintain that there is a place for maturation (I think it is necessary) but at the same time to refute the theory of preformation. Beilin has made me into a nativist, or preformist, and he has missed the crux of my problem, which is to try and explain how novelties are possible and how they are formed. For example, I must try to explain, starting with simple psychological function, how Cantor came to create the set theory. This is one of a thousand other problems.

Thus, to my regret, I did not find in Beilin's paper any reference to this problem of novelty—of the formation of novelties in general and the conditions necessary for the development of new structures. What I did find were the two alternatives of physical preformation in the external world and internal preformation or maturation. I uphold neither of these two solutions, and all my efforts are concentrated on going beyond both of them in order to explain the formation of novelties. If there are novelties, then, of course, there are stages. If there are no novelties, then the concept of stages is artificial. There lies the whole problem.

BEILIN

It would be difficult for me of course to respond really adequately to what Professor Piaget is saying—it would probably require another paper. But I would just like to comment on the idea of novelty. Novelty is of course a crucial issue; it relates to the whole problem of the emergence in life. But the question of novelty can be thought of in two ways. There is novelty with regard to individual functioning and there is novelty with regard to species functioning. So that to account for species novelty, one apparently would have to invoke the processes of evolution, whatever they are. But with regard to individual novelty, once one has a specification of what the species is like and the processes of evolution, then for most human functioning, the question of novelty would be within the general framework of what's available in the species.

Now, obviously, sometime in human experience within the species there are new kinds of structures, or processes, or forms of development. But these, I think, would be within the possibilities of species change and novelty for the species. Now I realize that there are a number of epistomological and philosophic problems here, and I wouldn't mean to even try to answer them now. The problem is really much more profound than we can really deal with in this short period of time. I appreciate very much Professor Piaget's remarks. I really didn't think that I would transform him into a maturationist—certainly not by my talk. But I would like to put the issue on the table and let us argue about it a little bit for awhile.

SMOCK

I think one of the problems we have in terms of species is that novelty within species is limited by our relatively stable environment, which might be considered a predetermined type of stability. That is, the environment predetermines exactly what kinds of potential assimilations are possible by a species. We will know very little about the possibility of new forms of thought until we can create some very special new kinds of environments in which, say, infants could be reared. For example, maybe space flight will reveal some unusual kind of environment in which we could rear infants and perhaps test some of these notions.

BENTLER

I have a reaction to Professor Beilin's remarks regarding the problem of quantity and quality, which is, of course, a fundamental issue in all of science and life.

In the first place, given the data that we have and the methods that we have for collecting data, we simply can't answer that problem. But, in principle, I suppose we believe in an invariant sequence of events such as manifested in the ideal case by a Guttman scale. You can have Guttman scales which have essentially virtually completely continuous characteristics and those that have very great discontinuities, and they can all represent stage notions. To illustrate what I mean, recall that my paper deals with the fact that one way to look at this scalogram problem, and to look at the means and the progression in means, is to look at the possibly more fundamental parameters, which I call variation parameters. As I said, suppose there is a constant increment in them. In that case, the effect on the means is very large in the middle range, but it gets smaller and smaller elsewhere. This is reflected of course in the data matrix itself. You still have Guttman scales, but the patterns change radically. Think about the limiting case in which you make the increment from one variation parameter to the next essentially infinitely small, so that you say: now growth is continuing in very, very small steps, but it is continuing. Then the effect of the transformation upon the means is again to make very, very small increments. And while there still may be larger increments in the middle than at the ends, the difference will be so small that you have a virtual continuity. Therefore discontinuities and continuities can be thought of in certain ways as continuities themselves.

For Beilin, this point raised the theoretical issue of whether the world is basically continuous or discontinuous. He suggested that what human beings do is make continuity out of discontinuity. For example, the work of Schrödinger and others in quantum mechanics indicates that the world, in the ultimate sense, is really discontinuous, and as you go further and further down to small units the discontinuity increases.

Bentler raised the question of what might be the minimal amount of information which is needed genetically in order to pass on and complete the unfolding structure. He suggested that there is a starting point and an increment and that this may be all the information you need. If this is true, the future, given the fact that there is a starting point and increment of a certain size, is essentially completely predetermined. On questioning, he denied that he was a preformationist but felt the issue he had raised would bear looking into.

De Vries pointed out that ordinal scales do not necessarily describe a developmental sequence and that this necessitates caution in their use. She noted that methods of using the Guttman scale technique in conjunction with other criteria have been developed which make it possible to say that a set of variables does in fact describe a developmental sequence.

In relation to this point, Bentler commented that if you randomly sample the population cross-sectionally, including children of successive age groups, and the sample is adequate, then, with the exception of the problem of the rate of growth, the Guttman scale will tell you what the direction is going to be. In his opinion, longitudinal studies are not necessary unless the data are not adequate.

Flavell raised an important issue when he noted that one of the major problems, and one that the conference had not dealt with, is that the proof of the invariant sequence is not, *ipso facto,* a proof of any sort of psychological connection. Unfortunately this point was not pursued further by the group.

Smock returned to the issue he had commented on earlier when he wondered if Beilin would agree that the patterning, the rule systems, lie in the transactions with the environment and that perhaps it was unnecessary to make the inside-outside distinction of the empiricist position. He suggested that all that genetics does is provide the starting point.

BEILIN

Genetics doesn't just provide a starting point. For example, take the developments in molecular biology; the coding in the gene does more than just provide a starting point—it really programs the entire development of the individual. The environmental materials out of which the construction has to be made are more or less constant, and the genetic programming provides the functional basis for taking the products and constructing a human being of a particular kind. Change the environmental conditions, and you get a very different kind of product. But it's always according to a certain set of rules;

you may try to alter the rules, but if you do that, then you'll get a human being or an animal of a different order.

Now, it's evident that there isn't that much specification about what the environmental elements have to be. A large variety of elements can initiate the processes and get the organism to develop in this defined fashion. To me at least, that says the programming is a much more significant element than the environmental experience. If a wide variety of environmental agents can trigger off the mechanism, then the mechanism is pretty well set with regard to the way it will function.

The Uses of Verbal Behavior in Assessing Children's Cognitive Abilities

JOHN H. FLAVELL
University of Minnesota

How do we go about trying to assess children's cognitive abilities? Typically, we say and do certain things in the child's presence, he is led to say and do certain other things in response, and then we try to make inferences about the meaning of his output in relation to our input. Although we may often wish it would be otherwise, his output is liable to reflect a fair amount of linguistic processing. It may reflect his interpretation of the words and sentences that we have addressed to him (language comprehension), and it may reflect his ability to make relevant verbal utterances in reply (language production). It even seems to be the case, unfortunately, that linguistic processing is likely to intrude despite our best efforts to preclude it, as in so-called "nonverbal" test procedures. Thus, a major part of our job in diagnosing a child's cognitive status in experimental or psychometric settings is apt to be that of interpreting his linguistic comprehension, production, or both. While a resolution of the thorny methodological problems raised by the necessity of making such interpretations is scarcely at hand, it is at least possible to look closely and carefully at the general issue of language-to-cognition inferences, in hopes that some distinctions might emerge that could one day contribute to such a resolution.

It may, for example, be useful to realize that language-to-cognition inferences vary considerably as to the relation between what is said or comprehended (language) and what is inferred (cognition). In particular, this relation may be relatively direct or relatively indirect. The direct-relation case is the more familiar one, and will be illustrated first. A Piagetian conservation-of-number task can serve as prototype. After the child has agreed that two identical rows contain equal numbers of objects, the investigator lengthens one row by spacing out its objects and then tries to ascertain by judicious questioning whether the child thinks the two sets remain numerically equal. The conserver is certain that they still are equal and the nonconserver thinks that one of them now contains more objects, usually the set that forms the longer row. The language-to-cognition inferences that the investigator makes in the task situation are quite direct, in the sense that he probes for the literal relation—different for nonconserver and conserver, obviously—between the key words and phrases he has addressed to the child ("same number," "just as much," "more," etc.) and the semantic interpretations of them which the latter spontaneously makes (row length versus genuine numerosity).

It should be said, parenthetically, that the inference process here will naturally be pursued further. There are additional cognitive implications that can be drawn from these contrasting semantic renderings; for instance, the possible presence of an underlying concrete-operational system in the case of the correct (conserver's) interpretation and the possible absence of this system in the case of the incorrect (nonconserver's) interpretation. It is precisely for this reason that Piaget's conservation problems, his earlier (1928) verbal probes for relational thinking (e.g., determining the meaning of "brother" and other relational concepts for the child), and numerous other Genevan tasks which entail linguistic processing are not "merely" vocabulary tests in disguise—"nothing but" measures of semantic development. For a Piagetian, really knowing what "number," "brother," and other key words mean implies an acquired intellectual substratum of a theoretically interesting sort, whereas really knowing what many other words mean ("coyote," "pipe," "banjo"—supply your own list) implies little of cognitive-developmental significance.

The main point for the present discussion, however, is that the child's linguistic processing does figure prominently in such tasks and, especially, that the language-cognition relation which the investigator looks at is of the relatively direct, verbal-symbol-presented-to-underlying-meaning-for-this-child variety. A direct relation between the verbal input and the child's interpretation may also hold in tasks designed to measure, not cognitive growth as that term is usually understood, but syntactic and other aspects of language development itself. For reasons just given, one would not be comfortable in categorizing a conservation task as primarily a test of language development. However, no discomfort would be felt in so labelling studies such as those recently carried out by Carol Chomsky (1968a). In one of her tasks, children of 5 to 10 years of age were instructed by the examiner to ask certain questions of a classmate present in the room, for instance, "Ask Joanna . . . (1) *who this is,*" or (2) *"her last name,"* or (3) *"what to put back in the box."* In each case, the child must recover from the examiner's imperative sentence the necessary syntactic information for posing the correct question sentence to the classmate, and the cues for recovering it are progressively more subtle and difficult to utilize as one goes from (1) to (3). Accordingly, all but the youngest subjects produce a correct "Who's that?" in response to imperative (1), since the fragment " . . . *who this is*" clearly specifies the correct subject *(who)* and other grammatical features of the question sentence. In contrast, many of even the oldest subjects incorrectly respond "What are you (sic) going to put back in the box?" when presented with imperative (3), because " . . . *what to put*" does not in any direct and obvious way reveal who the subject of the verb is to be—the child herself or the classmate. As in the conservation and other cognitive tasks described above, the focus of interest here is on the direct relation between what is said and how that which is said was understood by the child. The difference is that the child's knowledge of the nonspeech world is the ultimate diagnostic target in the cognitive tasks, whereas it is his knowledge of his native language in the Chomsky study.

Let us now examine task situations where the inferential route from the child's linguistic behavior to his underlying cognitive knowledge is less direct and straightforward. In one such task (Flavell et al., 1968, chap. 3; see also Glucksberg & Krauss, 1967), the child first learns to play a simple board game and then, with the game materials in view, tries to explain the game to a *blindfolded* listener. Under these circumstances young children tend to produce messages that are grossly maladapted to this particular listener's informational needs, even to the point of including utterances like, "You pick *this* up (points) and put it *there* (points)." We interpreted such communicative behavior as reflecting a relative inability to take the role of the listener, i.e., as a form of cognitive egocentrism. Thus, here as in the conservation and other tasks previously mentioned, the child's linguistic behavior is taken as a basis for inferences about his cognitive abilities.

Notice, however, that the sought after language-cognition relation is rather different in the case of the communication task. The child's semantic interpretation of "more," "same number," etc., is the immediate basis for that relation in the conservation case, whereas his semantic interpretation of "this" and "there" in the communication case is of no interest to the investigator—it is assumed that he has long since acquired the correct lexical meanings of these commonplace words. What *is* of interest, and what *does* give a clue to his thought processes, is the fact that he chose to utter these particular words in this particular situation. Our analysis of the child's use of "more" will at least initially lead us to its underlying semantic interpretation for him; in contrast, our analysis of his use of "this" will immediately lead us elsewhere, namely, to inferences about his insensitivity to communication requirements. The nonconserver could be said not to know the correct meaning of "more" but to know the appropriate occasions for its use, given his semantic reading of it: the experimenter asked him a question entailing that word and he gave a responsive and relevant answer. In contrast, the egocentric communicator could be said to know the correct meaning of "this" but not to know something about the appropriate occasions for its use, namely an audience that has the informational means for specifying its referent.

Another example from our communication studies (Flavell et al., 1968, chap. 4) may further clarify the distinction between direct and indirect language-to-cognition inferences. The subjects were third grade, seventh grade, and eleventh grade girls. Each subject was to pretend that she was talking to her father, trying to persuade him to buy her a television set for her own room. She was encouraged to say anything and everything she could think of that might move him to comply with her request. The younger children tended to produce repetitive and unsubtle appeals of the "hard sell" variety. For example: "Come on, I want a television for my own room. Come on. Please. Daddy, come on." The following excerpt nicely illustrates the sorts of approaches favored by the older children: "Oh, hello Dad. How are you today? Do you want your slippers changed or something? Here, have a cigarette? . . . Ah—let's see—hey, Christmas is coming . . . Now there's only one thing I want . . ." (the remainder of her message includes a listing of alleged benefits *to the father* of her having her own set). Certainly no one would want to argue that the authors of these two messages do not differ in their level of semantic development or linguistic fluency; I shall return to this point later in the paper. Nonetheless, it is clearly not the literal, denotative meaning for each child of her message constituents that we want to analyze here. It is rather the possible implications, concerning her level of social-cognitive developments, of having chosen to utter one set of constituents versus another. The older child's message can reasonably be interpreted as the handmaiden of a careful and sustained cognitive reading of the intended listener, a reading of those emotional and motivational attributes of the listener deemed relevant to the objective at hand. To make this interpretation, however, one has to look at the child's linguistic production from the standpoint of why it was made rather than what it said—of what it meant to have said it rather than what it meant to say.

Communication tasks are not the only settings in which the child's linguistic behavior receives this indirect type of interpretation. Moely et al. (1969) administered a memory task to 5 to 11 year old children. The child was presented with a set of pictures of familiar objects (table, car, etc.), was left alone in an observation room for 2 minutes to study them, and then was asked to name all the ones he could remember. Virtually all of the children were observed during the study period to whisper or mouth object names as they perused the pictures. However, the older children frequently did something in addition. They would deliberately avert their gaze from the pictures and rehearse the object names, presumably to find out how their efforts at memorization were faring. Even more obviously than in the two communication tasks, the data of interest here are not the child's semantic interpretations of "table," "car," etc.; these can for all practical purposes be regarded as constant across the age range tested. It is again a matter of how he uses words, not what he means by them. The older child simply appears to know something about how to memorize material that the younger child does not know, and the evidence for this cognitive difference happens to be provided by their verbal behavior.

There are, then, at least two different types of language-to-cognition inference. While I am far from sure that "direct" and "indirect" are the best terms for conveying the distinction between them (and hope, in fact, that the conference participants can suggest some alternatives), I am quite certain that the distinction itself is real. I should like to conclude the paper by first making two further points about this distinction and then offering a more general methodological suggestion concerning the uses of verbal behavior in cognitive-developmental assessment.

The first point is that the indirect type of inference making can lead to conclusions about underlying cognitive abilities that are every bit as valid and trustworthy as those which derive from the direct type. One knows that the child who said "this" to the blindfolded listener had at least momentarily failed to represent to himself the latter's information processing situation just as surely as one knows that the child who invariably uses length of row as the sole criterion of numerosity has an inadequate concept of number. The trustworthiness of our language-to-cognition inferences can indeed vary considerably from task to task, but the variance is largely within-category rather than between categories.

As a matter of fact—and this is the second point—a frequent cause of inferential uncertainty in both types of studies is the investigator's difficulty in determining which category of language-cognition relation is primarily responsible for the subject's behavior. Thus, one would hope that the child's verbalized judgments about row numerosities really do reflect his understanding of number (direct relation). It is conceivable, however, that these judgments could in a given instance reflect instead a tendency to say what the child thinks the experimenter wants to hear, a belief that a "trick question" has been asked, etc. (indirect relation). Similarly, one must satisfy himself that the inadequacies of a young child's communication efforts are not largely attributable to genuine defects in linguistic skill (vocabulary, fluency, etc.) rather than to an egocentric inability to keep his listener in mind. The methodological strategy for overcoming such problems is obvious in principle, although sometimes difficult to follow in actual practice. It is to arrange conditions in such a way that the type of language-cognition relation which the investigator is *not* interested in studying will not lead to intersubject variation in the behavior to be measured, i.e., such that it will be effectively controlled for or held constant. The aforementioned Moely et al. (1969) study illustrates a task situation in which this kind of control is very easy to establish: the experimenters simply used pictures of objects that all the children could correctly and effortlessly label. In communication tasks such as those devised by Flavell et al. (1968), proper controls are more difficult to institute. In some of our communication protocols, it was perfectly obvious that the child's principal difficulty was in assessing the listener's informational needs rather than in being linguistically capable, having properly assessed them, of saying the appropriate things; in others, however, no clear separation of these two variables seemed possible. A doctoral dissertation study by Ada Hegion, currently underway at our Institute of Child Development, may better accomplish the desired separation. Instead of asking the child to devise his own message, as we had done, Hegion successively presents him with all possible pairings of a set of five brief and simple messages of her own devising, under the instruction always to choose the more communicatively effective of the two. Since little strain is placed upon the subject's ability to understand each message in the purely semantic sense, and since no strain at all is placed on his ability to produce it on his own, we are hoping that his preferences will constitute relatively pure estimates of his role taking skill in communication settings.

This brings me to the methodological suggestion I wanted to make. It is simply that the student of cognitive development might well emulate his language-development brethren by constructing new and better tests of the child's receptive as opposed to productive capabilities, i.e., tests which do not require him to generate elaborate chains of responses—either verbal or nonverbal—on his own. Flavell et al.'s blindfolded-listener task was inadvertently productive by this definition, for instance, whereas Hegion's is intentionally receptive.

Certain theoretical problems in the Piagetian domain might prove more tractable if receptive tasks were used. For example, the research evidence is still unclear (Wallach, 1969) as to just what information is most important in determining the conserver's decision that the quantity of liquid has in fact changed after the liquid has been poured from, say, a wider to a narrower container (the information that determines *nonconservation* decisions here is better understood). Is it the fact that pouring the liquid back into its original container would reconstitute its initial perceptual appearance (and its initial perceptual equality with the comparison quantity)? Is it the recognition that no liquid has been gained or lost during the pouring? Is it the belief that the gains in liquid-column height in the new container are exactly compensated for by the losses in liquid-quantity width, thereby implying no change in quantity? Or could it be some other consideration entirely? Discovering the underlying conceptual basis for the child's decision is important, because it might illuminate cognitive-structural meaning and developmental origin of conservation. Experimenters have so far tried to discover this basis simply by asking the child why he judged as he did. As with the Flavell et al. blindfolded-listener task, however, this procedure may place more of a load on the child's productive capacities than is either desirable or necessary. Dr. Rochel Gelman of the University of Pennsylvania and I are currently planning a study that should, as in Hegion's procedure, lighten that load considerably: present conservers with pairs of already prepared conservation rationales and try to elicit their preferences. An interesting possibility that can be tested in this fashion is that the preferred rationale for conservation actually changes systematically with age, i.e., that the epistemic foundations of conservation may continue to undergo development even after the conservation judgment itself has become stable and constant. I think that receptive versus productive methods might prove fruitful in quite a number of the testing situations in which we pursue our self-appointed task of learning as much as possible about the growth and development of the human mind.

SUMMARY

Developmental psychologists frequently find themselves in the position of having to infer the child's cognitive level from his linguistic behavior. The substance of this paper is to suggest that these language-to-cognition inferences are of two major types: (1) *direct*—what the child actually and literally means by the verbal utterances he sends or receives; (2) *indirect*—roughly, the implications for his cognitive level of the way he utilizes his linguistic resources in goal-directed activities. The child's conceptual management of terms like "more," "same number," etc., in a number-conservation task is an illustration of the first; his ability to communicate with his listener's informational requirements in mind is an illustration of the second. It was further suggested that direct inferences are not inherently more trustworthy than indirect ones, that uncertainty as to which type of inference should be made from a given sample of linguistic behavior is a frequently encountered methodological problem, and that, more generally, measures of the child's receptive (in contradistinction to productive) linguistic behavior should be more widely exploited in the study of cognitive development.

Comments on Flavell's Paper
by George B. Flamer
CTB/McGraw-Hill[1]

Professor Flavell has identified an important and too often neglected problem that must be attended to if we are to establish an accurate psychology of cognitive development. Since I agree with Flavell's position, I would like to discuss a related problem which deserves close attention: that of determining what a subject thinks his task is and what his subsequent behavior means. Sometimes it is not clear that the subject is doing what the experimenter wants him to do or that the experimenter is interpreting the subject's responses correctly.

[1] Now at the University of Minnesota at Morris.

Although the data on conservation of number in preschool children seem quite consistent, I would like to examine the possibility that there are assessment errors of the false-negative variety (in Flavell's, 1968, sense of the term) in these findings. For several years I've felt that the "méthode clinique," while admittedly providing much unique, necessary, and extremely valuable information about cognitive development, is not entirely appropriate for use with young children. It is a method which relies heavily on language as the means of communication between subject and experimenter, and thus requires a relatively high degree of linguistic competence on the part of both. While aware of the many statements concerning the child's rapid acquisition of language, I still don't believe that it is easy to communicate accurately with young children. The meaning of a particular word or phrase that is intended by the adult using it may not even be a meaning the child knows. This is similar to, although more elementary than, the problem Piaget referred to in his opening address, of determining whether cognitive structures really exist in the child's mind or are only the invention of the psychologist.

In the case of conservation of number, when the child is asked (after one set of objects has been transformed), "Now are there the same number, or does one have more?", what might this question mean to him? Does the use of the word "now" imply (to the child) that the sets aren't the same anymore? Does "same" mean unchanged? Does "more" mean longer? Greater weight, volume, or area? Taller? Or what? To adults these words mean all these things within certain contexts; however, I don't think it's always clear what they mean to the young child. I do think this problem should be systematically investigated.

In a recent paper, Olson (1968) discusses some variables which seem to be related to the child's misinterpretation of adult statements. He argues that in situations where the child is asked to make a decision, the most salient perceptual cues interfere with his judgment. Olson also cites evidence which indicates that the preschool child is able to attend to only one dimension of a multidimensional figure at a time.

The results of an experiment by Mehler and Bever (1967) indicate that when children between about 2 years 8 months and 4 years 3 months were asked to choose the row with more clay pellets, they tended to base their judgments on length of the row rather than number of objects in the row. However, they also found, when the objects were M&M's (candies) and the children were asked to pick the row they wanted to eat, that they now tended to base their decisions on number. These results seem to support Olson's conclusions. Another surprising finding by Mehler and Bever was that the youngest children tested (2 years 4 months to 2 years 7 months) seemed to base their judgments on number of objects, whether the objects were clay pellets or M&M's.

Beilin (1968) has been critical of the Mehler and Bever study, but he did not try to replicate their study nor did he include their youngest and, I think, most interesting age group.

Bever, Mehler, and Epstein (1968) report another experiment in which they systematically determined whether the child's responses were based on number of objects, the length of the rows, or the spacing of the objects in the rows. Their results provided convincing confirmation of the earlier study by Mehler and Bever. Again it was found that 2-year-olds tended to make judgments based on number, 3-year-olds tended to be influenced by length, and at about 4, performance began to improve again.

Piaget (1968a) also has been critical of the Mehler and Bever studies, stating that their research "has nothing to do with conservation (p. 976)." I must agree with Piaget if he insists that we can talk about conservation of number only in terms of his traditional paradigm in which two sets of objects are initially judged equal and then transformed in space. Mehler and Bever never used that exact paradigm. However, they have done almost everything except use that particular paradigm, and it's difficult to see how their results are completely unrelated to the conservation problem or that the results of this series of studies should be ignored in any systematic account of cognitive development.

The Mehler and Bever studies indicate that young children are capable of some behaviors that Piaget's theory does not claim for them. The differences between Piaget's findings and those of Mehler and Bever need to be resolved. If they simply reflect differences in the methods used in the data collection, then we need to take the best of both methodologies, perhaps create some new ones, and combine them all to get a more accurate description of what really is "going on" in the child's mind. If we *are* misleading the child or asking him "trick questions" as Flavell suggested, then let's develop ways of asking questions where the meaning is clear. Flavell has recommended taking the *productive* control of language out of the young child's hands. Now I'd like to suggest that, in a sense, we also take the productive control of language out of the experimenter's hands. That is, that we exert the same care in making sure that our subjects understand us that Flavell advocates we use in making sure that we understand our subjects. It might be wise to *instruct* the child and ask our questions of him through means other than language. For example, if a child really doesn't believe that he has the option of using the response "no change" or "no difference" when asked if the two sets are the same, then maybe we ought to show him that this is a legitimate option. One way to do this might be to show him a short film of another child being instructed on and performing a similar task and making use of all legitimate responses for that task under appropriate circumstances. Of course, this would have to be done carefully so that subjects would not imitate the exact responses they had just observed. This technique also might be used to check the effectiveness of the instructions for a particular task by asking subjects to describe what they thought the child in the film was supposed to do.

Another general approach that investigators using Piagetian tasks might try would be to create situations where the subject is reinforced for paying close attention and responding correctly (as Mehler and Bever did by using M&M's). That is, make it worthwhile (without biasing responding) for the child to show you what he knows.

We have to develop unambiguous methods for demonstrating the rules of our game to the child so that he doesn't have to infer them for himself. We also need to determine all the possible response options for a given situation and then construct unambiguous ways for the child to show us which option he is using.

Recognizing that there is an intimate relationship between general cognitive development and language development, I'd like to ask that we make a concentrated effort to separate the effects of one on the other so that our knowledge of general cognitive development is not confounded by the child's linguistic competence. This may be more an ideal thought than a real possibility; however, if successful, it seems well worth the effort.

Open Discussion

The controversial Mehler and Bever studies mentioned by Flamer elicited comments from both Beilin and Inhelder. This matter was then dropped, and Flavell's final methodological suggestion was the last matter discussed before Inhelder and Piaget made closing remarks.

Beilin led off with his views on the Mehler and Bever work.

BEILIN

I'd like to comment on the Mehler and Bever studies. The question as to whether Mehler and Bever are correct or not can be made on two bases. The first is a question of the logic of their experiment and the second is in regard to the actual empirical collection of the data.

Assessing the Mehler and Bever study in terms of the logic of the experiment, I think it is fairly clear that, given the way they conducted their experiment, one could not possibly make the kinds of inferences they did. And the same thing is true of their second experiment. It is for this reason that I made no effort to replicate their study; there is no point in replicating a study that was basically illogically formed. I didn't really deny the fact that they got their results; the results are there, but they're uninterpretable in the sense in which they meant them. The methodology is of such character that it confounds every one of the variables that they're attempting to test. It's impossible to make an adequate inference about what, in fact, they're claiming does develop in the child. Others who have collected data from 2-year-olds, including Rothenberg, Linda Siegel, and the Geneva group, do not get the kind of results that Mehler and Bever obtained.

Inhelder reported that Mehler and Bever agree that conservation was not really involved in their tasks, but she added that the question of what was going on in these subjects is interesting and in need of investigation. She also noted that Sinclair had found that normal children over 4 years old could understand "same," "more," and "less," but that the ability to label the things this way comes much later. Retardates, however, don't understand either.

Moss recounted some of the misunderstandings of questions she found among preschool children while developing her Tests of Basic Experiences. Kamii reported that by using the clinical method, Sinclair quickly got talking from preschool disadvantaged children who had said little during several previous months in Kamii's class. From this she inferred that Flamer was wrong in criticizing the clinical method as too verbal.

FLAMER

I don't disagree with what you're saying, but I'm really not talking about the child's ability to talk or your using his language. The point is, if you use his words, do those words mean the same thing to you that they mean to the child? All I'm trying to suggest is that maybe there are other ways (other than through language) of determining what the child is trying to tell you. I want some additional confirmation. I'm not denying that the clinical method is a valuable technique and some absolutely necessary information comes out of it, but I'd like to be a little more sure that the child is saying the same thing I think he's saying and that he understands the same thing that I think I'm trying to tell him.

FLAVELL

It seems to me, if you look at the child's language production—especially in a situation where he's trying to justify his reasoning or otherwise communicate to you the basis for his judgment—you've got some funny things going on. Clearly it's possible for the child to have genuinely reasoned in a certain way and not be able in that situation to tell you. Now that doesn't mean he couldn't under any circumstances, but I think as a rule I understand more about my thinking than I am saying, and I think that's just as true of the child. Now, if you were actually to present him with those arguments that you already know young children sometimes give, and if he can understand those arguments, it seems to me he'll have a better chance of finding out which argument, if any, actually underlies the reasoning and is true. Certainly we know it's a chancey thing whether children are saying what they know or whether they *can* say what they know. And I think there's a good deal of evidence that people who comprehend things crystallize possible roads of thinking. I should think you might reject those ideas that don't make any sense to you and you might accept the ones that seem true. This kind of track hasn't been tried enough in our research.

Kamii asserted that a multiple choice situation suggests things to children that they would not otherwise have thought of. Flavell agreed, but noted that if you offer the child a group of two choice problems, you can arrange them systematically so as to get an unambiguous scale without requiring the child to say a word.

SMOCK

I want to ask Dr. Flavell if he sees the differentiation between receptive and productive as primarily a methodological problem as opposed to the possibility that there are some theoretical implications as to whether or not an individual might recognize an appropriate solution without being able to produce it. I think your last illustration implies that it's primarily a methodological variation that will help us learn more.

FLAVELL

That's a hard question, and I'm not sure that I can satisfactorily answer it. I certainly do mean methodological, but the second thing that you mention is a difficult issue. It seems to me that we need to get the best window we can find to what the child latently knows. And how do you do that? I'm not sure this method is going to work, but it seems to be one of the best to try.

DE VRIES

I think that part of our confusion over the child's verbal inconsistency is sometimes a lack of recognition that the inconsistency is really a characteristic of the child's level of development. I was really puzzled for a long time over the fact that when I gave a conservation of mass test with candy and said to the child, "Show me the one that has more to eat," he would pick one. And then when I asked him which one was bigger he would pick the other one. The analysis of these data shows that the lowest nonconservers and the top conserving group are consistent in their use of these terms. They say that the one that has more to eat and one that is bigger are the same. They see it as a simultaneous thing. But there's a group in between who says one thing is more in one way and one is greater in another. It seems to me that this may be an instance of the decentration process that is going on that may lead to the establishment of the conservation.

INHELDER

I am in full agreement with you that it's really in the intermediate stage that the child is becoming aware of more and more cues and not just of one. So it's not just an error of methodology as some have said.

Closing Remarks

by BARBEL INHELDER
and JEAN PIAGET

Professors Inhelder and Piaget were asked to make any statements they wished and thought appropriate at the short closing session of the conference. Professor Inhelder chose to leave the substantive remarks to Piaget and limited herself to the brief remarks below. Piaget's comments which follow were the final ones of the conference.

INHELDER

I wish to thank CTB/McGraw-Hill and particularly the organizers of this excellent symposium, Dr. Ford and Dr. Green, both for extending their invitation to this conference and because they had this meeting in the most beautiful place in the United States.

It was marvelous to meet old friends and to make new acquaintances. I realize that the Piagetian family is growing every year in a geometric progression. It is, of course, reassuring to know that Piaget's work and hypotheses are fruitful and lead to new research and that at least some of our exploratory research is confirmed by a large body of hard-nosed and carefully analyzed data like Dr. Lovell's and Dr. Tuddenham's. It is still more exciting to learn new methods, like the very elegant procedures for the mathematical analysis of cognitive data that Dr. Bentler has shown us.

Also it is very refreshing to be confronted with strong criticism, and I hope that the Piaget family will never become a church with its own Ten Commandments. It was very gratifying to see that so much research in this area is being conducted. I would be very grateful to all of you if reprints and copies of work in progress could be sent to us for our archives in Geneva, so that we can keep up to date with what is happening elsewhere in the world.

And, finally, please come to see us in Geneva so we may return your splendid hospitality.

PIAGET

First of all, I should like to join Bärbel Inhelder in thanking you for giving us the opportunity to take part in this symposium.

I should like to make two or three comments on the problems we have encountered. They will be very short, since my command of English is not sufficient for me to understand native speakers—I find it much easier to understand English when it is spoken by Russians or Frenchmen. If I have had a chance to study the papers in advance, I can follow, but unfortunately they arrived a little late. Because of this, I shall comment only on what I have read.

We have encountered many basic problems. First, there is that of the ordinal succession of stages, which belongs to the realm of general psychology. This general psychological problem has led us on to question the very existence of stages. I think that one of the best ways of finding a solution to this problem is, first of all, to study the succession of these stages in spontaneous development and then to compare these observations with those made during learning experiments, such as those described by Bärbel Inhelder, which she carries out with her collaborators. One theory prevalent today maintains that development is a succession of "bits" of learning.

By contrast, if stages do exist, then it is not development which is dependent upon the laws of learning, but the different forms of learning which are dependent upon development and governed by the laws, or limits, of the different levels, i.e., the different stages which may be observed in spontaneous development. This is one of the problems Inhelder spoke about this morning. It is very striking to see that when in learning situations we seek to make use of the many factors already observed in spontaneous development (i.e., to reproduce spontaneous development as closely as possible), we obtain proof of the importance of the selection of a learning procedure. It is quite impossible to gain positive results through the use of a learning procedure involving strategies of which the child, at his particular stage, is incapable. There are boundaries, or limits, which cannot be crossed.

There is a second problem, however, which has come under discussion during the last few days. This is ordinal succession, not in general development, but in the development of the individual—in other words, the problem of the possible use for diagnostic purposes of data obtained through the clinical method, the "psychometrization" of the clinical method, to use Tuddenham's expression. Now, we are no longer dealing with a problem of general psychology, but of differential psychology, psychology of the individual—of each individual. This, I must confess, is a problem I have unfortunately never studied, because I have no interest whatsoever in the individual. I am very interested in general mechanisms, intelligence and cognitive functions, but what makes one individual different from another seems to me—and I am speaking personally and to my great regret—far less instructive as regards the study of the human mind in general.

Nevertheless, an attempt such as Tuddenham's seems exciting because it appears to link these two areas of interest, although, as seems inevitable, it encounters certain difficulties. How can one apply in a "psychometrizable" form, in the form of tests, information gained through the clinical method?

The data I have obtained presuppose in each case a certain activity on the part of the subject. How much time should one allow a subject when he is working on a problem? How long does one give him—not simply to "mobilize" what he already knows, but to reach the level of which he is capable? What new inventions can be elicited on this occasion? This is the problem. In the discussion of Tuddenham's work, this problem was, in fact, brought up. But there is another one: will this activity which one tries to elicit enable the subject to reach solutions characteristic of various higher levels? Here, once again, we come up against the problem of stages and their boundaries. These very delicate problems have opened up new lines of research which, as yet, are far from exhausted.

Other problems have been raised by Elkind—in particular, that of preschool education, for which he has put forward a certain number of new ideas. It is obvious that if you try to teach too much at the preschool level and thus to accelerate development greatly by making a child acquire knowledge normally gained only after the age of 8 or 9 years, then you will fail. It is clear that this type of education is not ideal. But, on the other hand, I think that Elkind was a little too pessimistic in maintaining that preschool education is more or less pointless. Even if we do not teach directly what will be taught later on, we can pave the way by means of a preparation that may later be extremely useful for the child's further development. For example, we are not going to start teaching a 5 or 6-year-old numerical structures since the child has not by then acquired conservation of number. But if we prepare him fairly early on, using exercises in handling materials of classification and ordering, etc., then it is not impossible that we shall have helped the construction of number at a later stage. This problem may perhaps be linked very closely with that of the ordinal succession of stages in development which I feel needs extremely detailed study.

I shall not dwell upon the problem of developmental mechanisms which was discussed in connection with Beilin's paper, but I should like to say that the main problem here is not to determine whether the new knowledge acquired comes from the external environment or stems from genetic preformation, but to establish the method of construction of true novelties. During development, we witness a whole series of original and new constructions. Beilin answered me by talking about species-specific novelties. There are also, however, the novelties which are *invented* by the individual. The whole of human history is a history of *inventions* and *creations* which do not stem simply from the potentialities of the human race as a whole—we cannot yet even imagine to what heights human invention will lead us—but which are also empowered by initiatives, by individual activities (and, of course, interindividual activities, since one cannot dissociate the individual from his social environment). There is thus a basic problem in the solution of which I feel the biologists may be able to play an important part. They have not yet said their final word on this point and have not yet mastered the problem of novelties. Even DNA is not identical in all species, and how are transformations of the genetic system carried out? Darlington has spoken of an evolution of the genetic system itself. Here, we have a series of novelties—this is a central problem, initially biological and then psychological, which to me seems to dominate the whole question of development and stages.

Finally, my last comment. Engelmann said that I have proved nothing. He is quite right. There are many things that I have not proved. I think there are two ways of proving something: the first is to study one problem in as great detail as possible, using statistical methods, calculations of variations, and whatever else you may think feasible; the second is to keep moving from problem to problem, from field to field, seeking—and this is what counts—convergences and links between one field and another. Having for many years studied logico-mathematical operations with Bärbel Inhelder, we have recently moved on to other problems: mental images, memory, processes of spontaneous learning, and so on. And for the last 2 or 3 years, I myself have concentrated on causality, where there remains so much to do and unravel. When you pass from one field to another, either there is chaos or you find results which link up with observations already made, i.e., you find all sorts of convergences and analogies. I personally think it is far more satisfactory, as far as proof is concerned, to find these convergences and connections between fields than it is to work on only one problem using increasingly accurate statistical methods. Such statistical methods are of great value for critical purposes, but it is not with them that we should start off.

Those are the few points I wished to raise at the end of this symposium. Thank you once again so much for your welcome, your comments, your criticisms, and in fact for all the valid discussion of the past 2 or 3 days.

Retrospect and Prospect[1]

DONALD ROSS GREEN
CTB/McGraw-Hill

The preceding 200 or so pages represent the proceedings of a conference announced as "The CTB/McGraw-Hill Conference on Ordinal Scales of Cognitive Development" but referred to universally among those concerned with the management and execution of the affair as the "Piaget Conference." These two descriptions represent the basic theme of the conference. That is, as noted in the Preface, the conference was conceived and convened in the belief that there was a need to establish closer working relationships between the fields of measurement and development and in the hope that Piagetian theory with its implied possibility of ordinal scales provided the basis for such a rapprochement.

A dozen years ago in his APA presidential address on "The Two Disciplines of Psychology," Cronbach compared the "tight little island" of experimental psychology with "the sort of Holy Roman Empire" of correlational psychology (Cronbach, 1957). Among the "principalities" of the latter discipline were both psychometrics and developmental psychology. He noted in passing that there was another bipolar factor in the scientific values of psychologists independent of the dimension with which he was concerned. He described this second dimension of values as ranging from verbal to quantitative. This dimension is relevant here because test theory and developmental psychology have, in fact, gone their separate ways for a number of years in spite of their close partnership in the early years of this century, at least partly because the two approaches do place differential value on quantitative and verbal statements. Psychometric theory has come to involve increasingly sophisticated mathematical formulations of interrelationships among test scores; developmental psychology has come farther toward making a common cause with experimental psychology than it has with mental measurement, in spite of its ties to the latter from their common origins.

The measurement of intellectual status and growth is one of the classical domains of study in psychology. Indeed, one can argue that a large portion of the work in developmental psychology represents an outgrowth of that tradition. Psychometric theory has, of course, developed in the context of the measurement of intellectual functioning. Thus, both fields have a tradition of

[1] I would like to thank my colleagues George Burket and Samuel C. Reed for their helpful comments on this paper.

working with intelligence tests and both, by and large, seem to have taken the Binet type of instrument as their given starting point. Certainly, most developmental psychologists have been more prone to use these tests to study intellectual growth than they have been to spend time in questioning the rationale of the instruments. After all Binet and his successors chose those tasks most clearly related to age, and in any case, until a theory came along which was sufficiently explicit to be translatable into a really different sort of measuring instrument, one could hardly demand that such tests be built. Furthermore, there has been a lot to be learned from the use of extant tests (these possibilities are not yet exhausted) even though these instruments were developed empirically and without any clear theoretical bases for the selection of their items.

There is still, in fact, little reason to claim that the composition of current intelligence tests is based on anything but the fact that similar items have proved useful in the past. For psychometricians, as for developmentalists, tests were for checking theories, not vice versa. Theorizing about intelligence among psychometric scholars has been largely devoted to questions about the structure of abilities and traits. Psychometric models have rarely enabled one to say much about the course of intellectual development, although they are based on the assumption that the components of intelligence grow in quantity during childhood. Test theory has made dramatic progress in the last 50 years, but it has not concerned itself with the mechanisms of intellectual growth.

However, the effort to understand that topic has been the central theme of Piaget's work. Piaget also started in psychology with Binet, working on the standardization of traditional test items in the Binet laboratory, but he early became interested in understanding how children responded to these items. He was led by this work to abandon the use of such items and the whole testing enterprise in favor of his "méthode clinique," which was less concerned with quantification than with the meaning of children's answers to questions. Nevertheless, his work has stayed closer to measurement than that of many, and after more than 40 years, he has now developed a description of cognitive development which may offer a new basis for developing standardized tests of intellectual functioning.

Thus, it is not coincidental that his theoretical formulations now seem to offer the greatest hope of reestablishing a functional working partnership between the two areas of psychology. Because his theory of intellectual growth specifies a sequence of development of cognitive abilities, there are clear possibilities of benefit to both fields if instruments based on the theory can be developed.

For those interested in the theory, the benefits should be obvious: the refinement and systematization of the whole elaborate Piagetian framework would become immediately practicable. Developmental psychologists, like other kinds of psychologists, have not found it easy to come up with directly relevant criterion measures; a comprehensive set of standard scales plainly based upon the theory could meet that need.

Perhaps, however, the greatest potential benefit accrues to measurement because of the fact that such a test offers the possibility of avoiding two very serious pitfalls in the use of current measures of intellectual ability. A test which could place a person on a scale of intellectual development not based solely on norms would have a kind of meaning intelligence test scores do not now have but which is sometimes erroneously attributed to them. That is, one could say something about where an individual or group stood in relation to a standard of development which would give a real indication of what that meant he could do intellectually; present tests cannot really do this. At the same time, it would not be necessary to say anything about whether the person was better or worse than anyone else. It would still be possible to do so if one wished, but it would no longer be a requisite feature of a description of his abilities. Since the invidious and sometimes inappropriate comparisons which are part and parcel of our current norm-based tests have become, quite properly, major objections to their use in schools, the potential value of what would be essentially a criterion-referenced test of intellectual ability is substantial. In short, Piagetian theory appears to be an ideal context for a meeting of minds among psychometric and developmental psychologists, and hence the Piaget Conference with its hopeful title of Conference on Ordinal Scales of Cognitive Development.

Were the hopes realized? The answer seems to be "partly," although some might say that "only a little" is fairer representation of the outcome. The negative view can be expressed and disposed of quickly: it is fair to say that, by and large, those concerned with development and Piagetian theory talked about those concerns and did little to relate their discussion to measurement issues, while those concerned with measurement did not do much better with developmental issues, although probably developmental problems got more attention. However, there were some constructive exchanges of view; further-more, there were some who were, in effect, in the middle from the beginning (e.g., Tuddenham, whose self-classification of differential psychologist fell exactly in the middle of the scale between the quantitative and verbal extremes in Cronbach's chart). But most to the point is the fact that the problems discussed all had relevance to the central issue as that issue was seen by whoever had the floor, thus permitting others to see the problem in new lights.

From one point of view, the ideal outcome of the conference would have been the complete specification of the steps necessary to develop a set of scales along with a description of the numbers and kinds of scales needed. These scales would provide explicit data about the developmental status of an individual in reference to the invariant sequence of stages postulated by Piaget. Also helpful would be the specification of the nature of movement along the scale and the conditions which produce or increase that movement. Tuddenham reported on a nearly standardized set of Piagetian tasks he was developing and Lovell described briefly the new British Scale of Intelligence still under construction which will provide some information about developmental stages. However, neither instrument can be expected to provide a full description of the developmental status and growth of a person in the manner described above. There are a large number of difficulties, both psychometric and developmental, which preclude that outcome as things now stand, and it is to these problems that most of the attention at the conference was turned.

Piaget, in his opening address, began the conference in essentially that vein. He pointed to several basic questions about his theory whose answers would be necessary for full use of a scale of cognitive development based on his views. He asked if there are, in fact, the stages in the growth of intelligence he has described and if the structures he postulates really exist. Both he and Inhelder later tried to make it clear why they think that one must conclude that the structures are real and do form the basis for a sequence of stages in intellectual growth. He also commented on the related problem of the mechanisms for moving from one stage to the next. Finally, he said he had no adequate theory of the time lags, the décalages, that appear in his reports of the intellectual growth of children. He commented again on these matters in his closing remarks, elaborating on certain aspects of the last two matters in the light of Tuddenham's data and Beilin's remarks.

These questions are basic and were discussed at length throughout the conference. They are not measurement questions per se, but they are relevant when considering "Piagetian" scales. The first of them is plainly the fundamental one. Everyone agrees that time passes and children change, but not that these changes occur in a specified sequence of distinct stages. One can raise questions about the distinctness of the stages as well as the relationships between them, their number, the process of changing from one to another, and so forth, all of which are relevant to the matter of measurement.

The distinctness of the Piagetian stages is important because it is relevant to know whether different stages are different quantitatively and/or in nature. The ordinal character of cognitive development can refer mainly to a sequence in time, to discriminable increases in the quantity of one or more traits over time, or thirdly, to a structural hierarchy whose sequence has a logic beyond that of increasing quantity.

The first of these three possible meanings is the simplest and is included in the other two. A developmental theory which asserts C follows B and B follows A in time, but which does not characterize $A, B,$ and C as having any quantitative or logically necessary relationships to each other, would perforce lead to a "scale" whose ordinality was based only on its asserted connection to the time scale; it is also possible, of course, to develop instruments which are ordinal only in this manner from more adequate theories by simply not making use of the propositions about quantity or logical necessity to be found in the theories. Much of the Vineland Social Maturity Scale could be considered an ordinal scale of this type as can some, but not all, of the "growth gradients" offered by Gesell and Ilg (1943).

The second of these is the more traditional psychometric meaning and the one most developmentalists accept either explicitly or implicitly when they use concepts such as mental age.

The Piagetian position is the last of these three, and both he and Inhelder took some pains to be explicit about their view on this matter. This position seemed to be accepted by most of those at the conference, and some acted as though there was no issue. Furthermore, there were times when people appeared to be treating all these views as equivalent. Nevertheless, Piaget's view was disputed directly in one session and at several other points reference to the possibility of alternate views was made; for example, both Lovell and Inhelder referred to the topic during their comments on Goldschmid's paper, as did Nivette in his discussion of Bentler's paper.

The most direct confrontation was that between Engelmann and Kamii. Engelmann was arguing for the first of the three possibilities listed above although, even more, he was denying the logical necessities of the Piagetian view. Thus Englemann offered the principal example of a position in disagreement with that of Piaget about the existence of the stage sequence. The fact that Engelmann and Kamii drew contradictory conclusions from the same data suggests that disagreements about this will persist for some time. To be sure, the Englemann—Kamii study was hurried to meet the conference deadline, but the history of psychology does not suggest that such arguments are settled by "crucial" experiments.

The argument is obviously important if, as Engelmann maintains, the Piagetian sequence is not inevitable and can be rearranged and short cut by instruction, any interpretation of a scale based on Piagetian tasks would perforce be normative in nature, thereby losing one of the major advantages (if not *the* major advantage) that might be gained from such a scale. The amount of information contained in a score is much less in that case since you no longer know for certain what preceded and what will follow in that person's intellectual growth.

Note that it is not the measurement process that is at issue here, but the nature of the relationship among a set of psychological phenomena that is to be measured. And note also that to be able to talk of measuring relationships is unusual in psychometrics, because few standard measurement problems involve situations in which an underlying theory makes the measurement task one of determining these interrelationships. Thus, for example, it is normal for a test score to be a function of the number of correct perceptions of some situation or phenomenon, but it is not normal for a test score to be determined by which perceptions are correct and which ones are incorrect, as in a conservation task. Approaches to measurement which consider sequences of logically interrelated phenomena clearly need much more study. It would be interesting indeed if one could develop instruments whose interrelationships permitted statements of logical necessity or sufficiency.

Equally important are some similar issues raised by Beilin in his paper from the developmental point of view. He contrasted the Piagetian position with the quantitative one. For quite different reasons than Engelmann, he raised questions about the appropriateness of concluding that cognitive growth can be adequately measured by an ordinal scale. His central concern was the nature of the stage construct and its relation to the idea of developmental processes. His analysis of these matters led him to suggest that in using measurement procedures, such as scalogram analysis, to study performances on Piagetian tasks, too little attention has been given to the fit of these procedures with Piagetian theory. Unfortunately Beilin did not elaborate on these points and, perhaps because Piaget did not believe that Beilin defined certain questions about his theory correctly, there was no substantial discussion of this interesting and important issue.

These examples show that numerous questions in need of study arise when psychometricians look seriously at measures of development through the eyes of developmentalists and when developmentalists consider theories of cognitive growth from the viewpoint of psychometrics. They also show even more plainly that when one considers the measurement problems implicit in the theory, the Piagetian approach offers both domains rich food for thought.

The fact that the measurement issues discussed at the conference were not limited to traditional psychometric questions illustrates the fact that Piaget and his colleagues have been able to consider growth without making all the standard assumptions which most developmental theorists seem to have taken from psychometrics without question. Piagetian theory, as a meeting ground for the two kinds of psychology, does not fall along the verbal-quantitative dimension that has seemed to differentiate the two because the theory's epistemological emphasis points in new directions and thereby opens up many possibilities.

Extensive work needs to be done to realize these possibilities; Flavell's paper illustrates this point. The question of the language-to-cognition inference he explored comes alive as a question of theoretical as well as practical measurement import when examined in the context of Piagetian theory and his paper makes it clear that much can be learned from its pursuit, but that the pursuit has just begun. Piaget's efforts now make it possible to think of measurement arrangements in which logical networks determine the interpretation of a child's set of responses instead of relying on empirical comparisons of the responses of many children.

Hence it seems possible that further meetings of the sort represented by this conference could produce useful results; the two fields are indeed principalities of the same empire and have much more in common and much more to offer each other than appears at first blush.

Monotonicity Analysis: An Alternative to Linear Factor and Test Analysis

PETER M. BENTLER
University of California, Los Angeles

As is well known among psychometricians, but little popularized among test constructors and users, the multicategory and binary scoring schemes used in most psychological tests hinder the effective use of factor analysis in discovering dimensions underlying the interrelations of variables. Indeed, when the measurement scale is ordinal, and one has confidence only in the rank order of the values of a variable, the theory of reliability (e.g., Gulliksen, 1950; Lord and Novick, 1968) and factor analysis (e.g., Harman, 1967; Horst, 1965), as well as other methodologies (Stevens, 1968), generate inappropriate procedures for psychometric and statistical analysis. Reliability coefficients and factorial results are sensitive to monotonic (order-preserving) transformations of the variables, and thus results generated using linear psychometric models tend to be arbitrary, reflecting the arbitrary measurement scale selected for various variables. Monotonicity analysis represents a psychometric technique for determining the reliability and internal structure of variables which generates results that are meaningful and invariant under any linear or monotonic transformation of variables.

The example of a perfect Guttman scale can serve to point out the difficulties inherent in applying inappropriate reliability or factor theory to binary items, the type of items used in the majority of psychological tests. The items comprising a Guttman scale are such that when arranged in order of increasing difficulty, each examinee passes all items up to a certain point and fails all items thereafter. Thus, for the persons in Table A-1 the four items form a perfect Guttman scale. The items are all perfectly monotonically related to one another,

TABLE A-1   EXAMPLE OF A PERFECTLY HOMOGENEOUS SCALE

PERSON	ITEM NUMBER 1	2	3	4
1	+	+	+.	+
2	+	+	+	+
3	+	+	+	−
4	+	+	+	−
5	+	+	−	−
6	+	+	−	−
7	+	−	−	−
8	+	−	−	−
9	+	−	−	−
10	−	−	−	−
p(Yes)	.9	.6	.4	.2

TABLE A-2   CHARACTERISTICS OF TABLE (A-1) DATA

(A) HEIGHT	(B) LATENT CONTINUUM	(C) PROBABILITY OF "YES"	(D) ITEM NUMBER	(E) PERSON NUMBER	(F) ITEM
		0		1, 2	
		.1			I am over 6' tall.
6'		.2	4		
		.3		3, 4	
5'6"		.4	3		I am over 5'6" tall.
		.5		5, 6	
5'2"		.6	2		I am over 5'2" tall.
		.7		7, 8, 9	
		.8			I am over 5' tall.
5'		.9	1		
		1.0		10	

and can be said to be manifestations of a single latent trait on which each person and item can be perfectly represented as a single point. Thus, the data matrix of Table A-1 can arise from an error-free manifestation of the latent continuum presented in Table A-2. Let us suppose the continuum (b) is "height" (a), and the items as replied to by subjects were questions regarding their height, as shown in the last column (f) of table A-2. Then the items represent points on the continuum (d) and persons fall somewhere on the same continuum (e). Persons cannot be placed exactly on the continuum since four items only allow the continuum to be chopped into five segments. A person can, however, be placed into a segment, so that we know, for example, since persons 1 and 2 say they are over 6 feet tall, they fall into the topmost segment.

Although it is obvious that the items of Tables A-1 and A-2 are perfectly internally consistent, and fall on one latent continuum, reliability formulations of internal consistency as defined, for example, by the Kuder-Richardson 20 or Cronbach alpha formulas (Cronbach, 1951), would have one believe that internal consistency is imperfect, and factoring procedures would have one believe he is dealing with several dimensions (Horst, 1965). Clearly, traditional psychometrics are misleading. Finally, if we obtain only a few cuts (d) on the latent continuum (b), and wish to make no assumptions about the "true" distributions of items or persons, we cannot assume that the continuum represents anything more than an ordinal scale. The placement of the height (a) items on the continuum, as marked (b), has been sliced into equal-length segments. We can have confidence only in the rank order of the persons and items.

Early models for performing monotonicity analyses were presented by Guttman (1944) and Loevinger (1947), following the lead of Walker (1931), but these authors were not clearly aware they were dealing with the general problem of analyzing monotonic relationships. The development of a general methodology to handle latent dimensions was both spurred and hindered by the early work of Guttman and Loevinger. Guttman's coefficient of reproduceability was quite outside the traditions of test theory, dealing with answer patterns instead of correlations or variances. It became the target of well-known criticism (e.g., Festinger, 1947). The coefficient was defined for a scale, and for an item, as the proportion of responses to the items in a scale, or to a given item, which could be correctly reproduced from the knowledge of the rank position of persons on the scale. Being defined in this manner, however, there was no useful way of assigning monotonicity to pairs of items so that the predictability could be analyzed into component sources. In providing her coefficient of homogeneity for two binary items, Loevinger made a significant advance. This coefficient was ϕ/ϕ max, and has been espoused as useful recently by Horst (1966). Unfortunately, however, ϕ/ϕ max provided an inadequate conception of monotonicity for the general multicategory case, and even in the binary case needed replacement by $\phi/|\phi|$ min for negative relationships (Bentler, 1966; Guilford, 1965). Furthermore, in dealing with the monotonicity or homogeneity of a composite, both Loevinger and Horst overlooked some fundamental attributes which it would seem should be possessed by a homogeneity coefficient. Loevinger indicated quite reasonably that any coefficient of homogeneity for a scale should be based upon the interitem homogeneity coefficients she had previously described. She chose the index

$$H_t = \frac{V_t - V_{min}}{V_{max} - V_{min}}$$

where V_t refers to the variance of the total test scores, V_{max} refers to the maximum variance possible, given the same score distributions on the items, and V_{min} refers to the minimum variance possible for a test with the same item score distributions. In contrast to the general criticism given Guttman's work, Loevinger's was simply ignored. Her coefficient was probably not neglected because of its break with classical test theory, but because it largely duplicated the more well-known and controversial coefficient of reproduceability proposed by Guttman. In addition, the judgment of experts such as Guilford indicated that the coefficient was largely irrelevant to successful measurement—"that many a test with low H_t can still be highly reliable and useful" (1954, p. 387). The homogeneity coefficient proposed by Loevinger tended to give values much below that of the equivalent Kuder-Richardson reliability coefficients, and it is likely that few investigators wished to be caught presenting a small value when they could just as soon present a larger value by more traditional means. The reason for the small values, it seems, had not previously been made clear.

The rationale of any monotonicity analysis certainly applies equally well to a set of items having identical distributions as to items having differing distributions. In the general case, it may be shown by some simple algebra that Loevinger's coefficient reduces to $H_t = \bar{c}/\bar{c}_{max}$, the ratio of average interitem covariance to average maximum interitem covariance. In the binary case, when all item means are equal, the variances of all items are equal and the maximum value for all correlations is unity. In that case, the variance term can be factored out of the numerator and denominator of Loevinger's coefficient and canceled, and the coefficient may be written as $H_t = \bar{\phi}$, the average phi coefficient. It is then immediately obvious that no matter how many items might be included in a scale—even an infinite number of items—the scale would not become perfectly homogeneous by Loevinger's criterion unless all of the items were perfectly correlated. Loevinger's criterion is clearly at variance with classical test theory in this situation: linear test theory would say that a total score becomes perfectly reliable as the number of components increases to infinity, provided that the components have some reliability. Thus Loevinger's coefficient should be applicable to describing component homogeneity rather than total score homogeneity. No wonder Loevinger's homogeneity estimates tended to be so low!

Horst (1966) considered the V_{min} term in Loevinger's coefficient as superfluous, suggesting instead V_t/V_{max}. Unfortunately, it too suffers from being based on an inadequate coefficient (ϕ/ϕ max), and has the same drawback noted above for Loevinger's coefficient. In addition, this coefficient has the sad characteristic of being greater than zero even when all items are mutually independent. This is because the test variance V_t will always be positive, even when all covariances are zero.

Thus there were, and remain, a number of strong objections to the early monotonic scaling approaches. The models were severely restricted in application. They required error-free data, were applicable primarily to binary items possessing positive intercorrelations, and could not deal at all with the ever-present problem of multidimensionality. These early procedures proved sufficiently sterile to lead Torgerson to say "it is immediately apparent that a considerable amount of work needs to be done on these models before they will become of much practical use" (1958, p. 358).

The extensions of Guttman scaling to the multidimensional case (e.g., Lingoes, 1963; Coombs, 1964) did not improve the situation, for these writers continued to deal with what might most generally be called manifest structure analysis, still requiring error-free data. Latent structure analysis (Lazarsfeld, 1959), the most reasonable general alternative to these approaches, requires assumptions which an investigator may well not wish to make about the form of underlying trace lines or latent continua. Similarly, while the approach of finding latent factors which may relate non-linearly to manifest variables (McDonald, 1962, 1967; Shepard & Carroll, 1966), is reasonable, these procedures consider the metric of the manifest variables as important in their own right rather than accidental. There is no need to do so. One approach to rejecting the metric of manifest variables was presented by Horst (1965), but it went so far as to "throw out the baby with the bathwater." In factoring binary matrices, Horst suggested removing the latent Guttman scale (simplex) from the matrix of covariance and factoring the residuals. But factoring the residuals ignores precisely the latent variable of most interest, the simplex. Thus, this approach would best be avoided.

The work of Shepard (1962a, 1962b) provided a computational breakthrough, loosening the metric requirements involved in finding the smallest space for a set of variables using only rank-order information on distances among variables (e.g., Guttman, 1968). This remarkable feat in turn led to various modifications which attempted to apply the smallest-space principles to binary and multicategory data matrices, such as the ones presented in Table A-1 and later tables of this paper (e.g., Lingoes, 1968; Lingoes and Guttman, 1967). These procedures, while ingenious and worthy of exploration, apparently require a number of fairly arbitrary decisions by the user, do not necessarily converge to the smallest possible space, may not recover the latent ordinal dimensions, and are in some instances not invariant under monotonic transformations of the original variables. An early attempt to provide a general solution to monotonic scaling, which avoided the problems just mentioned, was presented by Bentler (1966) and applied in several instances of dichotomous data (Bentler, 1968a, 1968b; Goldschmid and Bentler, 1968a). That approach is now largely superseded by monotonicity analysis. The goal of monotonicity analysis is to recover all ordinal latent dimensions without any metric assumptions for binary variables, while for multicategory variables it seeks to recover latent continua using only ordinal assumptions about the variables. Thus, for the data for Tables A-1 and A-2, monotonicity analysis aims to demonstrate that the data are perfectly internally consistent and that one latent continuum accounts for all observed data. The solution to this problem requires defining monotonicity and dimensionality.

RANK-ORDER CORRELATION

Suppose for two variables X and Y we observe the following scores in the population of N persons:

	PERSON				
VARIABLE	1	2	i	j	N
X	X_1	X_2	X_i	X_j	X_n
Y	Y_1	Y_2	Y_i	Y_j	Y_n

Pairs of persons are randomly sampled from the population, yielding scores (X_i, Y_i) and (X_j, Y_j). The line segment joining these points has positive slope if $[(X_i - X_j)(Y_i - Y_j)] > 0$, and such a pair of observations may be called concordant in the sense that the difference scores on X and Y possess the same sign. Similarly, if $[(X_i - X_j)(Y_i - Y_j)] < 0$, the pair of observations may be called discordant and the line segment joining the points has negative slope (Kruskal, 1958). Since concordance and discordance are ordinally invariant, i.e., the particular ordinal scale used for X and Y is irrelevant, it is convenient to define a coefficient of rank-order correlation as

$$\Psi = \frac{\Pr(\text{con})}{\Pr(\text{dis})} \qquad \text{(A-1)}$$

the ratio of the probability of concordance to the probability of discordance. It is interesting to note that in the special case that X and Y are binary or dichotomous variables and the joint frequency distribution is the fourfold table

$$Y$$

The rank-order correlation becomes

$$\Psi = \frac{bc}{ad} \cdot \tag{A-2}$$

This special case of Ψ has recently received the praise and attention of statisticians (Plackett, 1965; Edwards, 1963; Mosteller, 1968).

Although Ψ represents an excellent coefficient of rank-order correlation, it is convenient to make a monotonic transformation of Ψ to obtain a coefficient whose range is $+1$ to -1

$$m = \frac{\Pr(\text{con}) - \Pr(\text{dis})}{\Pr(\text{con}) + \Pr(\text{dis}) + 2\sqrt{\text{PR}(\text{con})\Pr(\text{dis})}} \tag{A-3}$$

which may be more conveniently written, using Kendall's (1955) notation for frequencies, as

$$m = \frac{P - Q}{P + Q + 2\sqrt{PQ}} \cdot \tag{A-4}$$

We may call this coefficient a coefficient of rank-order correlation or monotonicity.

PROPERTIES OF THE MONOTONICITY COEFFICIENT

The monotonicity coefficient has been defined for the population, with components being probabilities; the sample analogue simply utilizes relative frequencies or frequencies rather than probabilities and it is the maximum-likelihood estimator of the population coefficient. When the probability of concordance equals the probability of discordance, $P = Q$ and $m = 0$. Thus, when random sampling of pairs of X, Y values would lead equally often to observations of positive and negative slope, we may say the variables are independent. When the probability of concordance is zero $m = -Q/Q = -1.0$, indicative of perfect negative monotonicity. For zero probability of discordance, $m = P/P = 1.0$, perfect positive monotonicity. Reversal in ranking of either pair of variables simply reverses the role of P and Q, and thus the coefficient changes sign but remains equidistant from 0.

It is interesting to note that in the special case of binary variables, m is equivalent to Yule's Y coefficient. Furthermore, when the marginal distribution for binary variables X and Y is identical and symmetric, so that each marginal equals .5, the coefficient m equals ϕ, the product moment correlation. With binary variables, we see from (A-2) and (A-4) that

$$m = \frac{bc - ad}{bc + ad + 2\sqrt{abcd}} \; . \tag{A-5}$$

But when the marginals equal .5, $b = c$ and $a = d$, so we may write

$$m = \frac{bc - ad}{a^2 + b^2 + 2ab} \; . \tag{A-6}$$

Phi can generally be written as

$$\phi = \frac{bc - ad}{\sqrt{(a + b)\,(c + d)\,(b + d)\,(a + c)}} \tag{A-7}$$

but when $b = c$ and $a = d$, the denominator reduces to $a^2 + b^2 + 2ab$, equivalent to m in (A-6). This equivalence is useful for the analysis of binary variables.

The sampling distributions of the rank-order coefficients m and Ψ have been studied extensively for the binary case, and the reader may consult Goodman (1964) for methods of obtaining confidence limits for these coefficients. Additional statistical work is required for the general case.

FURTHER DESCRIPTION AND AN EXAMPLE

An alternate way of describing the coefficients Ψ and m may be useful. Let (X_k, Y_k) represent a pair of scores on X and Y with a certain probability, $Pr(X_k, Y_k)$, of occurrence. Each of $k = 1, ..., s$ possible *types* of paired scores has its own particular probability of being observed, subject to the restriction $\sum_s Pr(X_k, Y_k) = 1.0$. Under the hypothesis of independence, the probability of a particular set of two pairs, say (X_i, Y_i) and (X_j, Y_j), being observed is the product of their separate probabilities $Pr(X_i, Y_i) \cdot Pr(X_j, Y_j)$. The probability of concordance is simply the sum of these products for all combinations of scores which have $[(X_i - X_j)(Y_i - Y_j)] > 0$, while the probability of discordance amounts to an equivalent sum for all combinations which have $[(X_i - X_j)(Y_i - Y_j)] < 0$. This situation can be clarified graphically. Table A-3 lists the various possible pairs of (X_k, Y_k) scores with their associated (marginal) probabilities. The probability of a particular combination of pairs, say (X_1, Y_1) and (X_k, Y_k), is the product of marginal probabilities as entered in the table. The probabilities of concordance and discordance represent sums of probabilities for which the scores are concordant or discordant, as described above.

An example shows the scores of 7 persons as follows:

	PERSON						
	1	2	3	4	5	6	7
X	3	3	2	2	2	1	1
Y	3	2	3	2	2	1	1

The possible pairs of scores are listed in Table A-4, along with their marginal and joint probabilities. Table A-5 presents the products $(X_i - X_j)(Y_i - Y_j)$ for the various combination. The probability of concordance is then simply the sum of entries in Table A-4 for which the corresponding elements in Table A-5 are greater than zero—that is, $\frac{2}{49} + \frac{2}{49} + \frac{2}{49} + \frac{2}{49} + \frac{4}{49} + \frac{2}{49} + \frac{2}{49} + \frac{2}{49} + \frac{2}{49} + \frac{4}{49} = \frac{24}{49}$. The probability of discordance is the sum of the probabilities of the two cases in which minus signs appear in Table A-5—that is, $\frac{1}{49} + \frac{1}{49} = \frac{2}{49}$. These two probabilities can be entered in Eqs. (A-1) and (A-3) for calculation of the Ψ and m coefficients. In this case $\Psi = 12$, and $m = .55$.

TABLE A-3   MARGINAL AND JOINT PROBABILITIES OF
PAIRS UNDER INDEPENDENCE

	SCORE COMBINATION				MARGINAL PROBABILITY
	X_l, Y_l	X_k, Y_k	$\cdots$	X_s, Y_s	
X_l, Y_l	$[Pr(X_l, Y_l)]^2$	$Pr(X_l, Y_l)$ $\cdot Pr(X_k, Y_k)$	$\cdots$	$Pr(X_l, Y_l)$ $\cdot Pr(X_s, Y_s)$	$Pr(X_l, Y_l)$
X_k, Y_k	$Pr(X_k, Y_k)$ $\cdot Pr(X_l, Y_l)$	$[Pr(X_k, Y_k)]^2$	$\cdots$	$Pr(X_k, Y_k)$ $\cdot Pr(X_s, Y_s)$	$Pr(X_k, Y_k)$
$\cdots$	$\cdots$		$\cdots$	$\cdots$	$\cdots$
X_s, Y_s	$Pr(X_s, Y_s)$ $\cdot Pr(X_l, K_l)$	$Pr(X_s, Y_s)$ $\cdot Pr(X_k, Y_k)$	$\cdots$	$[Pr(X_s, Y_s)]^2$	$Pr(X_s, Y_s)$
Marginal probability	$Pr(X_l, Y_l)$	$Pr(X_k, Y_k)$	$\cdots$	$Pr(X_s, Y_s)$	1.0

TABLE A-4 MARGINAL AND JOINT PROBABILITIES FOR EXAMPLE OF 7 INDIVIDUALS

| | SCORE COMBINATIONS | | | | | MARGINAL PROBABILITY |
	(3, 3)	(3, 2)	(2, 3)	(2, 2)	(1, 1)	
(3, 3)	$\frac{1}{49}$	$\frac{1}{49}$	$\frac{1}{49}$	$\frac{2}{49}$	$\frac{2}{49}$	$\frac{1}{7}$
(3, 2)	$\frac{1}{49}$	$\frac{1}{49}$	$\frac{1}{49}$	$\frac{2}{49}$	$\frac{2}{49}$	$\frac{1}{7}$
(2, 3)	$\frac{1}{49}$	$\frac{1}{49}$	$\frac{1}{49}$	$\frac{2}{49}$	$\frac{2}{49}$	$\frac{1}{7}$
(2, 2)	$\frac{2}{49}$	$\frac{2}{49}$	$\frac{2}{49}$	$\frac{4}{49}$	$\frac{4}{49}$	$\frac{2}{7}$
(1, 1)	$\frac{2}{49}$	$\frac{2}{49}$	$\frac{2}{49}$	$\frac{4}{49}$	$\frac{4}{49}$	$\frac{2}{7}$
Marginal probability	$\frac{1}{7}$	$\frac{1}{7}$	$\frac{1}{7}$	$\frac{2}{7}$	$\frac{2}{7}$	1.0

TABLE A-5 PRODUCTS $(X_i - X_j)(Y_i - Y_j)$

	(3, 3)	(3, 2)	(2, 3)	(2, 2)	(1, 1)
(3, 3)	0	0	0	1	4
(3, 2)	0	0	−1	0	2
(2, 3)	0	−1	0	0	2
(2, 2)	1	0	0	0	1
(1, 1)	4	2	2	1	0

For computational purposes it is easier to obtain the $N(N-1)/2$ cross-products $(X_i - X_j)(Y_i - Y_j)$, $i \neq j$. There P can be taken to be twice the number of such cross products which are positive, and Q twice the number that are negative. (It is not necessary to compute all N^2 crossproducts because of the symmetry of the results). Thus for example, we obtain for the $\frac{7(6)}{2} = 21$ comparisons:

PAIR	PROD.	PAIR	PROD.	PAIR	PROD.	PAIR	PROD.	PAIR	PROD.	PAIR	PROD.
(1, 2)	0										
(1, 3)	0	(2, 3)	−1								
(1, 4)	1	(2, 4)	0	(3, 4)	0						
(1, 5)	1	(2, 5)	0	(3, 5)	0	(4, 5)	0				
(1, 6)	4	(2, 6)	2	(3, 6)	2	(4, 6)	1	(5, 6)	1		
(1, 7)	4	(2, 7)	2	(3, 7)	2	(4, 7)	1	(5, 7)	1	(6, 7)	0

Then $P = 2(12)$, $Q = 2(1)$, so that $\Psi = 12$ and $m = .55$, as before.

METRIC MONOTONICITY

In certain cases it is desirable to obtain a coefficient describing the monotonicity of the variables while maintaining the metric of the original variables, as when the variables have a physical representation. The coefficients Ψ and m have simply ignored the metric of the original variables, giving unit weight to concordance and discordance irrespective of the magnitude of the product $(X_i - X_j)$ $(Y_i - Y_j)$. Maintaining the metric implies that the probabilities entering the concordance and discordance formulas be weighted by the magnitude of the product $(X_i - X_j)$ $(Y_i - Y_j)$. Thus, we define $P^* = \sum_p [(X_i - X_j)(Y_i - Y_j) \cdot \Pr(X_i, Y_i), (X_j, Y_j)]$, for the p products $(X_i - X_j)(Y_i - Y_j) > 0$. Similarly $Q^* = -\sum_q [(X_i - X_j)(Y_i - Y_j) \cdot \Pr(X_i, Y_i), (X_j, Y_j)]$, for the q products $(X_i - X_j)(Y_i - Y_j) < 0$ (the minus sign makes the sum positive). Then

$$\Psi^* = P^*/Q^* \tag{A-8}$$

and

$$m^* = \frac{P^* - Q^*}{P^* + Q^* + 2\sqrt{P^* Q^*}} \tag{A-9}$$

For the example given, from Tables A-4 and A-5 we see that $1(\frac{2}{49}) + 4(\frac{2}{49}) + 2(\frac{2}{49}) + 2(\frac{2}{49}) + 1(\frac{4}{49}) = \frac{22}{49}$ for the upper diagonal, or $P^* = \frac{44}{49}$. $Q^* = -[1(\frac{1}{49}) + (-1)(\frac{1}{49})] = \frac{2}{49}$, so that $\Psi^* = 22$. This value is quite different from the metric-free Ψ value of 12. Computationally, it is again easier to simply sum the appropriate products in the $N(N-1)/2$ comparisons and double the result. Thus, from the previous paragraph, we see $P^* = 2(1 + 1 + 4 + 4 + 2 + 2 + 2 + 2 + 1 + 1 + 1 + 1) = 2(22) = 44$ while $Q^* = 2(1) = 2$. The denominator, $N^2 = 49$, cancels out in the computation of Eqs. (A-8) and (A-9) and can be ignored (as could, indeed, the "doubling" operation).

It will be obvious that between metric-free Eqs. (A-1) and (A-4) and the metric Eqs. (A-8) and (A-9) lies the metric of ranks. If individuals' scores on the variables are first transformed to ranks, and Eqs. (A-8) and (A-9) are utilized, a formula is obtained which is ordinally invariant, but which operates in the metric of rank order. This coefficient would be analogous to Spearman's rank-order correlation, just as Eqs. (A-1) and (A-4) are analagous to Kendall's τ rank correlation and Eqs. (A-8) and (A-9) relate to the metric-specific linear product moment correlation. All three versions of Ψ and m bear future study. The developments of the rest of this paper are applicable to all three monotonicity coefficients, but the first has been found extremely useful in multidimensional analyses, so it will be emphasized from here on.

MONOTONICITY OF A SET OF VARIABLES

A useful approach to describing the monotonicity of a set of n variables involves some function of all $n(n-1)/2$ intervariable monotonicities. The arithmetic mean does the job well, so that we may define the set by the average monotonicity $\overline{m}$. In a similar vein, we may define a *homogeneity* coefficient as the monotonic internal consistency of a composite variable composed of n variables as

$$h = \frac{n\overline{m}}{1 + (n-1)\overline{m}} \tag{A-10}$$

After some algebra, we obtain an equivalent expression for h as

$$h = \left[\frac{n}{n-1}\right]\left[1 - \frac{l'Il}{l'Ml}\right] \tag{A-11}$$

where l is a column vector of ones, I is the identity matrix, and M is an n by n matrix containing l's in the diagonal and the intervariable monotonicities in the off diagonal. $l'Il$ is equal to n, and $l'Ml$ simply represents the sum of elements in the matrix M. The homogeneity coefficient is thus explicitly defined as a stepped-up average of intervariable monotonicities. As such, it describes the internal consistency of a composite which rank-orders individuals in terms of the total number of category boundaries, across all variables, beyond which they fall. If the categories for each variable are given ordinal, unit-incremented values, then the composite consists of the total score across all such categories, or any monotonic transformation thereof. An example is the total score on a Guttman scale.

Several consequences of this definition of homogenity are immediately apparent. First, homogeneity increases rapidly with an increase in the number of items. This fact reflects the consideration that the number of possible discriminable categories for differentiating individuals increases as more variables (items) are added. Indeed, as the number of items increases to infinity, we see from Eqs. (A-10) and (A-11) that $h \rightarrow 1.0$ as long as $\overline{m} > 0$. This property is reasonable and represents an analogue to the Spearman-Brown formula in linear theory (h was constructed with this analogue in mind). It will be remembered that for dichotomous items of equal difficulty, the monotonicity coefficient amounts to a product-moment correlation. Then the matrix M is simply the correlation matrix R, and h is equivalent to a Kuder-Richardson formula. [Indeed, it is possible to calculate a "revised K-R 20" in the manner of Horst (1953) by letting $R_{xx} = 1 - n\overline{S}^2 (1 - \overline{m}) / S_x{}^2$, where $\overline{S}^2$ is the average variable variance and S_x^2 is the variance of the composite. This coefficient, like h, but unlike the K-R 20, can always reach unity. Its use amounts to assuming that an estimate of average "true" variance is $\bar{m}\bar{S}^2$, rather than the average covariance.)

Weighting for Maximal Homogeneity: Dimensions
The unit-weight scheme used in defining a composite's homogeneity is, of course, only a special case of a general set of weights applied to variables which could be used to define the homogeneity of a weighted composite. Weights which make the observed score composite most homogeneous may be useful. We find the vector of weights v for the tth composite by defining

$$h_t = \left[\frac{n}{n-1} \right] \left[1 - \frac{v'Iv}{v'Mv} \right] \qquad \text{(A-12)}$$

for the general case. The problem is one of finding the vector v which will maximize h_t. We can do this by maximizing the ratio

$$a_t^2 = \frac{v'Mv}{v'Iv} \qquad \text{(A-13)}$$

subject to the restriction that $v'v = 1$. We define the Lagrange multiplier a_t^2 in

$$v'Mv = v'Mv - a_t^2 (v'v - 1). \qquad \text{(A-14)}$$

The vector of partial derivatives is

$$\frac{\partial v'Mv}{\partial v} = 2Mv - 2a_t^2 v. \qquad \text{(A-15)}$$

To find the vector which maximizes $v'Mv$, we set Eq. (A-15) equal to zero

$$(M - a_t^2 I) v = 0. \qquad \text{(A-16)}$$

A solution of Eq. (A-16) with $v'v = 1$ requires a_t^2 to satisfy the determinantal equation

$$|M - a_t^2 I| = 0 .$$
(A-17)

It is obvious that the solution for the largest value of a_t^2 is the largest root of M, and the vector v is the corresponding eigenvector of M. Thus we may write the set of eigenvalues and eigenvectors of M as

$$M = VA^2 V'$$
(A-18)

where A^2 is the diagonal matrix of roots and V the orthogonal, normalized set of eigenvectors of M. These roots and vectors provide successive composites of decreasingly less homogeneity. In each case, the homogeneity of the composite may be expressed in terms of the roots of M as

$$h_t = \left(\frac{n}{n-1} \right) \left(1 - \frac{1}{a_t^2} \right) .$$
(A-19)

If the manifest data represent one perfectly homogeneous scale, all cells in M contain entries of unity, M is rank 1, and the root of M is n, the trace of M. Then Eq. (A-19) becomes

$$h_t = \left(\frac{n}{n-1} \right) \left(1 - \frac{1}{n} \right) = 1.0 .$$
(A-20)

This result obtains for a perfect Guttman scale, for example.

The procedures described in this section represent a principal—component type of dimensional analysis of the intervariable monotonicities of the observed scores. The resultant matrix $L = VA$ may be considered to yield indices of monotonicity of variables with the components of M. An unambiguous criterion exists for termination of the weighting process for determining additional composites; it is given by $a_t^2 = 1.0$ or $\Sigma a_t^2 > n$, whichever is smaller. When a root of M equals unity, it is seen from Eq. (A-19) that the homogeneity of the observed scores is zero; when the root is less than unity, the composite has negative homogeneity. Finally, where the sum of the roots, Σa_t^2, is greater than n, the sum of diagonal elements of the matrix, all systematic monotonicity has been extracted. Transformations of the dimensions are, of course, permissible as in any standard factor analysis.

It should be noted that the homogeneity weighting procedures described here are independent of the scale of the original variables. No matter what the ordinal scale for the original items, the monotonicity matrix M remains identical, and hence component weights as determined in Eqs. (A-12) through (A-19) remain identical. This conclusion results from the basic definition of homogeneity given in Eq. (A-11).

CHARACTERISTICS OF MONOTONICITY ANALYSIS

The input to a monotonicity analysis is analogous to that of a factor analysis. Where factor analysis takes a matrix of correlations, monotonicity analysis takes a matrix of monotonicity coefficients. The dimensionalizing process is similar to that of factor analysis with unities in the diagonals (principal-component analysis). The process aims to place the variables in a Euclidian space of minimum dimensionality. Just as in factor analysis, a loading matrix is computed which represents projections of variables on dimensions. Changing the scoring direction of a variable simply changes the sign, but not the magnitude, of any projection. The initial matrix may be transformed to yield other more interpretable dimensions; these may be correlated or uncorrelated, dependent upon the goal of the investigator. Variables having high projections on a given dimension are, among themselves, highly monotonically related, and thus may be combined to yield one derived composite variable according to any scoring system (e.g., integer-incremental ordinal) which maintains the intervariable monotonicities. The final product is a composite ordinal-scale variable possessing higher monotonic internal consistency (homogeneity) than any variable from which it was derived. The homogeneity of the observed composite is determined by using Eqs. (A-10) or (A-11).

The function specified for maximization—the homogeneity coefficient—has explicit solutions. Thus the problem of local maxima or minima which plagues virtually all other nonmetric factor analyses is completely circumvented in this approach. The solutions are unique up to final transformations of the dimensions; these primarily serve interpretive meaningfulness. In addition, since only one roots-and-vector resolution is required of the matrix M, the computational labor is minimal in comparison to other nonmetric approaches. Finally, if r sets of variables are monotonically related within sets but orthogonal across sets, the result must be an r-dimensional solution. It seems that a similar conclusion is not possible for other approaches.

A word of caution is in order for the computer programming of monotonicity analysis. The M matrix is, in general, not Gramian. Thus negative roots are likely to appear. The roots and vectors routine must be able to handle negative eigenvalues (most are not), or must be one which successively determines eigenvalues in order of magnitude, so that the procedure can terminate when a negative root estimate is encountered. Negative eigenvalues A^2 must be rejected before performing the multiplication VA to obtain the loading matrix, so as to avoid taking the square root of negative numbers. Row sums of squares ("communalities") may be greater than 1.0; this should be no cause for concern.

A TWO-DIMENSIONAL EXAMPLE

To illustrate the capacity of monotonicity analysis to recover latent ordinal dimensions, a two-space example was constructed. Suppose the joint frequency distribution for 15 persons on variables X and Y is represented in Table A-6. Each number within the main box represents a person. We can assume that we have no metric for the variables, so that we cannot identify the scale used for either the X or Y axes. The 10-point notation represents an arbitrary ordinal scale to create a referent for Table A-7.

TABLE A-6 BIVARIATE FREQUENCY DISTRIBUTION

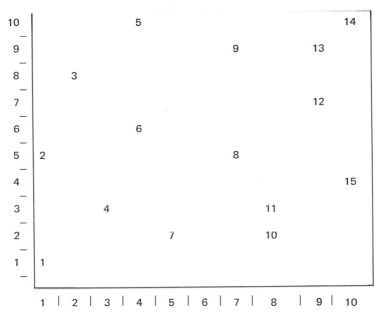

Binary Cuts

In test construction we write items which we hope will cut the latent continua at different points. With binary items, we expect our items to dichotomize the continua. If, for this example, we created four hypothetical binary items for each of the two continua, we should require a useful monotonicity analysis to recover the fact that our eight items actually represent exactly two ordinal dimensions.

Each of the two continua was artificially cut as depicted in Table A-7, generating four "items", eight items altogether. The scores 0 and 1 were assigned to the two segments for each item. Six items are scored so that the 1 score represents a higher number on the latent continuum than that corresponding to the 0 score. For items 3 and 7, however, the scoring direction was artificially reversed to make the problem more realistic. These various cuts of the continua, when referred to the original bivariate distribution in Table A-6, can be used to construct the 15 individuals' scores on the eight generated items by projecting the two-space location of an individual to the margins. These derived scores are presented in Table A-8. It should be pointed out that items 1 to 4 would represent one Guttman scale if the scoring for item 3 were reversed; similarly, for reversed scoring on item 7, items 5 to 8 represent a separate Guttman scale.

TABLE A-7   ARTIFICIAL CUTS FOR TWO-SPACE EXAMPLE

X CONTINUUM

ITEM	1	2	3	4	5	6	7	8	9	10
1	0					1				|
2			0		|		1			|
3			1			|		0		|
4	1				0			|	1	|

Y CONTINUUM

	1	2	3	4	5	6	7	8	9	10
5		0		|			1			|
6		0		|			1			|
7			1			|		0		|
8				0					| 1	|

The monotonicity matrix M, representing the interitem monotonicities for Table A-8, is presented in Table A-9. This matrix was entered into a principal-components analysis. The initial loading matrix, and the final loading matrix after rotation (transformation) by Clustran (Bentler, 1969b) appears in Table A-10. The final loading matrix represents the structure matrix obtained after rotation to the hypothesized two sets (1-4; 5-8) of variables. As expected, one obtains a negative sign for the loadings of variables 3 and 7, indicating that a scoring direction reversal for the original variables would be appropriate and would make these variables relate monotonically positively to the other variables in each set.

TABLE A-8   BINARY DATA MATRIX FOR TWO-SPACE EXAMPLE

				ITEM				
PERSON	1	2	3	4	5	6	7	8
1	0	0	1	0	0	0	1	0
2	0	0	1	0	1	1	1	0
3	1	0	1	0	1	1	0	0
4	1	0	1	0	0	0	1	0
5	1	0	1	0	1	1	0	1
6	1	0	1	0	1	1	1	0
7	1	1	1	0	0	0	1	0
8	1	1	0	0	1	1	1	0
9	1	1	0	0	1	1	0	0
10	1	1	0	0	0	0	1	0
11	1	1	0	0	0	0	1	0
12	1	1	0	1	1	1	0	0
13	1	1	0	1	1	1	0	0
14	1	1	0	1	1	1	0	1
15	1	1	0	1	1	1	1	0

TABLE A-9   MONOTONICITY MATRIX: BINARY EXAMPLE

	1	2	3	4	5	6	7	8
1	1.000	1.000	−1.000	1.000	.200	.200	−1.000	1.000
2	1.000	1.000	−1.000	1.000	.000	.000	−.117	−.117
3	−1.000	−1.000	1.000	−1.000	−.200	−.200	.225	.039
4	1.000	1.000	−1.000	1.000	1.000	1.000	−.478	.292
5	.200	.000	−.200	1.000	1.000	1.000	−1.000	1.000
6	.200	.000	−.200	1.000	1.000	1.000	−1.000	1.000
7	−1.000	−.117	.225	−.478	−1.000	−1.000	1.000	−1.000
8	1.000	−.117	.039	.292	1.000	1.000	−1.000	1.000

TABLE A-10   INITIAL AND FINAL LOADING MATRICES: BINARY EXAMPLE

	LOADING MATRIX			
	INITIAL		FINAL	
ITEM	I	II	I$'$	II$'$
1	.94	−.43	1.01	.58
2	.57	−.88	.99	.02
3	−.66	.77	−1.00	−.16
4	.99	−.36	1.01	.66
5	.85	.53	.35	1.00
6	.85	.53	.35	1.00
7	−.92	−.43	−.46	−1.01
8	.81	.60	.27	1.00

The total sums of squares of the two dimensions for the initial loading matrix is 8.37, greater than $n = 8$, the sum of the diagonals of the input matrix. Thus, no more than two dimensions need to be recovered. The loadings on the final dimensions, after transformation, are presented in the last two columns of Table A-10. The first four items "perfectly" define the first dimension (see the italicized values), and the second four items perfectly identify the second dimension; the .01 discrepancy from the ideal 1.00 loadings probably arises from computer rounding errors. Monotonicity analysis managed to recover completely and accurately the fact that two latent dimensions generated the data matrix of Table A-8.

Multicategory Cuts

Many psychologists prefer to deal with multicategory variables, such as Likert scales. We can illustrate the generality of monotonicity analysis by applying the technique to the two-space example of Table A-6 where the latent continua have been cut into separate multicategory variables. Table A-11 illustrates the data matrix generated this way. Items 1 and 5 represent the maximum-discrimination 10-point ordinal variables. Items 1 to 4 represent various cuts on the X continuum; item 3 again has the scoring reversed. Similarly, items 5 to 8 represent various cuts on the Y continuum, and item 7 has its scoring reversed. The monotonicity matrix M resulting from the data of Table A-11 is presented in Table A-12. The initial and final loading matrices are presented in Table A-13. The size of the two roots, or total sums of squares, again clearly indicates the 8 items fall into a two-dimensional space, since the total sums of squares as computed for the first two columns of Table A-13 is 8.01. After objective transformation by Clustran to the hypothesized clustering of variables in the two-space, the final loading matrix presented in the last two columns of Table A-13 is obtained. The loadings of appropriate items on dimensions, as indicated by the italicized values, again demonstrate that each of the two sets of variables is perfectly homogeneous. Thus, the items entering a composite constructed on the basis of the loading matrix are all perfectly monotonically related to each other.

Comparison With Factor Analysis

Although psychometricians generally recognize that factor analysis cannot recover latent continua of binary or multicategory items unless all the interrelations happen to be linear (they almost never are), it may still be useful to compare monotonicity analysis with factor analysis since, in practice, the injunctions against factor analysis are not heeded. The data matrices of Tables

TABLE A-11   MULTICATEGORY DATA MATRIX FOR TWO-SPACE EXAMPLE

	ITEM							
PERSON	1	2	3	4	5	6	7	8
1	1	1	5	1	1	1	5	1
2	1	1	5	1	5	3	3	2
3	2	2	5	1	8	4	2	3
4	3	2	5	2	3	2	4	2
5	4	2	5	2	10	6	1	4
6	4	2	5	2	6	3	3	2
7	5	3	5	3	2	2	5	2
8	7	4	4	3	5	3	3	2
9	7	4	4	3	9	5	2	4
10	8	4	3	3	2	2	5	2
11	8	4	3	3	3	2	4	2
12	9	5	2	4	7	3	2	2
13	9	5	2	4	9	5	2	4
14	10	6	1	4	10	6	1	4
15	10	6	1	4	4	2	3	2

TABLE A-12   MONOTONICITY MATRIX: MULTICATEGORY EXAMPLE

	1	2	3	4	5	6	7	8
1	1.000	1.000	−1.000	1.000	.108	.086	−.129	.178
2	1.000	1.000	−1.000	1.000	.138	.118	−.167	.222
3	−1.000	−1.000	1.000	−1.000	−.115	−.085	.155	−.172
4	1.000	1.000	−1.000	1.000	.109	.089	−.135	.186
5	.108	.138	−.115	.109	1.000	1.000	−1.000	1.000
6	.086	.118	−.085	.089	1.000	1.000	−1.000	1.000
7	−.129	−.167	.155	−.135	−1.000	−1.000	1.000	−1.000
8	.178	.222	−.172	.186	1.000	1.000	−1.000	1.000

TABLE A-13   INITIAL AND FINAL LOADING MATRICES:
MULTICATEGORY EXAMPLE

	LOADING MATRIX			
	INITIAL		FINAL	
ITEM	I	II	I$'$	II$'$
1	.75	.66	*1.00*	.12
2	.77	.64	*1.00*	.16
3	−.75	−.66	*−1.00*	−.13
4	.75	.66	*1.00*	.13
5	.74	−.67	.12	*1.00*
6	.73	−.69	.10	*1.00*
7	−.76	.65	−.15	*−1.00*
8	.79	−.62	.19	*1.00*

A-8 and A-11 were placed into one 15 (person) by 16 (items) data matrix. This data matrix was subjected to monotonicity analysis and factor analysis after appropriate computation of monotonicity and correlation matrices.

The results for monotonicity analysis are presented in Table A-14. The sums of squares of the entries in the first two columns (the two dimensions) again exceed $n = 16$, so all variables' monotonicity can be summarized (correctly) in 2-space. After Clustran transformation, the two latent dimensions are again identified, with only very minor rounding error. The italics indicate which items belong to which dimension.

TABLE A-14   MONOTONICITY ANALYSIS: 16-ITEM EXAMPLE

| | LOADING MATRIX | | | |
| | INITIAL | | FINAL | |
ITEM	I	II	I$'$	II$'$
1	.98	.41	*1.01*	.54
2	.63	.80	*1.00*	.03
3	−.71	−.71	*−1.00*	−.15
4	.94	.44	*1.00*	.49
5	.82	−.58	.26	*1.00*
6	.82	−.58	.26	*1.00*
7	−.87	.53	−.32	*−1.01*
8	.80	−.63	.21	*1.02*
9	.71	.71	*1.00*	.14
10	.73	.68	*1.00*	.18
11	−.72	−.70	*−1.00*	−.16
12	.71	.71	*1.00*	.15
13	.75	−.65	.16	*.99*
14	.73	−.67	.13	*.99*
15	−.77	.62	.19	*−.99*
16	.85	−.55	.30	*1.01*

Factor analysis, using Comrey's (Comrey and Ahumada, 1964) minimum residual method on the product-moment correlation matrix, found seven factors. The minimum residual method was used because it is the only available factoring method which avoids arbitrary estimates of communalities and of the number of factors. The major result of interest is that factor analysis yielded an incorrect number of dimensions, seven rather than two. Since we know that the 16-item data were generated from a basic two-dimensional space (something we would never know for empirical data), the results of the factor analysis can thus be seen to be completely misleading. Doing our best to recover the two dimensions, however, by transforming the first two factors into optimal closeness to the hypothesized two dimensional position (using Clustran) yields the matrix of the first two columns of Table A-15. Again, correct loadings are italicized. The loadings for the binary items (1-8) are nowhere near unity, as they were for Monotonicity Analysis. Indeed, one might be tempted to conclude items 1 and 8 are poor items since their loadings are only in the .50s. Such a conclusion would be patently false, as we know. The multicategory items (9-16) fared much better; indeed, in some cases the loadings approach 1.0. Items 11 and 16, however, have loadings sufficiently below the other loadings to lead one to suspect they are somehow "worse." Yet we know they are not.

TABLE A-15   FACTOR ANALYSIS: 16-ITEM EXAMPLE

| | FINAL LOADING MATRICES | | | |
| | ORIGINAL | | MODIFIED | |
ITEM	I	II	I	II
1	.54	.31	.50	.31
2	.86	.02	.84	.02
3	-.88	-.18	-.89	-.17
4	.74	.43	.76	.44
5	.23	.79	.27	.79
6	.23	.79	.27	.79
7	-.30	-.84	-.32	-.84
8	.12	.57	.11	.57
9	.98	.25	.97	.25
10	.99	.29	.96	.32
11	-.90	-.27	-.92	-.18
12	.96	.23	.84	.43
13	25	.98	.28	.98
14	.23	.94	.24	.93
15	-.27	-.97	-.31	-.97
16	.32	.85	.33	.85

To illustrate the effects of monotonic transformations of data on factor analysis (by definition there are none in monotonicity analysis), the data just described was subjected to some modifications. Items 10-12 of the data matrix were given monotonic transformations, so the rank order of individuals was maintained. The data were correlated and again analyzed using Comrey's minimum residual method. This time the procedure generated nine factors, again way off the true mark. Transformation by Clustran yielded the last two columns of Table A-15. The results are similar to those noted previously, but now item 12 appears much worse than it looked before. Changing the scale affected the results.

Effect of Random Error

Virtually all uses of monotonicity analysis involve data which are contaminated by error. Although a hypothetical error-free data matrix may be generated from a basic r-dimensional process, as we have illustrated for the case of two dimensions, the presence of random error or "noise" added onto that process produces a number of distortions which make recovery of the true latent process difficult. All types of multivariate analyses run into difficulties when faced with an error-contaminated data matrix. Interrelationships among variables become distorted, a person's true placement in r-dimensional space becomes difficult to identify, and the data matrix of observed scores may no longer be r-dimensional. Thus the recovery of latent dimensions and accurate placement of individuals on these dimensions becomes difficult as error modifies the true situation. It seemed worthwhile to investigate the effect of random errors on the two-space example, since errors could seriously distort the true picture, particularly in this example, where the number of individuals is extremely small relative to the number of items and dimensions. Multivariate analyses should ideally not be conducted on matrices which are this small.

An error-contaminated data matrix corresponding to the errorless binary data matrix of Table A-8 was constructed using a particular random model to generate the error. The 15 (persons) times 8 (items), or 120, observations were assumed to be independent observations of the basic bivariate frequency distribution described in Table A-6. In contrast to the error-free case discussed previously, a person's position in the space was now considered to be dynamically mobile rather than stationary. It was assumed that a person's position in space fluctuated from observation to observation. The direction of the fluctuation was considered to be random, in one of eight directions, as determined by a table of random numbers. The magnitude of the fluctuation was constructed so that on 50 percent of the 120 trials the person's position would be identical to his true position; and according to the normal curve on 20 percent, 14 percent, 9 percent, 5 percent, 1 percent and 1 percent of trials his position would be a distance of 1, 2, 3, 4, 5, or 6 units away from his true position, where the X and Y dimensions were divided into ten units. The actual amount of movement was determined by random sampling from a box of chips whose relative frequency represented the above proportions. Thus, the observed distribution of movement was generated by the two independent processes of direction and distance. The effects of this movement in the space were projected onto the eight variables described in Table A-7, so as to yield the data matrix of Table A-16. The latent error process just described generated 10 percent manifest error. That is, a comparison of Table A-16 with Table A-8 will show 10 percent of the observed 0, 1 scores to be in error (however, items 3 and 7 have had their scoring direction reversed, so that sets 1-4 and 5-8 represent error-riddled Guttman scales as scored). The monotonicity matrix computed from Table A-16 is presented in Table A-17. It can be seen that the effect of error was to reduce the average monotonicity of items within each of the two sets, the 1.0 monotonicities of Table A-9 having been replaced by lower values in several cases. In addition, the pattern of interrelationships between the two X and Y sets is also different.

TABLE A-16   DATA OF TABLE A-8, WITH 10 PERCENT ERROR

PERSON	ITEM							
	1	2	3	4	5	6	7	8
1	0	0	0	0	0	0	0	0
2	0	0	0	0	1	1	1	0
3	1	0	0	0	1	1	1	0
4	1	0	0	0	0	0	0	0
5	0	1	0	0	1	1	1	1
6	1	0	0	0	1	1	0	0
7	1	1	0	0	0	1	0	0
8	1	1	0	0	1	0	1	0
9	1	1	1	1	1	1	1	0
10	1	1	1	0	0	0	0	0
11	1	1	1	0	1	0	0	0
12	1	1	1	0	1	1	1	0
13	1	1	1	1	1	1	1	0
14	1	1	1	0	1	1	1	1
15	1	1	1	1	1	0	0	0

TABLE A-17   MONOTONICITY MATRIX: BINARY EXAMPLE
WITH 10 PERCENT ERROR

	1	2	3	4	5	6	7	8
1	1.000	.420	1.000	1.000	.101	−.089	−.172	−.402
2	.420	1.000	1.000	1.000	.240	.000	.200	1.000
3	1.000	1.000	1.000	1.000	.310	−.056	.072	.039
4	1.000	1.000	1.000	1.000	1.000	.089	.172	−1.000
5	.101	.240	.310	1.000	1.000	.478	1.000	1.000
6	−.089	.000	−.056	.089	.478	1.000	.614	1.000
7	−.172	.200	.072	.172	1.000	.614	1.000	1.000
8	−.402	1.000	.039	−1.000	1.000	1.000	1.000	1.000

Component analysis of the monotonicity matrix M yielded three dimensions possessing positive homogeneity. That is, three roots of the M matrix were greater than 1.0. Thus, the introduction of random error into the basic data matrix has generated another dimension; while this dimension accurately reflects the monotonicities of Table A-17, it does not accurately reflect the "true" latent space. The third dimension possesses a homogeneity coefficient of only .21, indicating its relative uselessness; note, however, that the distortion is less than that obtained even with perfect data using factor analysis. The loading matrix for the first two dimensions is presented in the left part of Table A-18. Transformation of the initial solution to a final structure solution using Clustran yields the rightmost two columns of Table A-18. The lowest loading identifying the relevant dimensions is .77, in the range of values observed for the error-free analysis using factor analysis. The average of the italicized loadings on the first dimension is .95, and the analogous average for the second dimension is .93. Thus clustering of items on dimensions is still identifiable with relative ease in the error-distorted case. The output of Clustran also produces a dimension homogeneity coefficient, using Eq. (A-19) with the relevant loadings of the final loading matrix. In this case the first dimension homogeneity is .97, while the second dimension homogeneity is .96, indicating that each of the two dimensions is highly, but not perfectly, internally consistent. The use of Eq. (A-11) for each of the four-item submatrices in Table A-17 yields identical values. This equivalence has been noted before, but whether it is general or only accidental is not known at this time.

TABLE A-18	INITIAL AND FINAL LOADING MATRICES:
BINARY EXAMPLE WITH 10 PERCENT ERROR

| | LOADING MATRIX | | | |
| | INITIAL | | FINAL | |
ITEM	I	II	I'	II'
1	.57	.74	.89	−.18
2	.88	.13	.80	.49
3	.83	.55	1.00	.13
4	.87	.73	1.13	.03
5	.87	−.41	.49	.89
6	.42	−.66	−.03	.77
7	.63	−.70	.13	.94
8	.54	−1.03	−.14	1.13

Assessing Cognitive Development via Measures of Optimal Performance

J. DOUGLAS AYERS
University of Victoria

Intelligence and aptitude tests have been designed with two main purposes in mind: to measure the child's current intellectual ability or status in order to plan his future school and work experiences, and to assess the child's intellectual strength and weaknesses, usually with a battery of aptitude measures, so that his behaviors can be better understood. Intelligence tests do a much better job of prediction than of diagnosis and this is probably why there has been a great deal of criticism regarding the validity of current instruments. However, many of the criticisms should be directed at the unwarranted conclusions drawn from test results rather than at the test results themselves. For example, the finding of relatively stable scores on intelligence tests over certain age ranges has sometimes led to unwarranted conclusions of fixed intelligence. Another type of criticism appears to arise from a misunderstanding of the nature and function of standardization. For example, there are criticisms that standardization procedures do not reflect the cultural training and background of all those for whom a test is to be used. Ferguson (1956) discards this criticism:

> Everything we know suggests that different environmental demands lead to the development of different ability patterns. The concept of a culture-free test is a misconception because the abilities of man are themselves not culture-free. (p. 129)

On the other hand, Tuddenham (1962) has made a very realistic comment on the limitations of current intelligence tests. He has pointed out that most of our tests have maximized the content aspect of ability at the relative expense of the process aspect and have focused on estimating the effectiveness of the individual at the time of testing rather than estimating the plasticity of central processes.

Another major limitation is revealed by the practices of school and clinical psychologists who have used tests that were developed primarily for predictive purposes to serve diagnostic functions. That is, they have collected information on the quality of a subject's intellectual functioning while he is solving tasks in addition to information regarding success or failure on the tasks themselves. In the light of these criticisms, it is suggested that a functional set of ordinal scales based on Piaget's model would overcome most of the current criticism of our tests as measures of status for either predictive or diagnostic purposes.

A scale developed from Piaget's conception of intelligence would be based on the presence or absence of specified hierarchically arranged operations and operational structures. The test would be automatically diagnostic, revealing the limit of the child's current development in various areas. As such then it would be extremely useful for assessing the readiness of particular children for specific educational experiences, especially those related to Piagetian developmental theory. Such an instrument might also be useful for evaluating the effects of intervention, either direct or indirect. Direct intervention might take the form of instruction on the essential skills involved in a concept, operation, or operational structure. In the case of indirect intervention the instrument would be used to evaluate the effectiveness of classroom instruction, especially when that instruction is based on cognitive theory.

It is proposed that in order to develop a functional set of ordinal scales of cognitive development that satisfy the criteria just outlined and others that will be specified in this paper, it will be necessary to develop procedures to determine the optimal performance of individual children. It is not enough to measure maximum performance as in traditional tests of ability, nor is it sufficient to determine typical performance as proposed by Chittenden (1969). In order to ensure optimal performance there must be a correspondence or match between the questioning of the measurement procedure and the cognitive capabilities of the individual child. It is not sufficient to focus on determining the characteristic or typical responses to Piagetian tasks. It is essential to ensure optimal performance, and this can probably only be accomplished by administering sequences of questions related to the prerequisite skills or subordinate capabilities of various operations and structures. Incidentally, when the Geneva interviewers prod a subject and rephrase questions until they are satisfied that the response they obtained is a true version of the child's view of the world, they would appear to be attempting to get at optimal performance rather than a typical performance. Essentially, the proposal is to develop and order the questions on a rational basis.

It is assumed, then, that it is necessary to match the testing via questioning with the cognitive capabilities of the individual child. This assumption and three subsidiary ones are presented at this time to provide an overview of the main arguments to follow. The three subsidiary assumptions to be developed and elaborated in order are:

1. Any measurement procedure must ensure that the child is brought to the point of generalization or transfer through appropriate practice exercises. (This is the major situational factor in testing that must be controlled.)
2. Traditional psychometric procedures, practices, and beliefs have not provided satisfactory instruments for measuring change in either achievement or ability, and there is less reason to expect that they will help in measuring the development of cognitive processes.
3. The child's environment is essentially haphazard with respect to learned experiences that must be related and coordinated in order to acquire higher order cognitive operations and structures.

CONTROL OF SITUATIONAL VARIABLES

In the traditional components of variance model the following relationship is assumed between true scores and error scores:

$$X_i = T_i + e_i$$

where X_i = the score of the ith person on the test

T_i = the true score of the same person on the test

e_i = the error component of the ith person on the test

Much more attention is typically paid to the error component than to the true-score component in the above model. For example, Thorndike (1949) and others emphasize the error component by subdividing it into three or four parts, and labelling the true score component "lasting and general characteristics of the individual." This conception tends to minimize the importance of constant bias due to test sophistication and other situational factors that are included in the true score variance. All too frequently no attempt is made to distinguish between the factors contributing to true ability and the factors associated with the systematic bias that can be attributed to situational factors. Obviously the bias due to these factors should be minimized in order to obtain more accurate estimates of true scores.

Vernon (1965) has proposed a determinants of test performance model in which it is assumed that true score variance can be divided into three parts: that which can be attributed to genetic influence, or, in Hebb's terms, Intelligence A; that which can be attributed to environment, labelled Intelligence B; and a component described as instrumental variance and labelled Intelligence C. Vernon's model provides a categorization of true-score variance that is consistent with Piaget's concept of intelligence being the product of the interaction of the organism and the environment.

Neither the Thorndike nor the Vernon conceptions emphasize sufficiently the importance or the variety of the factors that contribute systematic bias to true score variance. The importance of controlling these situational factors both in test development and in research methodology has been overlooked, perhaps because developers of traditional ability tests have been aware of the effects of situational variables and have attempted to control them in published tests. That situational factors have marked effects on test performance, either with new materials or with unsophisticated children, is indicated by the research that has been conducted in adapting European and American tests to African cultures (Irvine, 1966; Schwartz, 1961). Irvine (1965) has proposed that the following sources provide irrelevant variance in the scores of African subjects: (1) the content of the test itself, (2) the form and style of the test, (3) the transfer that takes place between practice items and actual test items, especially when the material is unfamiliar, (4) motivational influence of strange testers who at present tend to be Europeans, and (5) the particular cultural or educational bias of the test items. The effect of variations in content and task complexity will be discussed further in a later section. It is particularly important to note at this time that both the form and style of Piagetian tasks are new to most students and typically no provision is made for the equivalent of the sample and practice exercises provided with traditional tests. It is very doubtful that either of these crucial situational factors is controlled to any extent by the Piagetian procedure of providing several subtasks followed by questioning. It would appear to be best controlled by providing practice with the skills which are prerequisite to the actual task. The motivational influence of strange testers will be commented on later. The last factor listed by Irvine is not particularly relevant to the present discussion.

MEASUREMENT OF CHANGE

When it comes to measuring change in longitudinal studies, particularly if such studies are over long periods of time, all of our present instruments of aptitude and achievement are found wanting. These instruments have been developed to measure particular characteristics at specific points in time, and where instruments have been developed to cover a wide age range, one can seriously question the parallelism of the measures used. Sometimes tests which supposedly measure the same characteristics can be sufficiently different to hide any developmental trends. Usually, however, a test samples different characteristics at different ages. However, the greatest difficulty of all is encountered when we attempt to infer change by comparing two measures of status. Thorndike (1966) reanalyzed the Harvard Growth Study data and found that change scores are very sensitive creatures which are very responsive to changes in score scale and to changes in the function being measured.

Perhaps it must be concluded that, unless and until scales are developed that are truly homogeneous in the functions that they tap at all levels and are truly expressed in equal units, we will have to forego serious attempts to get a quantitative answer to the simple but tantalizing question: To what extent will children who have grown rapidly in intellect up to the present moment continue to grow rapidly in the future? (p. 127).

Bloom (1964) also states in his review of stability and change in human characteristics that measures of ability must meet the same criteria specified by Thorndike. Admittedly, it seems quite feasible to attempt to develop truly parallel measures for different ages, and where this is not possible, to find statistical procedures such as Thurstone's (1925) equal interval scale approach to control for the changing nature of the particular characteristic as well as the changing nature of the measurements of the characteristic. However, it is questionable that these approaches face the situation squarely. Piaget has shown that the child goes through a number of stages in the development of his thought processes. The characteristics that a child displays at one stage are qualitatively different from those displayed at a succeeding stage. In any case, to require that scales of cognitive development be homogeneous with respect to content and have equal units of measurement is unnecessarily restrictive. Change can be reported in descriptive terms within different stages of development, that is, in terms of particular abilities and patterns of operations or structures, probably related to age or schooling.

A FUNCTIONAL APPROACH TO COGNITIVE DEVELOPMENT

The need to get away from the idea of intelligence as a separate entity which simply unfolds as children grow has already been pointed out. A more appropriate model is to conceive patterns of individual differences in ability developing through interaction between the predispositions of the growing organism and its environment—in Piaget's terms, the development of more and more complex systems of thought schemata. These hierarchically arranged structures of abilities are referred to as plans by Miller, Gallanter, and Pribram (1960); as phase sequences by Hebb (1949); as learning hierarchies of intellectual skills by Gagńe (1968); and as overlearned acquisitions or abilities by Ferguson (1954, 1956). Intelligence, then, refers to the totality of intellectual skills, techniques, plans, or operations for coping with problems. Piaget says these structures have become operational: they are reversible. Ferguson says that abilities have obtained a crude stability or invariance, while Gagné makes no reference to stability, although it is implied.

As Piaget's position with regard to cognitive development is well known, a recapitulation will not be attempted. It is recognized that his behavioral descriptive system has made a tremendous contribution to developmental psychology, but the more functional-analytic approaches of Ferguson and Gagné provide clearer implications for the measurement of development in children. In fact, Ferguson's position emerged from a measurement orientation.

Essentially, Ferguson maintains that since abilities are clearly involved in the learning process, it follows that a particular learning task can at different stages of learning be described in terms of particular ability patterns. There is, then, a method for describing particular learning tasks and differentiating them from one another. Thus it may be possible to make progress in removing learning theory from the context of particular tasks. The main features of his theory which are critical to the present discussion are, first, the abilities of man subsumed under intelligence are attributes of behavior which, through learning, have obtained a crude stability or invariance in the adult. These abilities as they develop in the child also exhibit considerable stability over periods of time at particular age levels. Second, abilities emerge through a process of differential transfer and exert their effects differentially in learning situations. Those that transfer and produce their effects at one stage of learning may differ from those at another. Thus Ferguson assigns a more important role to learning than does Piaget. Also, in spite of his psychometric background, Ferguson does not view g and the various group factors as basic entities that predetermine development, but rather as factors attributable to transfer of training.

The cumulative learning model of Gagné (1968) is very similar to that of Ferguson. Gagné conceives of intellectual development as the building of increasingly complex and interacting structures of learned capabilities and the entities or skills which are learned, built upon each other in a cumulative fashion. Transfer of learning occurs among these skills. In addition, the structures of capabilities so developed can interact with each other in patterns of great complexity generating an ever-increasing intellectual competence. Thus, both Ferguson's and Gagné's models of development suggest that in order to measure and describe stages of development, it will be necessary to study the subordinate capabilities or prerequisite skills of each concept, operation, or structure.

A further implication of the Ferguson and Gagné models is that considerable learning is apt to occur during the simple review of the prerequisite skills of a particular Piagetian task. This is in contrast to the views of Piaget. Only when the schemas required for the solution of a problem are not too far removed in complexity from those available to the child will the inadequacy of the existing schemas force him to accommodate to the conditions of the problem. Thus the child reorganizes his schemas towards greater cognitive adaptation to his environment. Moreover, the child not only solves the problem, but also extends his capacity for further learning. In this view, then, the function of the testing procedure is to provide the right gap between the schemas available to the child and those demanded by the task.

Can this conjecture be used to explain research findings on intervention? Most intervention experiments have been unsuccessful in accelerating conservation through training. Acceleration has not resulted when training has either demonstrated conservation or provided practice with a task. When acceleration has been reported, it seems that some provision has been made for review of the skills prerequisite to the acquisition of a particular operation or structure. However, it may not be true acceleration through direct intervention, but simply facilitation of cognitive reorganization through review of previously learned skills, or, to put it another way, the child's previous experiences in an essentially haphazard environment have been recalled to the point of transfer. It might be noted that the conception of the child's environment as being haphazard is supported by Piaget's equilibration theory, which is essentially a probabilistic explanation for the acquisition of operations and structures.

THE PROPOSAL

When a child answers a series of questions associated with each of the related prerequisite skills of a particular task, the procedure is not necessarily direct intervention or instruction, but rather a testing procedure that ensures that the child's previously unrelated experiences are brought together at a point in time. It is a sort of quasi-training routine to help the child consolidate and coordinate his previously learned and essentially unrelated experiences. Such a procedure tends to provide a check on the comprehension of instructions as well as the equivalent of practice exercises that ensure that the child has been taken to the point of transfer. It probably also controls at least some aspects of the problems associated with variations in content or horizontal décalage as well as motivation.

That the proposed testing procedure was effective in measuring conservation of continuous substance has been shown by LaFrançois (1968). In this study a sample of sixty 5- and 6-year-old children who did not give any responses on a conservation of substance pretest, were randomly assigned to one of three experimental conditions: verbalizing, nonverbalizing, and no training period. The first two groups received quasi-training trials consisting of individual sessions with the experimenter where the subject was presented with a series of tasks ordered from simplest to most difficult. Figure B-1 shows the hierarchical organization of the subtasks and Figure B-2 illustrates the materials and instructions used for some levels of the hierarchy.

252

Figure B-1 Conservation of Continuous Substance:
Hierarchy of Prerequisite Skills

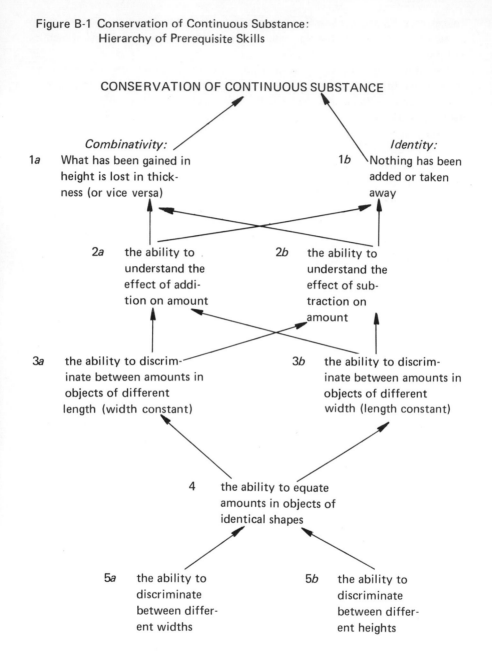

Figure B-2   Some Materials and Instructions Related to the Prerequisite
Skills for Conservation of Continuous Substances.

Illustrative materials and instructions for several
levels of the hierarchy are as follows:

Where Qi =   Questions by the experimenter where i stands for
a specific question for both the nonverbalizing
and the verbalizing groups

and   V   =   Added questions for the verbalizing group only.

4   The ability to equate amounts in objects of identical shapes

Material: Two wooden cubes of equal dimensions (set A, 2 inches)
and two wooden cylinders, also of equal dimensions
(set B, 1 X 3 inches)

Q3   Does this block (indicating one of A) have as much
wood in it as that one, or more, or less?
V—How do you know?

Q4   (Indicating one of B) Are these the same, or does
this one have more wood or less wood than that one?
V—How do you know?

3a The ability to discriminate between amounts in objects of different
length (width constant)

3b The ability to discriminate between amounts in objects of different
width (length constant)

Material: Two cylindrical wooden objects of different length but
equal width (set A, 1 X 6 inches, and 1 X 4 inches),
and two of equal length but of different width (set B,
1 X 5 inches, and $\frac{1}{2}$ X 5 inches).

3a Q5   Is this one (indicating the longer member of set A)
longer or shorter or as long as that one (indicating
the shorter member)?

Q6   Is it less wide or wider or the same?

Q7   Does it have as much wood as that one, or more, or less?
V—How do you know it has more?

3b Q8   (Presenting set B and indicating the narrower cylinder)
Is this one wider, or as wide, or less wide than that
one?

Q9   Is it as long, or longer, or less long?

Q10   Does it have more wood in it than that one, or less,
or the same?
V—How do you know it has less?

These prerequisite tasks were intended to lead logically to the operations which Piaget has labelled identity and combinativity, operations which are manifested in correct conservation responses. In addition the children in the verbalizing group were asked to give reasons for their responses to each subtask. Subjects in the third group did not participate in any of the quasi-training sessions, but were administered all the relevant tests.

Some of the significant findings were:

1. Of 60 nonconservers, age 5 and 6, 56 performed according to a perfect Guttman scale on the nine prerequisite skills outlined in Figure 1.
2. Two-thirds of those children who achieved conservation did so on the first trial and no students achieved conservation on the third and last trial. (One 5-year-old lost conservation on the retention test 3 weeks later.)
3. All the 6-year-olds and 82 percent of the 5-year-olds who verbalized explanations at each step achieved conservation, while less than 40 percent of the nonverbalizing group did as well.
4. Of those students who achieved conservation of continuous mass, 90 percent transferred to conservation of number correspondence, where very few had achieved it on the pretest.
5. Simple reversibility was not used as a justification for correct conservation responses by any subject. The explanation was always given in terms of combinativity or identity.

These findings appear to support the hypothesis that the child has already acquired all or nearly all of the prerequisite skills before the measurement session, as two-thirds of the children who achieved conservation did so on the first trial and none on the third trial. Perhaps the fact that one-third took two trials to achieve conservation might be explained by such factors as becoming acquainted with the tester or not immediately being able to coordinate all of the prerequisite skills on one exposure. For example, verbalizing explanations at each step apparently gave considerable support as a higher proportion of students achieved conservation in the verbalizing group than in the nonverbalizing group.

It appears that the children who achieve conservation by exposure to the measurement procedure have acquired a relatively sophisticated and stable concept. For example, all children justified correct conservation responses with identity or combinativity explanations. None used the simple reversibility explanation which Piaget and Inhelder (1941) indicate is not true reversibility. Secondly, there was a high degree of retention of the concept after a 3-week period.

The finding of high positive transfer to conservation of number correspondence seems to imply that most of the prerequisite skills for the two main tasks are common with the probable exception of several prerequisite skills required for number correspondence that most children have apparently acquired previously.

The finding that most of the students fall on a perfect Guttman scale with respect to the prerequisite skills, if confirmed for other operations and conservations, indicates that the measurement procedure is essentially diagnostic. It specifies the skills that the child has already incorporated in his cognitive structure and those he has yet to acquire.

The initial success in the measurement of conservation with a series of questions based on the prerequisite skills must be replicated for other conservations and operations. It will also be necessary to test for necessary conditions, such as sequence and number of steps. For example, if the number of steps could be reduced there would be a considerable saving in testing time. Another task is to determine the relationship among various operations and conservations, as this may help in determining the critical tests to include in scales of cognitive development. Finally, if optimal performance is to be a critical requirement in measuring cognitive development, the effect of knowledge of results, verbal support, and number of trials must also be studied.

February 9-11, 1969
Monterey, California

INVITATIONAL CONFERENCE ON ORDINAL SCALES OF COGNITIVE DEVELOPMENT

Sponsored by

CALIFORNIA TEST BUREAU
A Division of McGraw-Hill Book Company

Conference Co-chairmen
Donald Ross Green
Marguerite P. Ford

PROGRAM

SUNDAY, FEBRUARY 9

MONTEREY INSTITUTE OF FOREIGN STUDIES
Auditorium
440 Van Buren Street
Monterey

3:00 p.m.

OPENING SESSION
Chairman: Dr. Donald Ross Green
California Test Bureau

WELCOME:
Dr. Joseph L. Dionne
California Test Bureau

REMARKS:
Edward E. Booher
McGraw-Hill Book Company

INTRODUCTION OF JEAN PIAGET:
Dr. Marguerite P. Ford
Pacific State Hospital

Professor Jean Piaget
University of Geneva

"THE THEORY OF STAGES IN COGNITIVE DEVELOPMENT"
Sylvia Opper, Translating
Cornell University

CALIFORNIA TEST BUREAU
Del Monte Research Park
Monterey

5:00 p.m.

RECEPTION

MONDAY, FEBRUARY 10

LA PLAYA HOTEL, Carmel

9:00-11:30 a.m.

SESSION II
Chairman: George Flamer

David Elkind
"Piagetian versus Psychometric
Approaches to Intelligence"
Discussant: Read Tuddenham

Peter Bentler
"An Implicit Metric for Ordinal
Scales: Implications for Assessment
of Cognitive Growth"
Discussant: James Nivette

2:00-4:30 p.m.

SESSION III
Chairman: Marguerite Ford

Read Tuddenham
"Theoretical Regularities and
Individual Idiosyncrasies"
Discussant: Douglas Ayers

Kenneth Lovell
"Some Problems Associated with Formal
Thought and Its Assessment"
Discussant: Thomas Sticht

7:30-10:00 p.m.

SESSION IV
Chairman: George Flamer

Marcel Goldschmid
"The Role of Experiential Factors
in the Rate and Sequence of Cognitive
Development"
Discussant: Kenneth Lovell

Siegfried Engelmann
"Does the Piagetian Approach Imply
Instruction?"
Discussant: Constance Kamii

TUESDAY, FEBRUARY 11

LA PLAYA HOTEL, Carmel

8:30-11:00 a.m.

SESSION V
Chairman: Marguerite Ford

Barbel Inhelder
"Cognitive Development and
Diagnostic Procedures"
Discussant: David Elkind

Harry Beilin
"Developmental Stages and Developmental
Processes"
Discussant: John Flavell

1:00-3:00 p.m.

SESSION VI
Chairman: Ross Green

John Flavell
"The Uses of Verbal Behavior in
Assessing Children's Cognitive
Abilities"
Discussant: George Flamer

Closing Remarks by: Barbel Inhelder

Closing Remarks by: Jean Piaget

The proceedings of the conference will be published in book
form by the College Division, McGraw-Hill Book Company.

CONFERENCE ON ORDINAL SCALES
OF
COGNITIVE DEVELOPMENT

PARTICIPANTS

J. Douglas Ayers
University of Victoria

Harry Beilin
City University of New York

Peter M. Bentler
University of California at Los Angeles

David Elkind
University of Rochester

Seigfried Engelmann
University of Illinois

George B. Flamer
CTB/McGraw-Hill

John H. Flavell
University of Minnesota

Marguerite P. Ford
Pacific State Hospital

Marcel Goldschmid
McGill University

Donald Ross Green
CTB/McGraw-Hill

Bärbel Inhelder
University of Geneva

Constance Kamii
Ypsilanti Public Schools

Kenneth Lovell
University of Leeds

James Nivette
CTB/McGraw-Hill

Sylvia Opper
Cornell University

Jean Piaget
University of Geneva

Thomas Sticht
Human Resources Research Office
    George Washington University

Read Tuddenham
University of California at Berkeley

CONFEREES

Nicholas Alliotti	University of Georgia
Millie Almy	Teachers College, Columbia
Edward G. Barnes	Southeastern Educational Laboratory
Hilton M. Bialek	HumMRO, George Washington University
Harry L. Bowman	Southeastern Educational Laboratory
W. J. Bridgeman	Miami University
Catherine Bruch	University of Georgia
George Burket	CTB/McGraw-Hill
Joe L. Byers	Michigan State University
Clinton I. Chase	Indiana University
Edward A. Chittenden	Educational Testing Service
Mary V. Colburn	Atlanta Public Schools
Rheta De Vries	University of Chicago
Joseph Dionne	CTB/McGraw-Hill
Stephanie Dudek	Allan Memorial Institute
Glen T. Evans	Ontario Institute for Studies in Education
Ruth Formanek	Hofstra University
Thomas M. Goolsby, Jr.	University of Georgia
Selma Greenberg	Hofstra University
Grace M. Heider	University of Kansas

Raymond C. Hummel	University of Pittsburgh
Thomas Innes	University of Tennessee
Henry F. Kaiser	University of California at Berkeley
John B. Kerby	Menlo Park Schools
William Kline	CTB/McGraw-Hill
Esther Kresh	Pittsburgh Public Schools
Henriette M. Lahaderne	I.D.E.A., Los Angeles
William E. Lamon	University of California at Santa Barbara
William F. Landers	Texas Tech
Jonas Langer	University of California at Berkeley
Audrey Little	University of Western Australia
Robert W. Locke	McGraw-Hill Book Company
Robert Long	CTB/McGraw-Hill
M. Ray Loree	University of Alabama
Carson McGuire	University of Texas at Austin
C. E. Meyers	University of Southern California
Margaret H. Moss	SEIMC, Washington, D.C.
Frank B. Murray	George Peabody College
Corrinne Mumbauer	University of Minnesota
Samuel Orpet	Long Beach State College

Quynh Chau Pham	Defense Language Institute
Samuel Reed	CTB/McGraw-Hill
G. Thomas Rowland	New York University
Arthur B. Silverstein	Pacific State Hospital
Charles D. Smock	University of Georgia
Beth Stephens	Temple University
Carolyn Stern	University of California at Los Angeles
Masako Tanaka	Educational Testing Service
Fred T. Tyler	University of Victoria
Gordon Wainwright	CTB/McGraw-Hill
Pearline Yeatts	University of Georgia

REFERENCES

Anthony, E. J. The significance of Jean Piaget for child psychiatry. *The British Journal of Medical Psychology,* 1956, **xxix,** 20-34. (a)

——. Six applications de la théorie génétique de Piaget à la théorie et à la pratique psychodynamique. *Revue Suisse de Psychologie,* 1956, **15,** 269-277. (b)

——. The system makers: Piaget and Freud. *British Journal of Medical Psychology,* 1957, **30,** 255-269.

Ayers, J. D. Assessing cognitive development via measures of optimal performance. See Appendix B this volume, pp. 245-255.

Baldwin, A. L. *Behavior and development in childhood.* New York: Dryden, 1955.

Bandura, A., and Walters, R. H. *Social learning and personality development.* New York: Holt, Rinehart & Winston, 1963.

Beilin, H. Cognitive capacities of young children: A replication. *Science,* 1968, **162,** 920-921/924.

——. Stimulus and cognitive transformation in conservation. In D. Elkind and J. H. Flavell, *Studies in cognitive development: Essays in honor of Jean Piaget.* New York: Oxford University Press, 1969.

Beilin, H., and Franklin, I. C. Logical operations in area and length measurement: Age and training effects. *Child Development,* 1962, **33,** 607-618.

Bentler, P. M. Multidimensional homogeneity scaling. Special scientific meeting, Psychometric Society, 1966.

——. Heterosexual behavior assessment—I. Males. *Behavioral Research and Therapy,* 1968, **6,** 21-25. (a)

——. Heterosexual behavior assessment—II. Females. *Behavioral Research and Therapy,* 1968, **6,** 27-30. (b)

——. A data transformation model for factor analysis. *Mathematical Biosciences,* 1968, **2,** 145-149. (c)

——. Some extensions of image analysis. *Psychometrika,* 1969, **34** (1), 77-83. (a)

——. CLUSTRAN, a program for cluster transformation in multivariate analysis. *Behavioral Science,* 1969, in press. (b)

——. Minimum rank, minimum trace factor analysis. In preparation. (c)

Berlyne, D. E. Curiosity and education. In J. D. Krumboltz (Ed.), *Learning and the educational process.* Chicago: Rand McNally, 1965, pp. 67-89.

Bertalaffny, Ludwig von. *Modern theories of development.* New York: Harper & Bros. (Torchbook ed.), 1962.

Bever, T. G.; Mehler, J.; and Epstein, J. What children do in spite of what they know. *Science,* 1968, **162**, 921-924.

Bijou, S. W. Ages, stages, and the naturalization of human development. *American Psychologist,* 1968, **23**, 419-427.

Bijou, S. W., and Baer, D. M. *Child development.* Vol. 2. New York: Appleton-Century-Crofts, 1965.

Bloom, B. S. *Stability and change in human characteristics.* New York: Wiley, 1964.

Bovet, M. Etudes interculturelles du développement intellectuel and processus d'apprentissage. *Revue Suisse de Psychologie,* 1968, **27**, No. 3/4, 189-199.

Brison, D. W., and Sullivan, E. V. (Eds.), *Recent research on the acquisition of conservation of substance.* Toronto: The Ontario Institute for Studies in Education, Educational Research Series No. 2, 1967.

Bruner, J. *The process of education.* Cambridge: Harvard University Press, 1962.

Bruner, J. S.; Olver, R. R.; and Greenfield, P. M. (Eds.), *Studies in cognitive growth.* New York: Wiley, 1966, pp. 225-256.

Burks, B. S. The relative influence of nature and nurture upon mental development: A comparative study of foster parent-foster child resemblance and true parent-true child resemblance. *Yearbook of the National Society for Studies in Education,* 1928, **27**, 219-316.

Burt, C. *Mental and scholastic tests. (4th Ed.)* London: Staples Press, 1962.

Burt, C., and Howard, M. The relative influence of heredity and environment on assessments of intelligence. *British Journal of Statistical Psychology,* 1957, **X**, 33-63.

Chittenden, E. A. Implications of Piaget's research for testing young children. Paper presented at the meeting of the American Educational Research Association, Los Angeles, February 1969.

Chomsky, C. The acquisition of syntax in children from 5 to 10. Unpublished doctoral dissertation, Harvard University, 1968. (a)

Chomsky, N. *Aspects of the theory of syntax.* Cambridge: M.I.T. Press, 1965.

———. *Language and Mind.* New York: Harcourt, Brace & World, 1968. (b)

Comrey, A. L., and Ahumada, A. An improved procedure and program for minimum residual factor analysis. *Psychological Reports,* 1964, **15**, 91-96.

Coombs, C. H. *A theory of data.* New York: Wiley, 1964.

Cronbach, L. J. Coefficient alpha and the internal structure of tests. *Psychometrika,* 1951, **16**, 297-334.

———. The two disciplines of scientific psychology. *The American Psychologist,* November 1957, **12** (11), 671-684.

Deal, T. N., and Wood, P. L. Testing the early educational and psychological development of children—ages 3-6. *Review of Educational Research,* 1968, **38,** 12-18.

Dodwell, P. C. Children's understanding of number concepts: Characteristics of an individual and of a group test. *Canadian Journal of Psychology,* 1961, **15,** 29-36.

Edwards, A. W. F. The measure of association in a 2 x 2 table. *J. Royal Stat. Soc. A,* 1963, **126,** 109-114.

Elkind, D. Quantity conceptions in junior and senior high school students. *Child Development,* 1961, **32,** 551-560.

——. Piaget and Montessori. *Harvard Educational Review,* 1967, **37** (4), 535-545.

——. Piagetian and psychometric conceptions of intelligence. *Harvard Educational Review,* 1969, **39** (2).

Elkind, D.; Barocas, R.; and Rosenthal, B. Combinatorial thinking in children from graded and ungraded classrooms. *Perceptual and Motor Skills,* 1968, **27,** 1015-1018.

Emmerich, W. Personality development and concepts of structure. *Child Development,* 1968, **39,** 671-690.

Engelmann, S. Cognitive structures related to the principles of conservation. In D. W. Brison and E. V. Sullivan (Eds.), *Recent research on the acquisition of conservation of substance. Educational research series no. 2.* Toronto: Ontario Institute for Studies in Education, 1967.

——. Teaching formal operations to preschool advantaged and disadvantaged children. Toronto: *Ontario Journal of Educational Research,* Spring 1967, **9,** 3.

Erikson, E. E. Comments. In J. M. Tanner and B. Inhelder (Eds.), *Discussions on child development.* Vol. 4. New York: International Universities Press, 1960.

Ferguson, G. A. On learning and human ability. *Canadian Journal of Psychology,* 1954, **8,** 95-112.

——. On transfer and the abilities of man. *Canadian Journal of Psychology,* 1956, **10,** 121-131.

Festinger, L. The treatment of qualitative data by "scale analysis." *Psychological Bulletin,* 1947, **44,** 149-161.

Flavell, J. H. *The developmental psychology of Jean Piaget.* New York: Van Nostrand, 1963.

——. Cognitive development. A chapter to appear in P. Mussen (Ed.), *Carmichael's manual of child psychology,* 1968 (mimeo. copy).

Flavell, J. H.; Botkin, P. T.; Fry, C. L.; Wright, J. W.; and Jarvis, P. E. *The development of role taking and communication skills in children.* New York: Wiley, 1968.

Fournier, E. Un apprentissage de la conservation des quantités continués par une technique d'exercises operatoires. Unpublished doctoral dissertation, Université de Montréal, 1967.

Fowler, W. The effect of early stimulation in the emergence of cognitive processes. In R. D. Hess and R. M. Meyers (Eds.), *Early education.* Chicago: Aldine, 1968, pp. 9-36.

Gagné, R. M. Contributions of learning to human development. *Psychological Review,* 1968, **75**, 177-191. (a)

———. Learning hierarchies. *Educational Psychologist,* November 1968, **6** (1). (Newsletter of Division 15 of the American Psychological Association). (b)

Gellman, R. Conservation, attention, and discrimination. Unpublished doctoral dissertation, University of California, Los Angeles, 1967.

Gesell, A., and Ilg, F. *Infant and child in the culture of today (II).* New York: Harper & Row, 1943.

Glick, J., and Wapner, S. Development of transitivity: Some findings and problems of analysis. *Child Development,* 1968, **39**, 621-638.

Glucksburg, S., and Krauss, R. M. What do people say after they have learned how to talk? Studies of the development of referential communication. *Merrill-Palmer Quarterly,* 1967, **13**, 309-316.

Goldschmid, M. L. Different types of conservation and non-conservation and their relation to age, sex, IQ, MA, and vocabulary. *Child Development,* 1967, **38**, 1229-1246.

———. The role of experience in the acquisition of conservation. *Proceedings, 76th Annual Convention, APA,* 1968, 361-362. (a)

———. The relation of conservation to emotional and environmental aspects of development. *Child Development,* 1968, **39**, 579-589. (b)

———. Cognitive development and preschool education. *Psychologia Wychowawcza,* in press.

Goldschmid, M. L., and Bentler, P. M. The dimensions and measurement of conservation. *Child Development,* 1968, **39**, 787-802. (a)

———. *Manual: Concept assessment kit—conservation.* San Diego, Calif.: Educational and Industrial Testing Service, 1968. (b)

Goldschmid, M. L., and Buxton-Payne, G. Comprehension of relational terms and the development of conservation in very young children. Montreal: Unpublished paper, McGill University, 1968.

Goldschmid, M. L.; Kasimer, G.; Cayne, H.; and Burck, C. Accelerating the acquisition of conservation in mentally retarded and emotionally disturbed children. Montreal: Unpublished paper, McGill University, 1968.

Goldschmid, M. L., and MacFarlane, B. The assessment of six Piagetian concepts in the same subjects: Classification, conservation, perspective, probability, seriation, and transitivity. Montreal: Unpublished paper, McGill University, 1968.

Gollin, E. S., and Saravo, A. A developmental analysis of learning. In J. Hellmuth (Ed.), *Cognitive Studies.* Vol. 1. Seattle: Special Child Publications, in press.

Goodenough, F. New evidence on environmental influence on intelligence. *Yearbook of the National Society for the Study of Education,* 1940, **39**, 307-365.

———. *Mental testing.* New York: Rinehart & Co., 1949.

Goodman, L. A. Simultaneous confidence limits for cross-product ratios in contingency tables. *J. Royal Stat. Soc. B,* 1964, **26**, 86-102.

Goodnow, J. J. A test of milieu effects with some of Piaget's tasks. *Psychological Monographs,* 1962, **76** (Whole No. 555).

———. Problems in research on culture and thought. In D. Elkind and J. Piaget (Eds.), *Studies in cognitive development.* New York: Oxford University Press, 1969, pp. 439-464.

Goodnow, J. J., and Bethon, G. Piaget's tasks: The effects of schooling and intelligence. *Child Development,* 1966, **37**, 573-582.

Gottlieb, F. J. *Developmental genetics.* New York: Reinhold, 1966.

Green, B. A. A method of scalogram analysis using summary statistics. *Psychometrika,* 1956, **21**, 79-88.

Greenfield, P. M. On culture and conservation. In J. S. Bruner; R. R. Olver, and P. M. Greenfield (Eds.), *Studies in cognitive growth.* New York: Wiley, 1966, pp. 225-256.

Guilford, J. P. *Psychometric methods.* New York: McGraw-Hill, 1954.

———. The minimal phi coefficient and the maximal phi. *Educational and Psychological Measurement,* 1965, **25**, 3-8.

———. *The nature of human intelligence.* New York: McGraw-Hill, 1967.

Gulliksen, H. *Theory of mental tests.* New York: Wiley, 1950.

Guttman, L. A. A basis for scaling qualitative data. *American Sociological Review,* 1944, **9**, 139-150.

Guttman, L. A new approach to factor analysis: The radex. In P. F. Lazarsfeld (Ed.), *Mathematical thinking in the social sciences.* Glencoe, Ill.: The Free Press, 1954. (a)

——. The basis for scalogram analysis. In S. A. Stauffer et al., *Measurement and prediction.* Princeton: Princeton University Press, 1954. (b)

——. A generalized simplex for factor analysis. *Psychometrika,* 1955, **20**, 173-192.

——. A general nonmetric technique for finding the smallest coordinate space for a configuration of points. *Psychometrika,* 1968, **33** (4), 469-506.

Hallam, R. N. Logical thinking in history. *Educational Review,* 1967, **19**, 183-202.

Harman, H. *Modern factor analysis.* Chicago: University of Chicago Press, 1967.

Hatwell, Y. *Privation sensorielle et intelligence.* Paris: P. U. F., 1966.

Hebb, D. O. *The organization of behavior.* New York: Wiley, 1949.

Hooper, F. H. Piagetian research and education. In I. E. Sigel and F. H. Hooper (Eds.), *Logical thinking in children.* New York: Holt, Rinehart & Winston, 1968, pp. 423-435.

Horst, P. Correcting the Kuder-Richardson reliability for dispersion of item difficulties. *Psychological Bulletin,* 1953, **50**, 371-374.

——. *Factor analysis of data matrices.* New York: Holt, Rinehart & Winston, 1965.

——. *Psychological measurement and prediction.* Belmont, Calif.: Wadsworth, 1966.

Hoselitz, B. F. Theories of stages of economic growth. In B. F. Hoselitz (Ed.), *Theories of economic growth.* New York: Free Press, 1960, pp. 193-238.

Hughes, M. M. *A four-year longitudinal study of the growth of logical thinking in a group of secondary modern schoolboys.* Master's thesis, University of Leeds, 1965.

Hunt, J. McV. *Intelligence and experience.* New York: Ronald Press, 1961.

——. Intrinsic motivation and its role in psychological development. In D. Levine (Ed.), *Nebraska symposium on motivation.* Lincoln: University of Nebraska Press, 1965, pp. 189-282.

Hyde, D. M. An investigation of Piaget's theories of the development of the concept of number. Unpublished doctoral dissertation, University of London, 1959.

Inhelder, B. *The diagnosis of reasoning in the mentally retarded.* New York: John Day, 1968.

Inhelder, B., et al. Développement et apprentissage. *Revue Suisse de Psychologie,* 1967, **26**, (1), 1-23.

Inhelder, B., and Piaget, J. *The growth of logical thinking from childhood to adolescence.* New York: Basic Books, 1958. (a)

———. *The growth of logical thinking.* London: Routledge and Kegan Paul, 1958. (b)

Inhelder, B., and Sinclair, H. Learning cognitive structures. In J. Langer; P. Mussen, and M. Covington (Eds.), *Trends and issues in developmental psychology.* New York: Holt, Rinehart & Winston, 1969, pp. 2-21.

Irvine, S. H. Adapting tests to the cultural setting: A comment. *Occupational Psychology,* 1965, **39**, 13-23.

———. Towards a rationale for testing attainments and abilities in Africa. *British Journal of Educational Psychology,* 1966, **36**, 24-32.

Jackson, S. The growth of logical thinking in normal and subnormal children. *British Journal of Educational Psychology,* 1965, **35**, 255-258.

Jensen, A. R. How much can we boost IQ and scholastic achievement? *Harvard Educational Review,* 1969, **39** (1), 1-123.

Jones, H. E. The environment and mental development. In L. Carmichael (Ed.), *Manual of child psychology.* New York: John Wiley, 1954, pp. 631-696.

Kaiser, H. F. Scaling a simplex. *Psychometrika,* 1962, **27**, 155-162.

Kamii, C. K. Evaluating pupil learning in preschool education: Socioemotional, perceptual-motor, and cognitive objectives. In B. S. Bloom; J. T. Hastings, and G. Madaus (Eds.), *Formative and summative evaluation of student learning.* New York: McGraw-Hill (in press).

Kamii, C. K., and Radin, N. L. A framework for a preschool curriculum based on Piaget's theory. In I. J. Athey and D. O. Rubadeau (Eds.), *Educational implications of Piaget's theory: A book of readings.* Waltham, Mass.: Blaisdell (in press).

Kaplan, B. The study of language in psychiatry. In S. Arieti (Ed.), *American handbook of psychiatry.* Vol. 3. New York: Basic Books, 1966.

Kendall, M. G. *Rank correlation methods.* London: Griffin, 1955.

Kendler, H. H., and Kendler, T. S. Vertical and horizontal processes in problem solving. *Psychological Review,* 1962, **69**, 1-16.

Kessen, W. "Stage" and "structure" in the study of children. In W. Kessen and C. Kuhlman (Eds.), Thought in the young child. *Monographs of the Society for Research in Child Development,* 1962, **27**, 65-86.

Kettlewell, H. B. D. Selection experiments on industrial melanism in the lepidoptera. *Heredity,* 1955, **9**, 323-342.

Kimball, R. L. *A background concept study in Malawi.* Domasi: Science Centre, 1968.

Kofsky, E. A scalogram study of classificatory development. *Child Development,* 1966, **37**, 191-204. Reprinted in I. E. Sigel and F. H. Hooper (Eds.), *Logical thinking in children.* New York: Holt, Rinehart & Winston, 1968, pp.210-224.

Kohlberg, L. Early education: A cognitive-developmental view. *Child Development,* 1968, **39**, 1013-1063.

Kohnstamm, G. A. An evaluation of part of Piaget's theory. *Acta Psychologica,* 1963, **21**, 313-356.

————. Experiments on teaching Piagetian thought operations. In Ojemann and Pritchett (Eds.), *Emphasis on guided learning.* Report of a conference organized by the Educational Research Council of Cleveland, Ohio. Cleveland, Ohio: E. R. C., 1966. Reprinted in *Cognitive studies,* Vol. 1. Seattle: Special Child Publications, 1968.

————. *Piaget's analysis of class inclusion: Right or wrong?* The Hague: Mouton, 1968.

Kruskal, W. H. Ordinal measures of association. *Journal of the American Statistical Association,* 1958, **53**, 814-861.

LaFrançois, G. R. A treatment of hierarchy for the acceleration of conservation of substances. *Canadian Journal of Psychology,* 1968, **22**, 277-284.

Lasry, J-C. Enseignement operatoire de la notion d'inclusion. Unpublished doctoral dissertation, Université de Montreal, 1968.

Lazarsfeld, P. F. Latent structure analysis. In S. Koch (Ed.), *Psychology: A study of a science.* Vol. 3. New York: McGraw-Hill, 1959.

Leik, R. K., and Matthews, M. A scale for developmental processes. *American Sociological Review,* 1968, **33**, 62-75.

Lingoes, J. C. Multiple scalogram analysis: A set-theoretic model for analyzing dichotomous items. *Educational and Psychological Measurement,* 1963, **23**, 501-524.

————. The multivariate analysis of qualitative data. *Multivariate Behavioral Research,* 1968, **3**, 61-94.

Lingoes, J. C., and Guttman, L. Nonmetric factor analysis: A rank reducing alternative to linear factor analysis. *Multivariate Behavioral Research,* 1967, **2**, 485-505.

Loevinger, J. A systematic approach to the construction and evaluation of tests of ability. *Psychological Monographs,* 1947, **61**, No. 285.

Lord, F. M. and Novick, M. R. *Statistical theories of mental test scores.* Reading, Mass.: Addison-Wesley, 1968.

Lovell, K. A follow-up study of Inhelder and Piaget's *The growth of logical thinking. British Journal of Psychology,* 1961, **52**, 143-153. (a)

————. *The growth of basic mathematical and scientific concepts in children.* London: University Press, 1961. (b)

————. Psychological aspects of research in education. *In education in Africa-action and research.* London: Heinemann, 1969.

Lovell, K., and Butterworth, I. B. Abilities underlying the understanding of proportionality. *Mathematics Teaching,* 1966, **37**, 5-9.

Lovell, K.; Mitchell, B.; and Everett, I. R. An experimental study of the growth of some logical structures. *British Journal of Psychology,* 1962, **53**, 175-188.

Lovell, K., and Shields, J. B. Some aspects of a study of the gifted child. *British Journal of Education Psychology,* 1967, **37**, 201-208.

Lunzer, E. A. Problems of formal reasoning in test situations. In P. H. Mussen (Ed.), European research in cognitive development. *Monograph of the Society for Research in Child Development,* 1965, **30** (2).

————. Formal reasoning. In E. A. Lunzer and J. F. Morris (Eds.), *Development in learning 2.* London: Staples, 1968.

McDonald, R. P. A general approach to nonlinear factor analysis. *Psychometrika,* 1962, **27**, 397-415.

————. Numerical methods for polynomial models in nonlinear factor analysis. *Psychometrika,* 1967, **32**, 77-112.

Mehler, J., and Bever, T. G. Cognitive capacity of very young children. *Science,* 1967, **158**, 141-142.

————. Reply. *Science,* 1968, **162**, 979-981.

Mehrabian, A. *An analysis of personality theories.* Englewood Cliffs: Prentice-Hall, 1968.

Mermelstein, E., and Shulman, L. S. Lack of formal schooling and the acquisition of conservation. *Child Development,* 167, **38**, 39-52.

Miller, G. A., Gallanter, E., & Pribram, C. H. *Plans and the structure of behavior.* New York: Holt, 1960.

Moely, B. E.; Olson, F. A.; Halwes, T. G.; and Flavell, J. H. Production deficiency in young children's clustered recall. *Developmental Psychology,* 1969, **1** (1), 26-34.

Montessori, M. *The Montessori method.* New York: Schocken, 1964.

Moore, O. K. Orthographic symbols and the preschool child: A new approach. In E. P. Torrence (Ed.), *Creativity: 1960 proceedings of the 3rd conference on gifted children.* Minneapolis: University of Minnesota, Center for Continuation Studies, 1961.

Morf, A. Apprentissage d'une structure logique concrète (inclusion): Effets et limites. *Etudes d'Epistemologie Génétique,* **IX**, P. U. F., 1959.

Morrison, D. F. *Multivariate statistical methods.* New York: McGraw-Hill, 1967.

Mosteller, F. Association and estimation in contingency tables. *Journal of the American Statistical Association,* 1968, **63**, 1-28.

Nagel, E. Determinism and development. In D. B. Harris (Ed.), *The concept of development.* Minneapolis: University of Minnesota Press, 1957.

Nassefat, M. *Etude quantitative sur l'évolution des opérations intellectuelles: Le passage des opérations concrètes aux opérations formelles.* Neuchâtel: Delachaux & Niestlé, 1963.

Neimark, E. D., and Lewis, N. Development of logical problem solving: A one-year retest. *Child Development,* 1968, **39**, 527-536.

Odier, C. *Anxiety and magical thinking.* New York: International University Press, 1956.

Olson, D. R. Language acquisition and cognitive development. Paper presented at *International Conference on Social-Cultural Aspects of Mental Retardation.* Nashville, Tennessee: George Peabody College, June 1968.

Peluffo, N. Culture and cognitive problems. *International Journal of Psychology,* 1967, **2**, 187-198.

Piaget, J. *Judgment and reasoning in the child.* New York: Harcourt, Brace, 1928.

———. *Play, dreams and imitation in childhood.* New York: Norton, 1951.

———. *Les relations entre l'affectivité et l'intelligence dans le développement mental de l'enfant.* Paris: C. D. U., 1954.

———. The general problems of the psychobiological development of the child. In J. M. Tanner and B. Inhelder (Eds.), *Discussions on child development.* Vol. 4. New York: International Universities Press, 1960, pp. 3-27.

———. Development and learning. In R. E. Ripple and V. N. Rockcastle (Eds.), *Piaget rediscovered.* Ithaca, New York: Cornell University, 1964. (a)

———. Relations between the notions of time and speed in children. In R. E. Ripple & V. N. Rockcastle (Eds.), *Piaget rediscovered: A report of the conference on cognitive studies and curriculum development.* Ithaca, New York: School of Education, Cornell University, 1964. (b)

———. *The child's conception of number.* New York: Norton, 1965.

———. Genesis and structure in the psychology of intelligence. In D. Elkind (Ed.), *Six psychological studies by Jean Piaget.* New York: Random House, 1967, pp. 143-158. (a)

———. On the nature and nurture of intelligence. Address delivered at New York University, March 1967. (b)

———. Intelligence et adaptation biologique. In F. Bresson et al. (Eds.), *Les processus d'adaptation.* Paris: P. U. F., 1967, pp. 65-82. (c)

———. The mental development of the child. In D. Elkind (Ed.), *Six psychological studies by Jean Piaget.* New York: Random House, 1967, pp. 3-73. (d)

———. *Biologie et connaissance.* Paris: Gallimard, 1967. (e)

———. Quantification, conservation, and nativism. *Science,* 1968, **162**, 976-979. (a)

———. Le structuralisme ("Que sais-je" series). Paris: P. U. F., 1968. (b)

Piaget, J., and Inhelder, B. *Le développement des quantités chez l'enfant.* Neuchâtel: Délachaux et Niestlé, 1941.

———. *Le développement des quantités physiques chez l'enfant.* Neuchâtel: Délachaux & Niestlé, 1962.

Plackett, R. L. A class of bivariate distributions. *Journal of the American Statistical Association,* 1965, **60**, 516-522.

Price-Williams, D. R. A. A study concerning concepts of conservation of quantity among primitive children. *Acta Psychologia,* 1961, **18**, 297-305.

———. Abstract and concrete modes of classification in a primitive society. *British Journal of Educational Psychology,* 1962, **32**, 50-61.

Rapaport, D. The theory of ego autonomy. *Bulletin of the Menninger Clinic,* 1958, **22**, 13-35.

Russell, W. A. An experimental psychology of development: Pipe dream or possibility? In D. B. Harris (Ed.), *The concept of development.* Minneapolis: University of Minnesota Press, 1957.

Schönemann, P. Scaling a simplex symmetrically. *Research Bulletin 68-31.* Princeton: Educational Testing Service, 1968.

Schrödinger, E. *What is life?* New York: Doubleday, 1956.

Schwartz, P. *Aptitude tests for use in the developing nations.* Pittsburgh: American Institutes for Research, 1961.

Shaffer, L. F. Children's interpretations of cartoons. *Contributions to education.* New York: Teacher's College, Columbia University, 1930, No. 429.

Shepard, R. N. The analysis of proximities: Multidimensional scaling with an unknown distance function—I. *Psychometrika,* 1962, **27**, 125-140. (a)

———. The analysis of proximities: Multidimensional scaling with an unknown distance function—II. *Psychometrika,* 1962, **27**, 219-245. (b)

Shepard, R. N., and Carroll, J. D. Parametric representation of nonlinear data structures. Paper presented at *International Symposium on Multivariate Analysis,* 1966.

Shoemaker, H. A. The functional context method of instruction. *Professional Paper 35-67,* Human Resources Research Office: George Washington University, 1967.

Sigel, I. E. Reflections. In I. E. Sigel and F. H. Hooper (Eds.), *Logical thinking in children.* New York: Holt, Rinehart & Winston, 1968, pp. 503-528.

———. The Piagetian system and the world of education. In D. Elkind and J. H. Flavell (Eds.), *Studies in cognitive development: Essays in honor of Jean Piaget.* New York: Oxford University Press, 1969.

Sigel, I. E., and Hooper, F. H. (Eds.), *Logical thinking in children: Research based on Piaget's theory.* New York: Holt, Rinehart & Winston, 1968.

Sigel, I. E., and Mermelstein, E. The effects of nonschooling on Piaget's conservation tasks. Paper presented at the meeting of the American Psychological Association, Chicago, 1965.

Sigel, I. E.; Roeper, A.; and Hooper, F. H. A training procedure for acquisition of Piaget's conservation of quantity: A pilot study and its replication. *British Journal of Educational Psychology,* 1966, **36**, 301-311. Reprinted in I. E. Sigel and F. H. Hooper (Eds.), *Logical thinking in children.* New York: Holt, Rinehart & Winston, 1968, pp. 295-308.

Silvern, L. C. Systems engineering of education I: The evaluation of systems thinking in education. *ETC,* Los Angeles, Calif., 1965.

Sinclair, H. *Acquisition du language et développement de la pensée.* Paris: Dunod, 1967.

Skeels, H. M. Adult status of children with contrasting early life experiences. *Monographs of the Society for Research in Child Development,* 1966, **31** (3, Whole No. 105).

Smedslund, J. The acquisition of conservation of substance and weight in children. *Scandinavian Journal of Psychology,* 1961, **2**, 71-84. (a)

———. The acquisition of conservation of substance and weight in children. III. Extinction of conservation of weight acquired "normally" and by means of empirical controls on a balance scale. *Scandinavian Journal of Psychology,* 1961, **2**, 85-87. (b) Reprinted in I. E. Sigel and F. H. Hooper (Eds.), *Logical thinking in children.* New York: Holt, Rinehart & Winston, 1968, pp. 277-280.

Sonquist, H. D., and Kamii, C. K. Applying some Piagetian concepts in the classroom for the disadvantaged. In J. L. Frost (Ed.), *Early childhood rediscovered: Readings.* New York: Holt, Rinehart & Winston, 1968, pp. 169-180.

Sonquist, H. D.; Kamii, C. K.; and Derman, L. A Piaget-derived preschool curriculum. In I. J. Athey and D. O. Rubadeau (Eds.), *Educational implications of Piaget's theory: A book of readings.* Waltham, Mass.: Blaisdell (in press).

Spearman, C. *The nature of "intelligence" and the principles of cognition.* London: Macmillan, 1923.

Stambak, M., et al. Les dyspraxies chez l'enfant. *Psychiatrie de l'Enfant,* 1964, **7**, fasc. 2, 381-496.

Steffe, L. P., and Parr, R. B. *The development of the concepts of ratio and fraction in the fourth, fifth and sixth years of the elementary school.* Madison: University of Wisconsin Center for Cognitive Learning, 1968.

Stendler Lavatelli, C. A Piaget-derived model for compensatory preschool education. In J. L. Frost (Ed.), *Early childhood rediscovered: Readings.* New York: Holt, Rinehart & Winston, 1968, pp. 530-544.

Stevens, S. S. Measurement, statistics, and the schemapiric view. *Science,* 1968, **161**, 849-856.

Strodtbeck, F. L. The hidden curriculum of the middle-class home. In H. Passow, M. Goldberg, and E. H. Tannenbaum (Eds.), *Education of the disadvantaged.* New York: Holt, Rinehart & Winston, 1967, pp. 244-259.

Suchman, J. R. A model for the analysis of inquiry. In H. J. Klausmeier and C. W. Harris (Eds.), *Analysis of concept learning.* New York: Academic Press, 1966.

Sullivan, E. V. Piaget and the school curriculum: A critical appraisal. *Bulletin No. 2,* Toronto: The Ontario Institute for Studies in Education, 1967.

Sutherland, N. S. Discussion. In J. Lyons and R. J. Wales (Eds.), *Psycholinguistics papers.* Edinburgh: Edinburgh University Press, 1966.

Tanner, J. M. Physical and physiological aspects of child development. In J. M. Tanner and B. Inhelder (Eds.), *Discussions on child development.* Vol. 1. London: Tavistock, 1956.

Tanner, J. M. and Inhelder, B. (Eds.), *Discussions on child development.* Vol. 4. London: Tavistock, 1960.

Taylor, J. E., and Fox, W. L. Differential approaches to training. *Professional Paper 47-67,* Human Resources Research Office: George Washington University, 1967.

Terman, L. M., and Merrill, M. A. *Stanford-Binet intelligence scale: Manual for the third revision.* Boston: Houghton Mifflin Co., 1960.

Thorndike, R. L. Intellectual status and intellectual growth. *Journal of Educational Psychology,* 1966, **57**, 121-127.

Thurstone, L. L. A method of scaling psychological and educational tests. *Journal of Educational Psychology,* 1925, **16**, 433-451.

Torgerson, W. S. *Theory and methods of scaling.* New York: Wiley, 1958.

Tuddenham, R. D. The nature and measurement of intelligence. In L. Postman (Ed.), *Psychology in the making.* New York: Knopf, 1962, pp. 469-529.

Uzgiris, I. C. Situational generality of conservation. *Child Development,* 1964, **35**, 831-841.

Vernon, P. E. Ability factors and environmental influences. *American Psychologist,* 1965, **20**, 723-733.

Vinh-Bang, N. P. Evolution des conduites et apprentissage. In A. Morf, J. Smedslund, Vinh-Bang, and J. F. Wohlwill (Eds.), *L'apprentissage des structures logiques. Etudes d'epistemologie génétique.* Paris: P. U. F., 1959, **9**, pp. 3-13.

Waddington, C. H. *The nature of life.* New York: Atheneum, 1962. (a)

————. *How animals develop.* New York: Harper & Bros, 1962. (b)

————. *Principles of development and differentiation.* New York: Macmillan, 1966.

Walker, D. A. Answer pattern and score-scatter in tests and examinations. *British Journal of Psychology,* 1931, **22**, 73-86.

Wallace, J. G. *Concept growth and the education of the child.* Slough, Bucks: National Foundation for Educational Research in England and Wales, 1965.

Wallach, L. On the bases of conservation. In D. Elkind and J. H. Flavell (Eds.), *Studies in cognitive development: Essays in honor of Jean Piaget.* New York: Oxford University Press, 1969, pp. 191-219.

Wallach, L.; Wall, J. A.; and Anderson, L. Number conservation: The roles of reversibility, addition-subtraction, and misleading perceptual cues. *Child Development,* 1967, **38**, 425-442. Reprinted in I. E. Sigel and F. H. Hooper (Eds.), *Logical thinking in children.* New York: Holt, Rinehart & Winston, 1968, pp. 308-324.

Warburton, F. W. Construction of the new British Intelligence Scale: Progress report. *Bulletin of the British Psychological Society,* 1966, **19**, 68-70.

Wechsler, D. *The measurement of adult intelligence.* Baltimore: Williams & Wilkens, 1944.

————. *Wechsler intelligence scale for children.* New York: Psychological Corporation, 1949.

Werner, H. The concept of development from a comparative and organismic point of view. In D. B. Harris (Ed.), *The concept of development.* Minneapolis: University of Minnesota Press, 1957, pp. 125-148.

White, R. W. Motivation reconsidered: The concept of competence. *Psychological Review,* 1959, 66, 297-333.

Wohlwill, J. F. A study of the development of the number concept by scalogram analysis. *The Journal of Genetic Psychology,* 1960, **97**, 345-377. Reprinted in I. E. Sigel and F. H. Hooper (Eds.), *Logical thinking in children.* New York: Holt, Rinehart & Winston, 1968, pp. 75-104.

Wohlwill, J. F., and Lowe, R. C. Experimental analysis of the development of the conservation of number. *Child Development,* 1962, **33**, 153-167. Reprinted in I. E. Sigel and F. H. Hooper (Eds.), *Logical thinking in children.* New York: Holt, Rinehart, & Winston, 1968, pp. 324-339.

Wolff, P. H. The developmental psychologies of Jean Piaget and psychoanalysis. *Psychological Issues,* 1960, **2**, (1, Whole No. 5).

Young, G. and Householder, A. S. Discussion of a set of points in terms of their mutual distances. *Psychometrika,* 1938, 3, 19-22.

Zimiles, H. Problems of assessment of academic and intellectual variables. Paper presented at the meeting of the American Educational Research Association, Chicago, February 1968..

INDEX